Narrow Escapes

A Boy's Holocaust Memories and Their Legacy

Narrow Escapes

A Boy's Holocaust Memories and Their Legacy

by Samuel P. Oliner

Foreword by John K. Roth

PARAGON HOUSE
St. Paul, Minnesota

Published in the United States of America by

Paragon House
2700 University Avenue West
St. Paul, Minnesota 55114

Portions previously published under the title *Restless Memories* (1979, 1986)

Library of Congress Catalog-in-Publication Data

Oliner, Samuel P.
Narrow escapes :a boy's Holocaust memories and their legacy / by Samuel P. Oliner ; foreword by John K. Roth.
p. cm.
"Portions previously published under the title Restless memories"--CIP t.p. verso.
ISBN 1-55778-792-1 (alk. paper)
1. Oliner, Samuel P. 2. Jews--Poland--Biography. 3. Holocaust, Jewish (1939-1945)--Poland--Personal narratives. 4. Poland--Biography. 5. Holocaust survivors--Biography. I. Oliner, Samuel P. Restless memories. II. Title.

DS 135.P63 045 2000
940.53'092--dc21
[B]

00-039152

10 9 8 7 6 5 4 3 2 1

For current information about all releases from Paragon House,
visit the web site at http://www.paragonhouse.com

To my family martyred on August 14, 1942,
in Poland. May their untimely death, as well as the
death of six million other Jews and five million
gentiles, serve as warning of what can
happen again if we don't truly become our
brothers' and sisters' keepers.

ACKNOWLEDGMENTS

I want to express my sincere appreciation to the many individuals who encouraged me to write this account and to those who subsequently read it.

I acknowledge Ms. Lynn Crosbie, who devoted considerable time to editing my initial manuscript and notes, making sense out of chaos, and then encouraging me to seek a publisher. I recognize with thanks Mr. Seymour Fromer, Director of the Judah L. Magnes Museum in Berkeley, who made the publication of the original manuscript, *Restless Memories: Recollections of the Holocaust Years*, possible. My special thanks go to James Hamby; Pearl Oliner, my loving wife; my three caring sons, Aron, David, and Ian Oliner; Jack Shaffer; Judy Shaffer; William Helmreich; Mona Skolnick; Sabra Chodor; and Shirley Ohrenstein for reading that manuscript and making valuable comments. I especially appreciate the encouragement of my colleagues. Among these are John Gai, Stephen Stamnes, Paul Crosbie, and Betsy Watson.

I also want to acknowledge and thank my recently discovered distant cousins, Joe and Jean Gerhard. As a survivor of the Holocaust who lived in the Zyndranowa region, Joe was able to provide me with substantial information and clarification of the facts about how members of my Zyndranowa family lived and perished in the last days of August 1942. Mr. Teodor Gocz, a member of the Lemko minority ethnic group in Poland, who lives in the village of Zyndranowa and who knew me as a child, helped me to recall some of my childhood memories. He also worked with me to establish a small Jewish regional museum, a kind of memorial to local Jews. It is located in the house that once belonged to Zalman Polster, my grandfather's brother.

The individuals who helped improve this book are Steven Newman and Paula Friedman who carefully read the new epilogue and made valuable suggestions. To Kia Ora Zeleny, a sociology graduate student, I owe a special debt of gratitude. She patiently and methodically checked the manuscript for errors and greatly assisted in refining the new epilogue. In addition, I wish to express my deep appreciation to Laureen Enright of Paragon House, who saw the merits of this volume and graciously made helpful suggestions, from which the new manuscript has benefited. Joanna Fryz-Boatright, a Polish graduate student in psychology at Humboldt State University, has made invaluable suggestions about the Polish translations that appear in the book.

I am particularly grateful to Professor John K. Roth, a caring and compassionate man, philosopher and eminent scholar of the Holocaust, who kindly agreed to write the forward for *Narrow Escapes*. He has been generous with advice and has made positive observations about the value of this work.

Finally, I also express thanks to Riley Quarles, Coordinator of the Courseware Development Center at Humboldt State University for his work on the graphics.

CONTENTS

1. Garbacz mass grave - execution August 14, 1942
2. Barwinek Forest mass grave - execution August 13, 1942

FOREWORD

JUST PEOPLE

Narrow Escapes defines Samuel Oliner's life in more ways than one. Not only is he a Holocaust survivor who barely eluded the genocidal "Final Solution" that Nazi Germany unleashed on the European Jews during the Second World War. Oliner is also a groundbreaking Holocaust scholar who has focused attention on the rescuers—small in number but immensely significant nonetheless—who risked their lives to give Jews life-saving narrow escapes during those dark times.

Oliner's personal experience of the Holocaust produced memories that have never left him. The title of an earlier version of this autobiography—*Restless Memories: Recollections of the Holocaust Years*—reflected that fact. Oliner's significant epilogue in this new edition both updates his story and helps to show how those restless memories led to a remarkable career. I say "helps to show" because modesty is one of Oliner's virtues. Although he minimizes his many contributions to Holocaust scholarship, *The Altruistic Personality: Rescuers of Jews in Nazi Europe*, which he published with his wife, Pearl M. Oliner, in 1988, is only one of his writings that remain "must reading" for anyone concerned with the ethical questions and implications raised by the Holocaust.

A Boy's Holocaust Memories and Their Legacy, as his autobiography is now subtitled, sheds important light on the difficult post-Holocaust path that took Oliner from the Holocaust's despair to his well-deserved position of scholarly and moral leadership. That path includes periodic visits to Oliner's native Poland. On Saturday, June 25, 1994, for example, he returned to Zyndranowa, a village three miles from the Slovak border in southern Poland, where he was born in

1930. On that June day, Oliner spoke at the dedication of the Zalman Jewish Museum, which he had generously helped to build. Situated in a house that had once belonged to Oliner's relatives and named after his grandfather's brother Zalman Polster, the museum honors Jews whose families lived in Poland for 800 years before the Holocaust decimated them.

Oliner's narrow escapes and restless memories focused the speech he gave in Polish on that day. In June 1942, he recalled, the Germans ghettoized his family. Two months later, the Bobowa Ghetto was "liquidated," the Nazi euphemism for *murdered*. As the killing action began, Samuel heard his stepmother say that he must "run and hide" and save himself "to tell the future generations what had happened."

Run he did. Then, with the help of a Polish gentile woman named Balwina Piecuch, her son Staszek, who has been Samuel's long-time friend, and others akin to the rescuers that the sociologist Samuel Oliner would later study with such commitment, the young Samuel Oliner also found places to hide and ways to save himself. Eventually he more than fulfilled his stepmother's plea to tell future generations what had happened. Sadly, that narrative had to include the fact that there were no havens for most of Samuel's immediate family. The Holocaust destroyed nearly all of them, but nevertheless Oliner's narrow escape made it possible for him to conclude his June 1994 remarks at Zyndranowa by thanking those who—then and now—were caring people.

Above all else, Samuel Oliner is a caring person. I first learned that fact on Thursday, April 10, 1980. On that day, I flew to San Francisco, but the meeting awaiting me was very different from the one I expected. That afternoon I was to participate in a panel on "Perspectives on the Holocaust" at a gathering of the Pacific Sociological Association. Recollections of those talks have faded, but what preceded I remember vividly.

Arriving at the Sheraton-Palace Hotel shortly before noon, I located the room for the afternoon symposium and then went to lunch. On the way, I met the panel's chairman. Strangers at that point, the two of us decided to share a table. Pleasantries exchanged, our conversation grew more intense. My companion inquired why I was so interested in Adolf Hitler's attempted annihilation of the Jews. My identity as an American, a philosopher, and a Christian, I explained, was what impelled me to explore how the Holocaust happened. When I returned the question, the response provided my first glimpses of Samuel Oliner's complex past.

His book, *Restless Memories*, reached me later. My reading made me realize how much I had been privileged to meet a very special person. Over the years, our friendship has grown and deepened. I was honored when Samuel asked me to join the Advisory Board for the Altruistic Personality Project, which has studied those who rescued Jews in Nazi-occupied Europe. His invitation to contribute introductory words to a reprinting of *Restless Memories* moved me even more, and my gratitude for his life, his survival, is profound as I draw upon them in this foreword.

Narrow Escapes records memories that are restless because Oliner's identity involves three-lives-in-one, all of them indelibly marked by the Holocaust. First, there is Samuel Oliner, the American professor of sociology. His is not the typical immigrant's story, for, among other things, he became a preeminent scholar of the Holocaust and the rescuers of Jews in particular. One reason why his scholarly career led that way is that Samuel is also a Polish boy named Jusek Polewski, a twelve-year-old orphan who worked as a farmhand while trying to elude the Germans and their antisemitic Polish sympathizers. Life was at stake, because hidden inside Jusek Polewski—that young sociologist who had to learn how communities as well as individuals behave—there was a Jewish boy named Shmulek Oliner.

Shmulek's world became cruel beyond imagining. Herded into the Bobowa Ghetto and then transported to a nearby forest where they were shot on August 14, 1942, Shmulek's family was among the 2.7 million Jews who were killed in that year alone, the Holocaust's most lethal. After the massacre, Shmulek-Jusek-Samuel alone remained to bear Jewish witness to the fate of Bobowa's Jews. Every reader of *Narrow Escapes* will learn how eloquently the three of them have done so.

These pages are filled with courage, honesty, and more pain than any life should have to bear. Reading and rereading them, I remember a phrase that Jusek Polewski heard in mid-1943. The farmers for whom Jusek worked, Mr. and Mrs. Padworski, had received a letter from a Warsaw friend. It described that April's heroic uprising in the Warsaw Ghetto and the merciless Nazi response that followed. As Samuel Oliner tells the story, Mrs. Padworski, moved by the hapless condition of Warsaw's Jews, said to her husband within Jusek's hearing: "The vision of it all, why it just make me feel so sorry for those poor people. They were just people, you know, with their hatreds and loves…their children…just like us…They do fight very bravely."

Just people—that phrase moves me as I trace the restless memories and narrow escapes of Samuel Oliner, the Holocaust orphan who became such a sensitive social scientist. The phrase affects me because the salient feature of the Holocaust is that the victims, killers, bystanders, resisters, and rescuers were people—just people, but not simply so, for that phrase conveys at least three meanings. One suggests a fundamental equality whose recognition—including respect for particularity and difference among people—might have prevented the Holocaust. A second recognizes the blindness and corruption, the arrogant racism and antisemitism, that inflicted Auschwitz on the world. The third suggests a qualitative difference between people: namely, that some are characterized by justice and caring much more than others.

Shmulek, Jusek, Samuel—all three have been concerned about "just people" in each of those ways. They would agree, however, that no concern can be of greater importance than the one that focuses on lives characterized by justice and caring. Hence, *Narrow Escapes* honors the Oliner family and millions of Jews like them—decent people who deserved to live but whose Jewish particularity was destroyed by the arrogance of German power and by the indifference of gentile bystanders, forces that were too strong for the valiant but limited resisters and rescuers who tried their best to intervene in Nazi-occupied Europe.

The author's triple consciousness does something else as well. This book is more than a memorial to the dead. It is a testament of survival, and thus its chapters also remember those who made survival possible. Once orphaned, Shmulek Oliner had neither Jewish family nor Jewish friends to help him. If his looks could pass as Polish, he still had always to be on guard. Word or deed—not to mention the telltale circumcision that he dared not reveal—might make him suspect in circumstances where Polish betrayal could put him in German hands and end his life.

A farmer named Woitek directed Shmulek-turned-Jusek to the Padworskis, who lived near the Polish village of Biesnik. Needing help for their farm—before the occupation it belonged to a Jewish family—they hired Jusek. Until the war's end, the Padworski's home was his. It could not be Shmulek's, however, because Jusek was never completely confident that he could reveal his Jewish identity even to these benefactors. To this day, Samuel Oliner is unsure whether the Padworskis knew he was Jewish, though he suspects they did. Fully aware that his presence had endangered their lives, he left the Padworski farm in 1945 with tears of gratitude in his eyes. Even though he returned to Poland, he never saw either of them again. "Somehow," his epilogue poignantly reflects, "my feelings toward them have not yet been sorted out." The farmer Woitek treated Jusek fairly. The Padworski's did, too. Samuel Oliner remembers them thankfully, and yet honesty requires him to retain the restless question: Would they have been just people if Shmulek had asked for their help?

Where "the good peasant woman Balwina" and her son Staszek are concerned, however, such questions do not make memories restless—and yet they do. Shmulek found his way to her door soon after the slaughter on August 14, 1942. A friend of Aron Oliner, Shmulek's father, Balwina knew the boy was Jewish and cared for him. She taught him survival skills to add to those Shmulek had already acquired. When the danger of discovery became too great, Shmulek left Balwina as Jusek Polewski. With Staszek as the intermediary, they kept in touch. Balwina was no longer alive when Samuel Oliner visited Poland in 1983, but his contacts with Staszek continued, and Oliner's telling of them in *Narrow Escape*'s epilogue provides some of the most touching moments in this narrative.

Narrow Escapes ends differently than its predecessor, *Restless Memories*, and yet the two endings point in similar directions. The earlier version of Oliner's story concluded with Samuel's wishing he could return to Balwina's door and say, "Here I am. It's Shmulek."

Balwina's life was just. So many others were not. But why are people just people? The multiple questions within that question keep Samuel Oliner's memories restless. As a result, he has spent his life trying to discern why some people proved to be much more just and caring than others during the Holocaust.

Perhaps such questions cannot be answered finally, not even by study as careful as Samuel Oliner's. Yet, his research emphasizes the following important discoveries: (1) Rescuers, women and men alike, came from different social classes and diverse occupations. (2) They had deeply internalized values such as helpfulness, responsibility, fairness, justice, compassion, and friendship. (3) They had friends in groups outside of their own family circles or immediate communities. (4) They were tolerant of differences and felt responsible for many kinds of people. (5) They had high levels of self-confidence and self-esteem and were not afraid to take calculated risks. (6) They knew what was happening around them, and, in addition, benefitted from a supportive emotional network; typically their rescue efforts met with approval from family members or others who could be trusted. Once, Samuel Oliner shared with me his belief that, if he were in need of help and could identify persons with these qualities, his chances of receiving assistance would be excellent.

The ending of *Narrow Escapes* is different but related. Oliner concludes this edition of his story with a reference to the Hebrew saying, *Tikkun Haolam*, which urges mending of the world. When he invokes those Hebrew words, I cannot help but think that he is urging his readers to live in ways that do not leave Balwina and Shmulek—and their counterparts among us—so much alone. *Narrow Escapes*, indeed Samuel Oliner's entire life, urgently bears witness: The mending of a world scarred by the Holocaust depends on what kind of "just people" we help each other to be.

John K. Roth
Russell K. Pitzer Professor of Philosophy
Claremont McKenna College

INTRODUCTION

I was born in 1930 of Jewish parents in Zyndranowa, a village near the town of Dukla in southern Poland. I was nine years of age when the Nazis invaded Poland. In 1942 my family was exterminated along with the other inhabitants of the Bobowa and Gorlice ghettos, but I was able to escape. With the help of a Polish woman, Balwina Piecuch, and her family (see photo page 144) I assumed a Polish identity and found a job as a cowhand on a farm not far from where I was born. Although I lived in constant dread of discovery and suffered many narrow escapes, I did not experience the concentration camp brutality. Yet the memories of my boyhood haunt me and I have felt compelled to write them down and share them.

My memories encompass the complex family relationships which were the stuff of my boyhood, the Nazi occupation and my life as an ersatz Pole during the war. While my story is a strictly personal one in that it is simply an account of what happened to one boy, I believe it also reveals something of Jewish and Polish life during this period. Unlike many other survivors, I lived the war years among ordinary Poles and thus had an intimate view of how at least some reacted to the events.

Like many other survivors of the Holocaust, I feel an urgent need to bear witness to those years. I owe a debt to those who perished.

I also share a dim hope that knowledge of the past may somehow avert a similar future, despite considerable evidence to the contrary. Indeed, it has been suggested by some that, given an already established historical precedent, it may be easier to try again in the future with any target designated for extermination by virtue of color, ethnic identification, or whatever reason. I prefer to believe, because I have little choice, that those who remember the past will do all they can to prevent its recurrence; I fear the future if we dare to leave it in the hands of those who ignore or remain uninformed about the past.

In the epilogue I try to bring the story of my personal and professional life up to date, focusing on my academic work in the area of rescuers who risked their lives on behalf of Jews in Nazi-occupied Europe.

In 1990, a Mr. Teodor Gocz from the village of Zyndranowa, who knew me and my family, contacted me as a result of reading about me in a Polish newspaper. He informed me that one of the four Jewish homes belonging to my family in the village of Zyndranowa still remained standing. It had belonged to my maternal grandfather's brother, Zalman Polster, who was exterminated with other Jews. Afterward, the house was occupied by another Zyndranowa resident. Subsequently, this resident died, and the building became totally dilapidated. (See photo, front cover.) Mr. Gocz suggested that I help to rebuild it and make it into a local, regional Jewish museum. I was very moved by this suggestion, because for me it meant that I might be able to rescue the memory of those loved ones who perished in that region of Poland close to the Slovak border. After obtaining funds, I was able to have the museum rebuilt, and then we were able to gather enough Jewish artifacts including various enlarged photographs of Jews who had lived in the region and who had perished.

On June 25, 1994, Mr. Gocz arranged a grand opening of the Zalman museum to which I was invited along with my rescuer's son Staszek and his family. Upon my arrival and to my great astonishment, there were hundreds of people including the Polish minister of culture (who came from Warsaw especially for the occasion) and German, Slovak, and Polish television and newspaper journalists. I had expected only the village elders, Mr. Gocz, and some villagers. I was asked to give some remarks, which appear on pages 200-202. In closing, I said, "I want to conclude these remarks here today on this very special occasion by saying that it is somehow fitting that someone in Poland saved my life and now a wonderful, caring group of people had such a wonderful vision to save the memory and culture of the people of the Hitlerian mass murder."

I reemphasize that I am grateful to Mr. Gocz for this honor he has bestowed upon my dead family. In addition, I want to honor those altruistic souls, Gentiles and Jews alike, who risked much to help others. They are living testimony to the human capacity to resist perversion even in an environment saturated with evil and madness. It is a strange irony of history that the names and deeds of the righteous are more quickly forgotten than those of tyrants and killers. By writing these words in this book, I am trying to ensure that we remember not just the evil but the goodness, such as was demonstrated by Balwina Piecuch, Mr. Gocz, and the other ordinary people who took a moral stand and made a difference.

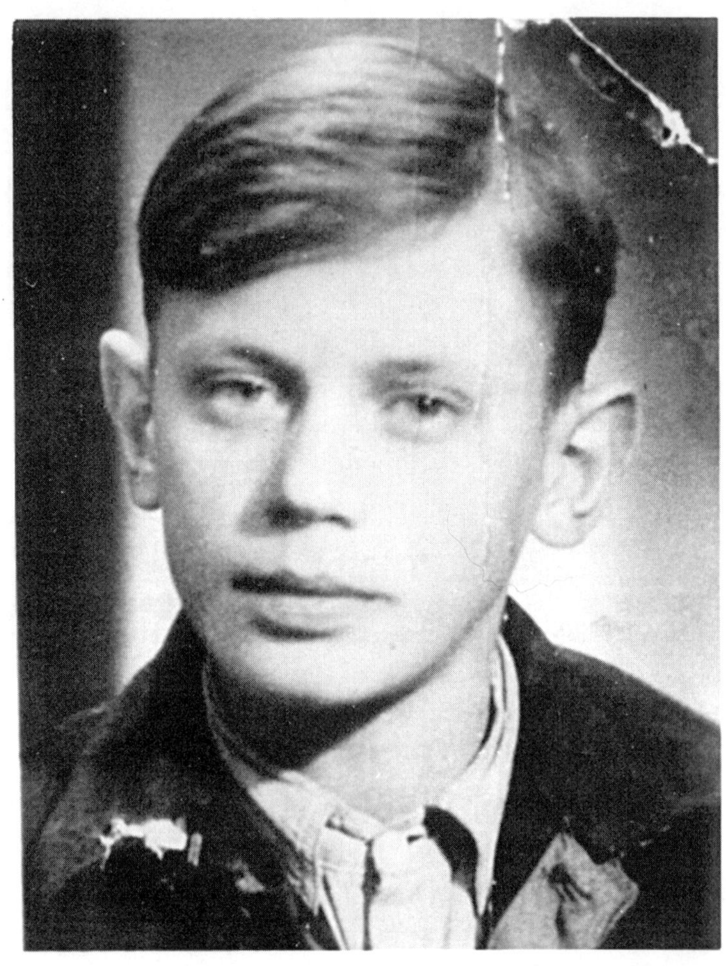

Photo 1943
Samuel P. Oliner, also known as Juzek Polewski between 1942-1945

THE ESCAPE

ESTER WAS MY STEPMOTHER, my father's second wife. She was dressed in the rags she had sewn and patched and somehow managed to make presentable, and her face was grey and a little swollen. Her eyes frightened me. The dark rings under them made them look like holes in her head, and when I was in the house they seemed to follow me, accusing me of something. I felt she hated me for some unknown reason.

Avoiding her, I crossed the room with a burlap sack on my shoulder. My father looked up from where he was sitting at the wooden table along the far wall. He looked right at me and his face was hard and expressionless. With him was my grandfather Herman Polster, my father's father. During those trying times, they spent their days going to Shul (temple), reading the scriptures and meditating. "God will save us," my father said day in and day out; "God has always taken care of the Jews." My grandfather said very little. His farm had been taken away by the Germans. His shoulders were withered and bent like a burned-up match and he spent much of his time just staring at things and coughing from asthma.

Unlike the rest of the family, I had blond hair. Once I got through a hole in the barbed wire fence surrounding the ghetto and was quite free to walk about and steal things.

This made me proud and I couldn't see why the rest of the family didn't seem to appreciate my good luck.

In the burlap sack was a rabbit I had stolen in the Polish sector and then killed. I dumped the rabbit on the floor and threw the sack over by the door. Without a word, my stepmother picked up the rabbit by a hind leg and took it to a far corner. There she immediately started to dress it.

I waited for someone to say a word of hope or approval to me.

My father said: "Ester, must you clean that animal here in the house where we live?"

Without looking up or stopping her work, my stepmother replied:

"And would you have me clean it on the doorstep for all our starving neighbors to see? It would be a cruel trick to play on those poor people." She was referring to the wandering beggars who looked into people's windows and if they saw food knocked on the door and begged for something to eat.

He turned back to the table, where the scriptures lay open. My grandfather just sat and stared. I was never sure what he was looking at, because he didn't seem to see anything. On the straw mattress along the wall where we all slept together at night, my younger stepsister Jaffa played with my stepbrother Shaia. They pulled out bits of straw through the holes in the mattress and let them fall from their little hands. Another family lived with us in this tiny room; on a mattress along the opposite wall a woman was asleep. She had two small sons.

"Where are the boys?" I asked.

Without looking up from the rabbit, which was bleeding on the floor, my stepmother said: "They are out with their father. He is a heartbroken man."

She covered the remains of the rabbit with a rag. In the morning she would scrub the floor with soap and water, if soap could be found. Otherwise, she would scrub the floor with water and sweep it clean with a homemade broom. On a tin can heated with coals, she began to cook our supper.

"This sort of thing I don't like," said my father, his head bent over the scriptures. "To see my family eat the food of the gentiles. "

"Shmulek has brought us food for our bellies," said my stepmother, turning her dark approving eyes on me.

"I don't like it."

My stepmother continued to cook the rabbit and my father said no more. My stepsister was named Jaffa after my real mother, who had died. What my father had to do with Ester, his second wife, was none of my business. She sometimes cried in the middle of the night, and in the darkness I heard her sobs. My father never cried.

Still standing in the middle of the room, where I had dropped the rabbit, I felt hurt and angry. There was nothing for me in this overcrowded, crumbling one room house; I ran outside. Tears came to my eyes and I clenched my teeth. The alley outside the door was cobblestone, broken in spots and very uneven. It was late afternoon and cold for July. Moss grew on the dark wet stone. The sky between the rooftops overhead was grey. The buildings covered by tin, shingle or tar-paper roofs looked as if they were about to fall in on me.

The sides of the alley were strewn with bits of dirt, rubbish, and black and soggy leaves. During the early part of the day children played games with rocks. I wanted no part of such games. I was twelve and felt like a man.

As I looked down the alley, the cold air made me shiver. The smell of the cooking rabbit came from inside the house. Such food or any other meat was rarely eaten in the ghetto and my mouth watered. I felt a wave of self-pity. I didn't want to go back into the house. It was a house of despair, but I did not want to remain outside, either. I kept wondering why the Nazis made us leave the villages which had been home to us for decades. The streets of the Bobowa ghetto were frightening. The men walked hunched in the shadow of the decrepit buildings and scarcely spoke to each other. Mothers tried to find food for their babies, and the babies cried from hunger. Very few Jews would have delicious rabbit for supper. If a Jew was discovered in the Polish sector, he was immediately turned over to the Gestapo. If it was the Nazis who found him, he was most likely shot on the spot. Some Poles made it their business to be on the alert for Jews because it was profitable to report them to the Gestapo. They were known as *Szmalcowniks.*

For two months now, we had lived in the ghetto. Two months of hunger, sickness, and fear. The Nazis said they were preparing a new life for us, and that the ghetto was only a temporary measure.

Some people were even talking about resettlement in the East. This the rabbis and members of the *Judenrat* repeated and the Jewish people believed. The ghetto was surrounded with barbed wire and there was only one main gate. The Nazis said they had our best interests at heart, and sometimes the heavy gate of wood and wire would swing open. Jeeps came through carrying young German men in uniform barely old enough to have hair on their face. They had blue eyes and pink faces, and as they drove through the streets they would take fun in shooting at people who happened to be along the way. When I saw these Germans, their pink faces reminded me of the flesh of swine.

A cold breeze blew and dust scuttled past me down the alley. The smell of rabbit made me hungry. By now the sun had gone down, and in the strip of grey sky at the end of the alley I could see the moon. It was flat and cold-looking, like a round silver coin. There were no sounds in the air and the buildings were black. No one would bother to call me for supper, and I didn't have the courage to go back into the house. The cold air made me shiver.

Then there was the sound of a stone rattling along the cobblestones, and a man came around the corner of the alley. I didn't know his name. He carried his small son against his chest, and his steps were slow and weary. The slightly older son tagged along by his father's pant leg. We had lived with them for two months and I didn't even know the names of the boys. The man shuffled along in the deepening gloom, coming at last to the doorstep. Shoulders hunched under the ragged cloth jacket, he cast a brief glance at me. One of the reasons I avoided the streets of the ghetto was that the people you met spoke with their eyes. It made me upset and angry and I looked off in the other direction. The man climbed the doorstep and went into the house. His young son climbed after him.

The rabbit was on the makeshift table. A candle lit what was to be our dinner. Candles were hard to come by. I didn't know how Ester got them. The family, including the woman who had been asleep on the mattress, was gathered around the table and my father's head was bowed over his clasped hands. No one moved or said anything as we joined the table. I sat on a wooden crate I had found in another alley. My stomach was so empty that my whole body felt weak. The candle was burning down. My father prayed a long time without moving and the rest of us awaited his signal. Finally he said, "Forgive us, oh Lord, for eating this unkosher food, but we must do it to keep our bodies from falling apart."

He raised his head and stared at the rabbit. No one made a move toward it. My belly quivered and I had to swallow my saliva. Then father gave the signal and the supper began. No words were spoken and the bones were chewed clean.

A single rabbit does not go very far among nine people and when we were finished my belly still ached from hunger. In a small sack in the corner my stepmother had some flour for bread. We had to save it for another day. The *Judenrat* kitchen (a communal kitchen for the poor) gave us some food, but hardly enough.

"I went to see the rabbi this afternoon," said the father of the two boys. His eyes were on the table. "The rabbi says the persecution will not last forever. God is just testing the Jewish people's faithfulness to Him. He says the Messiah will come and that God will protect us." The man's wife got up from the table. She went over to her mattress and took the two boys with her. "He says we should pray and have faith, the Lord knows what He is doing."

"God will help us. He will protect us," said my father. My stepmother let out a low sigh. "He will forgive our lack of faith," said my father.

Ester got up from the table. She cleared away the bones and put the tin plates by the door to be washed in the morning. The candle was sputtering. During those times, when I sneaked out of the ghetto in order to steal things for the family, I often took the opportunity to walk about the Polish countryside. This was done illegally, of course, but I looked Aryan enough not to arouse suspicion. During those walks I often wondered why the Nazis had packed us all into small places. Back in the ghetto, I asked this question of the elders and their reply was: "Only God knows why the Nazis have taken us from our homes." But some did say that the Germans are a very civilized people who would not hurt the innocent. After all, we Jews have not done anything harmful to the

Germans. We are guilty of nothing. That felt reassuring.

The candle sputtered one last time and went out and everyone prepared for bed. Tomorrow would be Friday, and *Shabbat* would begin. Before the war *Shabbat* was a joyous occasion. Shops and factories closed down early on Friday afternoon and women started to cook special meals. Special breads and cakes would be baked too. Pleasant aromas would come from Jewish homes and the time would be one of peace and happiness.

Shabbat was no longer a joyous event, nonetheless it was strictly observed.

I lay on the edge of the mattress with my coat over my pajamas to keep warm. Ester was beside me. My father was already snoring and I was aware of the silence of the deadly quiet night. Even the babies, who could often be heard crying at this time of night, were quiet. The Polish peasants told tales about men covered with hair, who prowled on nights like this. I shivered from the cold and discomfort. I felt as if I were being watched, as if someone were making special plans for me. I prayed to God that it be He.

Dreams were spinning wildly in my head. I saw a gaping hole in the ground that seemed to draw me into its murky darkness. Somehow, I knew the hole was my mother's grave and that it was waiting for me. The grave was empty and I was soaked with perspiration. There were loud noises and a terrible confusion. There was an explosion and I awakened so suddenly I fell off the edge of the mattress. Outside the house it was still dark and I could hear gunshots and people screaming. My father and the other man we lived with were at the window, staring out into the darkness. "The Nazis are here!" said my father. Ester gasped and one of the children started to cry. From outside came the sound of deep, snarling voices: *"Alle Juden raus . . . raus!"* People were screaming right outside our door. Children were crying.

Ester cried, "My God, my God, what are they going to do to us now? What are those Germans going to do to us?" There was a noise right outside the door and Ester started sobbing, gathering the children fearfully into her arms. My father ran outside to see what was going on. Immediately, my grandfather started praying:

"God help us. God, what's happening? God protect us."

I jumped up from the mattress. Someone ran into me and I tripped on some twisted blankets and fell. Everyone was running around in the dark and before I could get up someone stepped on me. I got up and pushed my way to the door. Outside, people were milling everywhere, yelling and crying. Men in military uniforms were herding them with clubs and rifle butts to the marketplace called Rynek (city square). My father ran back into the house.

"The trucks are coming to get us. At the marketplace they're beating us and loading us onto huge army trucks. I guess we are just leaving, to where I don't exactly know.

"What are they going to do to us? What are they going to do to us?" cried Ester. I went over to her and said: "Mother, don't be afraid. God will save us."

"Oh, God! Help us, save us. What are they going to do to us?"

Still wearing my pajamas, I ran out of the house. The houses were one story high, with sloping roofs, and I climbed up on the roof and stayed there for a while hugging close to the tar paper and listening to the cries and sounds of terror. The sky was pink, the color of a baby's skin; everything else was black. I crawled to the edge of the roof and looked down. A woman was trying to hide her small child in a garden overgrown with weeds. The weeds were very tall and she crouched down, protecting the small body with her own. The child started crying. She shushed and fumbled to keep it quiet, but it was too late. A Nazi hit her with his rifle butt and stabbed the child with his bayonet.

The soldiers were going from door to door, shouting, *"Alle Juden raus!"* and pushing the people toward the market place, a square in the middle of the ghetto. I was still in my pajamas. I saw a soldier throw a small child through the window of a tall house. Another soldier was dragging a woman by the arm. She was holding back and fighting him, begging him to leave her alone. She was wearing only a nightgown; her legs and feet were bare. The soldier yanked her ahead of him and hit her in the face with his rifle butt. I was crying quiet stinging tears and could not seem to catch my breath.

After a while, I got down off the roof and sneaked back into the house. My father was gone. Ester was holding the small children to her breast and rocking back and forth. She stared at me wildly for a moment, as if I were some sort of alien, and then she leaned forward and savagely whispered:

"Antloif mein kind und du vest bleiben beim leben," ("Run, my child; run away so that you will save yourself.")

"But Mother, where shall I go?"

"Go. Go anywhere. Hide. Hide. Hide. They're killing us all. I am sure of it now. The trucks are taking people from the marketplace to unknown places of slaughter." I backed away from her and turned toward the door.

"Shmulek...." I turned around. She stared at me for a long time, and her dark accusing eyes sent shivers up my spine. I wanted to run and I wanted to stay. I didn't know what I wanted to do.

"Shmulek...I love you. I know God will protect you."

Bursting into tears, I ran toward her, but she pushed me away. "Go. There is no time. Go quickly and hide. Run into the countryside. Save yourself." She had a premonition that this was the end.

I ran outside, still in my pajamas. People hurried past the end of the alley, clutching their few belongings. In groups and in pairs, they hurried past, pushed from behind by the uniformed Germans. A young girl broke away from the rest. She threw down the bundle she was carrying and ran down the alley. A Nazi guard saw her and aimed his rifle. Then, seeing me, he swung the rifle in my direction. I ducked around a corner just as a shot rang out; above my head a board exploded into splinters. Breathing hard, I climbed up onto the roof where I had hidden earlier. The flat sloping roof had been used as a storage place and I covered myself with old boards and pieces of rubbish.

The sun climbed slowly and the tar paper got warm and soft. Gradually, the shouting, screaming, and occasional gunshots subsided. All day long, there was the sound of heavy trucks. Hiding where I was, under planks and rubbish, I felt sick. Dust made my throat and chest hurt and the smell of tar paper heated by the sun made me sick. I drifted into a daze, a sort of dreaming wakefulness and flies crawled on my ear. Whenever there was a noise close by, my heart beat so hard I thought it would burst.

By late afternoon the ghetto was quiet. The people had stopped crying, the Nazis had stopped shouting, and the trucks had stopped roaring in the streets. The ghetto was like a ghost town. A small, quiet breeze drifted dust on my neck from the thin boards that covered me. At one time, long, long ago, these breezes had been redolent with animal smells and alive with the sound of human voices; now, I felt there was no one left for the breezes to touch. Like the blood flowing through my veins, a feeling of great loneliness filled my body, and I wondered if I were actually dead. Maybe I was dead and my lot through eternity was to lie under these boards and listen to the breeze in absolute stillness.

I began to hear quiet sounds. I heard Polish words and muffled laughter, shuffling and scurrying. I slowly crawled out from under the boards; I was as still as I could be, and I was aching with an awful longing. At the edge of the roof, I looked down in time to see two Poles emerging from a house about half a block away. I recognized one man. Before the war, my father had done business with him on market day. He was a Pole from a neighboring village, and I watched him emerge from the house with some curtains in his hand. The other man was dragging a ragged mattress behind him.

I waited until they had gone out of sight. Then, making sure no one else was on the street, I climbed down from the roof. My pajamas were a dead giveaway that I was a Jew, and so I searched through some houses until I found some clothing. A strange feeling crept over me as I put on a pair of pants with neat patches sewn on the knees. A breakfast of bread, baked under crude conditions and with black crust on the sides, was laid on the table. The floorboards were splintered but swept clean; in the corner was a forgotten prayer book. My mouth was dry, my knees weak. I felt like a grave robber and prayed for forgiveness. The ghosts of the people who had lived there spoke to me with their unseen eyes. They seemed to say it was all right to take the clothes, that it was better to keep a fellow Jew warm than to clothe a rampaging Pole as they themselves had no further use for the material. A wooden shutter creaked outside the broken window and my body was filled with fear. I couldn't stand to remain in the house another moment.

Much as I wanted to run to my father's house, I was afraid and chose the other direction. The *shtetl* consisted of wood and brick buildings with narrow alleys of cobblestone or dirt. The roofs of tin glinted in the afternoon sunlight; it was a sight, with no one, it seemed, to see it but me. Then I heard the sound of boot heels and I peeked cautiously around the corner of a building. Six Germans, or Ukrainians in German uniform, were walking down the main street.

They split up and searched from house to house, cellar to cellar. Flattened against the wet decayed wall of a building, I watched a soldier approach one particular house. Moss grew on the roof and moisture made dark streaks down the wood of the outer wall. As he pushed open the door, a young woman rushed out. She threw herself at him, insisting there was no one else in the house. He laughed and grabbed her waist, pulling her to his chest. Her body sagged and she didn't fight him, but I could see her eyes squeezed tightly shut. Then there was the cry of a baby. The soldier, who was a Ukrainian in the service of the German army, hit the woman and knocked her down; then he turned and strode into the house. The woman) jumped to her feet and rushed after him, but as she reached the doorway a pistol shot went off inside the house, and she fainted right there on the doorstep.

I left the wall where I was hiding and ran. Bile was coming up in my throat. I was in a daze and I ran and ran, stumbling on the broken uneven road. Finally I stopped and leaned against a wall to catch my breath. In front of me was an old shop with boards nailed over the windows. My chest hurt, my knees were weak and I started to slide along the wall. Suddenly I remembered the picture.

Of all my possessions, I valued most the picture of my mother. It was in my father's house. In the confusion of my mind, the picture stood out as being of vital importance and I was sure I couldn't take another step without it. The ghetto was a very dangerous place to be in and my stepmother had said, "Go!" but I simply had to retrace my steps. The marketplace was on a sort of plateau. It consisted of four of cobblestones and trees, shaped like a square. This area I avoided because it was where the Jews had been loaded onto German military trucks. Keeping an eye open for the Nazis and Polish looters as well, I arrived at my father's house. It was a sad-looking structure, with a low roof and rotting door posts. Saddest of all was the stillness in it. Swallowing my fear, I entered the door I had gone through so many times in the past two months. The room was empty: only twisted bedding and a wreckage of personal belongings remained. Some looters had been there already. Something tore loose within me and I sank to the floor. Small childish sobs wouldn't come. My chest felt crushed with the agony of an entire people. On my hands and knees, blinded by tears, I searched for the photograph. Nowhere was it to be found. I had lost my family and even the picture of my mother.

As I wormed through hedges and crawled along the sides of buildings, one thought filled my mind: ESCAPE. As I neared the barbed wire fence that partially surrounded the ghetto, I saw a young Polish boy. He had a fat, white face and crooked teeth, and I'd had several fights with him in the past. Of course, he spotted me, and immediately sounded off. *"Jude! Jude!"* Frantically, I searched for a way of escape, but I was at the edge of the ghetto and there was no going back nor any way out. Trapped, I rushed at the boy, desperately intent on choking the voice that was giving me away. The boy's eyes widened with fear. He dodged me and ran off screaming that a Jew was trying to kill him. Shaking like a leaf, I stumbled into one of those old broken-down houses on the edge of the ghetto and hid in a small closet.

Very quickly it grew dark outside and I spent the night in the house. There were dark and fearful sounds to keep me awake: the wind kicking garbage about, the noise of a board turned over, or of a door pushed open and then closed. Once I heard a sob and then, sometime later, there was a small, thin laugh in the darkness. Loudest of all was the pounding of my heart as I waited for some Nazi to open the door of the closet with his cold blue rifle barrel. Only toward dawn did I manage to drift in and out of sleep.

Sleep was no more comforting than reality. It was filled with the faces of my family staring at me: not just my father and my stepbrother and stepsister, but my real mother as well. Also Feigele, my oldest sister, and Moishe, my oldest brother, whom I hadn't seen since I was put in the ghetto. All the while the dark accusing eyes of Ester stared at me as she clutched her children and said, "I love you."

In the morning I realized I should have escaped during the night. The golden opportunity had come and gone. Now the Nazis were up and about, once more mopping up the ghetto; if I were killed, it would be my own fault. I was so scared I could barely open my mouth, but I practiced being calm in case I had to speak to anyone.

Pushing open the closet door, I looked out into the room. Through the window the sun made yellow squares on the floor. The window panels were filmy and glared in the sunlight. I sneaked to the door of the house: pushing it open, I peeked outside. Mist was rising from the lane, which was dark and muddy. My clothing was caked with mud from the day before and the cool air made me shiver. The buildings along the lane were black and empty.

I left the house cautiously. I breathed deeply and my belly growled. The ache of hunger was intense, making my feet numb and my head empty. As I stood there, wondering which way to go, a Nazi came around the corner of a building.

"Halt!" he said, yanking the rifle off his shoulder and pointing it at me. "Who are you?"

"Oh, I'm not Jewish."

Astonished at my own voice, I waited, holding my breath and expecting the Nazi to pull the trigger at any moment. He was a big man, with short blond hair and slightly brown teeth. Looking me over from head to foot, he tried to make up his mind. Just then, another kid ran from the tangled hedge next to the house, crying for his mother in Yiddish, "Mamma, Mamma, Mamma."

The guard took off after him and I ran in the opposite direction. Very clearly the shots rang out. I ran along the barbed wire fence and then ducked down a narrow lane. The somber windows of the empty houses stared at me as I slipped and skidded in the mud. Across a narrow footbridge past a rickety wooden fence covered with vines was the main road. Throwing caution to the wind, I raced across the bridge. Not far from the main gate someone had cut a hole in the fence. It was my luck to notice it and I ran through it and into the Polish sector of Bobowa.

The Poles were conducting their business as if everything was normal. Dogs barked and wooden carts creaked along the road. A man in a homespun shirt was harnessing his horse. Noticing my hurry, he stopped and looked at me. "Hey, are you a Jew?" He came toward me and I dodged down an alley. Dogs ran after me, barking at my heels. I stopped long enough to throw rocks at them and then I went through town as quickly as possible without arousing further suspicion.

The country surrounding Bobowa was mildly hilly with scattered villages in the valleys. The Carpathian winters were very cold. Roads were poor the year round, deeply rutted, at certain points sloping into ravines. It was now summertime and the roads were very muddy. The mud was cold and my feet were bare following the road away from Bobowa. I didn't look back. I wondered what had happened to my parents and to the Jews of Bobowa. Where could they have been taken. Then I remembered the rumors in the ghetto about resettlement somewhere in the East. But where in the East? I kept thinking. Will I ever see my family again? I kept hoping. My mind felt empty and dead. Wild grasses grew green along the hillsides. Cattle were in the high pastures; as I trudged along I wished I were a cow with food and shelter and nothing in the world to worry about.

Toward noon I came upon a farmer digging a ditch along the road. He wore a coarse homespun jacket and wooden shoes. His face was brown from exposure to the weather; a rough, grey stubble was on his chin. Taking courage, I approached him.

"Please, sir, could you give me some bread? I haven't eaten in two days."

He leaned on the wooden shovel he had been working with and sized me up. I was certain he could tell I was a Jew. But I was too tired and hungry to run. Besides, where was I to go? The world seemed nothing but a cold and muddy road cut through hillsides of green and brown grass. When the farmer smiled, I saw that many of his teeth were missing.

"Come to my house and I'll give you some bread."

We walked toward a farmhouse on the side of a hill. A little trail of smoke came from the chimney. Behind the house was a shed, called *stodola,* for the animals.

"It looks like the Germans have cleaned out the wretched Jews from Bobowa," said the farmer. His footsteps were slow and methodical, but I had to hurry a little to keep up with him.

"What did they do with them? Where did the Germans take the Jews?" I asked.

"Oh, Jacek, my neighbor, told me they took them all to Garbacz."

"Where's that?" I tried not to sound too interested. The farmer squinted a little as he strode along.

"About fifteen kilometers up in the woods, not far from the village of Mszanka."

"And there, what are they going to do with them?"

The farmer laughed as if I had said something funny. "The Germans took care of everything," he said. "They shot every last one in a huge mass grave. "

I stumbled and nearly fell and heard my voice burst out: "They shot them all?"

"Yes. Every one."

"But how can they shoot so many people?"

"They kept shooting them with machine guns all day long and some of them just fell into the graves from the planks that were put across the mass grave."

"Does that mean that some people were alive when they fell into the grave?"

"Naked bodies, both dead and alive were piled up one on top of another and covered up with chemicals and earth. Some, who were still alive and were on top of the pile of bodies, crawled out and ran away. A peasant saw one of these people; he looked totally insane—as if his brain had snapped."

DEATH IS ONLY FOR A LITTLE WHILE

I WAS BORN IN 1930 in the village of Zyndranowa, where houses had no electricity or plumbing. Although the village was located high in the Carpathian Mountains, near the Czechoslovakian border, the country around Zyndranowa was relatively flat. Small patches of woods provided lumber for buildings, fencing and firewood, and there was ample land for crops and pasture.

Before the war, my mother's father, Isak Polster, who was Herman Polster's brother, owned a small farm in this village. He was a tall man, slim and bearded (see photo page 104, dated approx. 1934-37). A sensitive person, learned in the tradition of Judaica, he looked stately even when wearing crude working clothes. Using the crudest of instruments, Isak tilled the soil with his one-eyed horse, whom he treated with respect. At the crack of dawn he took the sacks of seed out to the field and by the day's end he came back, sunburned and tired, along with his younger son, Mendel.

In a gray, large log house set among trees, my grandfather Isak lived with my grandmother Reisel. A wooden fence surrounded their yard. On this fence honeysuckle grew and there I learned to look for sparrows who hopped among the vines seeking insects and other food. A little way past this fence was a cabin built of logs where my parents lived, and it was there that I was born. My father owned a little land in the area and had also a general store in the village. He always had something to do and rarely did I see him during my early childhood.

My mother was a quiet, soft woman. I remember her pleasant fragrance and gentle voice. Every Friday she would bake special things for *Shabbat,* and I took great pleasure eating her cookies, *rogelech* and *kichelech. Shabbat* was a day we all looked forward to. The very best of meals were prepared for this occasion and the whole family would sit down together. We ate and said prayers. Together we sang songs. As kind and thoughtful as my grandfather was, he couldn't seem to get along with his wife. They slept in the same room, raised a family, and lived their daily lives without talking to each other. If communication was absolutely necessary, they achieved it indirectly, speaking to one another in the third person, but even they could not help but be amicable during *Shabbat.* No matter how unhappy or poor a man was, he always tried to get into the spirit of festivity at this time. (Exactly when my grandparents stopped talking to each other, I don't know. Nor do I know the cause. This was a topic my family didn't discuss. Most important to me at this time was that both grandparents loved me very much.)

Living with my grandparents were their two sons, Mendel and Mordecai. With my parents and me, in the log cabin, were my older sister, Feigele, and my older brother Moishe. There was always the good feeling of having one's family close by.

When I was about six years old, my mother got sick. Mendel and Mordecai were jovial and friendly, but I had the feeling that something was seriously wrong. She coughed a lot and got very thin.

One day I ran to her bedside and looked into her dark eyes. "Mamma, what's wrong?" She said nothing, and only looked at me. She was like an angel to me—my mother—dark and beautiful. It was she who soothed my aches and I wanted desperately to make her well.

At last she said, "It's nothing, my son. You go run outside and play."

"But mamma!"

She started coughing; with tears in my eyes I ran outside. The sun was hot on the logs of the cabin. Strips of bark were curled out away from the wall. Dust was warm and deep between my bared toes and insects buzzed in the air. A breeze stirred the leaves on the trees alongside grandfather Isak's house and I couldn't believe there could be sickness on such a fine day. Mendel was harnessing the horse. My father came out of the barn carrying a load of straw, which he put in the back of the wagon; then he went into the cabin. When he came back outside, mother was in his arms. She looked as light as a baby with her arms around his neck. He carried her to the wagon and made her comfortable on the straw. Then he and Mendel climbed onto the wagon seat. The horse quivered when the reins struck its back. Its brown hide twitched; then it broke into a slow walk, straining against the harness. Grandmother Reisel came from the big house wiping her hands on her apron. She had a rather square body, grey hair tied in back of her head, and deep lines on her face. She stood next to me and watched the wagon down the lane; then she put her hand on my shoulder.

"Where are they taking her?" I asked.

Without a word, she pulled me toward her and I buried my head in her apron. Behind us I heard footsteps and then my grandfather's voice: "I see they've finally gone."

"If Isak's good-for-nothing son Mordecai were here," said my grandmother, "he could have gone with them."

The sun climbed in the sky. The day warmed up, briefly, then quickly cooled; the passage of time was dreadfully slow.

When the wagon returned, my mother was not in it. Darkness had fallen. I was in the kitchen of the big house and the lamp on the table made shadows on the walls. My father came into the house and stood next to my grandmother. She would not look at him. He said, "I did all I could." She pounded the dough she had been kneading. Her mouth was set in a straight hard line.

"Where's Mamma?" I cried, running to him.

"I'm going to the cabin," he said. "The boy can spend the night here."

"What about the other two?" asked my grandmother, still pounding the dough.

"I will send them over."

He left the house stomping his boots loudly on the porch. When he stomped like that it usually meant he was angry and we were in for a rough night. Now my mother was gone. My brother, my sister and I were staying at the big house, and my father would be angry all alone. I was very scared. No one would tell me what was the matter with mother. All I knew was that she had gone away from home and I began counting the days since she had left. With a rock I made marks on a board at the back of the barn. Soon the board was covered with marks.

At first my father said, "She is in a hospital." Then he said, "She is in a rooming house in Dukla."

One day I rounded the corner of the barn and came upon Mendel and my sister Feigele. She had long dark hair and a chest as big as mother's. Her eyes were dark as night, her skin smooth as the cream of milk, and Mendel often seemed to have trouble breathing when she was near. She was standing next to the side of the barn holding chicken eggs in her apron, and Mendel was leaning against the wooden rail of the fence. Feigele was crying. At first I thought Mendel had hurt her, but then I knew he would not do such a thing.

Above all else he was a gentle, loyal person who was always kind to everyone in spite of the extremely hard life he led as a farmer. With the exception of Friday and Saturday, he worked sixteen hours a day with hoe and pick in hand.

Then I heard Feigele say "mother." With one hand she held an apron full of eggs, with the other she covered her face. Upon seeing me, she quickly wiped her face, took the apron in both hands, and walked past me toward my grandparents' house. Mendel turned around slowly. In order to see me he had to turn past me a little because one of his eyes had been damaged in an accident.

"What's wrong with Feigele? What happened to mamma?"

The muscles of Mendel's jaw bulged out and I could see he was upset. I watched his damaged eye, which looked white, and waited for him to say something, but he turned his shoulder and walked away slowly.

Since my mother had been gone, Feigele, Moishe, and I spent most of our time at the big house. My father was there occasionally, but grandfather Isak didn't have much to say to him and Reisel didn't speak to him at all if she could help it. Most of the time, she wouldn't even look at him.

It was at the evening meal that my grandmother announced that she would accompany my father to Dukla the following day. Isak sat at the head of the table. He neither looked at Reisel nor spoke to her directly.

"Will Reisel go alone?" he said.

"I would like to go with her," said Mordecai. He had a shaggy head that usually found its way into dark places. Certainly, he didn't spend much time in the fields.

Isak said. "When there is work to be done you're nowhere to be found, but let there be business in Dukla and you want to be the first in line."

"I would like the company of Mendel," said grandmother.

Mordecai hit the table with his fist.

"Mendel this, Mendel that. If he is so good in the fields, let him spend his time there. Jaffa is my sister, too, and I have as much right as anyone to see her. "

"The table is no place for a fist and a voice raised against one's brother," said Isak.

"I, also, would like to go," said Mendel. "But I will gladly stay home and work in the fields."

"You see?" said Mordecai. "Mendel is such a good son. He will tend the crops!"

"I would like Mendel to go with me to Dukla," said grandmother. "The crops can wait for one day."

Mordecai got up from the table and left the house. Grandfather Isak called after him, but there was no response. I ate quickly to avoid the tension as much as possible. Feigele was evidently not hungry. Mendel went out to look for Mordecai and Feigele excused herself. Only Moishe and I remained at the table with my grandparents. "Come, Moishe, eat your food," said my grandmother. "You need good food to grow up strong like your uncle Mendel. Come, eat while it's still hot."

"Where's Papa?" asked Moishe.

"Don't worry about him. He can take care of himself."

Mendel returned and sat down at the table. He worked very

hard and he was hungry. I was the first one finished, and, after waiting a few minutes, was excused. Before long, Moishe was also excused, and we went to the bedroom. Through the wall we could hear the voices from the other room.

"Where is that black sheep Mordecai?"

"I don't know. I searched outside and called his name, but he was nowhere to be found. Possibly, he went off into the fields. "

"In the dark?"

"I don't know. The shepherds say they've seen him up in the pastures with peasant women. From time to time, he has been seen with gypsy women, too. The shepherds tell stories of his doings."

"No peasant would be out on a night like this. The moon is full, and peasants are superstitious. They are afraid of the evil eye.

Grandmother Reisel said, "No good will come of Mordecai's foul doings."

"Maybe he did have the right to go to Dukla," said Mendel. "Jaffa is his sister, too. We may not see her again."

"Let us not talk of such a thing," replied grandmother.

"But you know the doctors said there is no cure."

Grandmother now said, "It is the fault of that stingy husband of hers. A business he has and land as well, but he says he can't afford anything better than a room in Dukla! Imagine shutting Jaffa off in a smelly room, separated from parents and children! If anything happens to her it will be his fault and no one else's. May the good Lord hang a weight of shame on him!"

"But, Mother, she has a sickness for which there is no cure. The doctors tried everything, and there is nothing they can do."

After a long silence we heard grandmother say, "Tomorrow we will do what we can."

Soon, the door of the room Moishe and I were in opened, and my grandparents and Mendel prepared for bed. All of us slept together in this one room, and I hid my face in the pillow so that no one would hear me cry. I didn't know why I cried. Certainly, I couldn't understand why my mother hadn't returned. Peeping up from the pillow, I could see Feigele along the far wall. When she was upset, her appetite failed her and all she would do is sleep.

Early the next morning, the horse and cart took off for Dukla. On the wagon seat were my father, my grandmother, and Mendel. Mordecai was off somewhere. Moishe and I began to cry.

" Don't worry," said grandfather. "Everything will be all right."

As the wagon bounced down the lane, he watched it steadily for a while, then he went out to the field, where he spent most of the day.

All day long I waited for the cart to return. My grandmother had made some sandwiches for lunch but they tasted dry and harsh. The morning turned into afternoon and then it began to get dark. Grandfather lighted the kerosene lamps in the house. I waited outside on the porch. A dog barked on a neighboring farm.

Finally, I saw a black object on the horizon, and I waited as the wagon approached the farm. In the dusk, I thought I could see my mother on the wagon seat. Oh, the joy that surged through my body! As the cart neared, however, I saw that the figure was my grandmother's. It was then that I had a terrible feeling. I wanted to run to the cart, but my feet stuck to the floor of the porch. The cart pulled up in front of the barn and my father climbed down. He walked straight to the little log cabin. Mendel got down from the wagon, too, but he walked around to the other side to help grandmother. She had remained seated, and he had to take her by the arm and gently urge her to move down. With trembling knees, I ran to the cart. Grandmother was smoothing her dress and Mendel was leading the horse towards the open barn door through which the yellow lantern light spilled onto the ground, "How is mamma? Is she coming home?"

Grandmother began to cry. She turned to me and said, "Your mother is dead.

I simply couldn't believe such a thing. How could one's Mother die? How could she bake special cookies and cakes for *Shabbat* if she wasn't coming home again? Through my tears I managed to say, "My mother is dead. But that is only for a short time, isn't it?"

Grandmother put her arms around me. "Yes. For a very, short time. Everything will be all right."

That night I went to bed wondering how short a time, death

would be. I was seven, and it did not occur to me that death was forever! The days dragged into weeks and the weeks into months; and I still kept believing my mother would return.

CHEDER AND MR. HERSHEL

AFTER MY MOTHER'S DEATH IN 1937, my father decided to leave the farm at Zyndranowa and go to the village of Mszanka to live with his father who had a small farm. This was perhaps a logical decision. When he wasn't attending to business in Zyndranowa he spent his time alone in the log cabin. Isak spoke to him very little and Reisel ignored him as much as possible. Now that my mother was dead, he didn't have to take any abuse from her parents.

Feigele, Moishe, and I were to stay with my maternal grandparents in Zyndranowa. Before my father could leave, the very important matter of my education had to be decided. I was seven years old and had not yet attended *cheder* (Hebrew school). Most children—at least the ones from towns—started *cheder* at the age of three or so. A Jew had to know how to pray, and to do this he had to know how to read Hebrew. Also, a Jewish man was judged not only by how good a provider and businessman he was, but also by how well versed he was in the Torah and in the Jewish tradition. Since I was illiterate at seven, my education was not off to a very good start.

"Shmulek will grow up to be a stupid goy!" lamented my grandmother.

I was in the kitchen of the big house having a crust of bread and warm milk. It was one of those rare occasions when my father was also at my grandparents' table.

"Then it is decided. He will attend *cheder,*" said my father. He was a big man with muscles on his chest and arms, and sometimes he looked at Reisel as if he would like to crush her.

"And where will he do this? There is no *cheder* in Zyndranowa, as you must know."

"Dukla has a *cheder.* I will send him there."

Reisel looked at my father. Her eyes seemed to have sparks in them. I grew very nervous but actually, it was all right with me if I never went to *cheder.* I got along very well without knowing the Jewish rituals one learned there. I would much rather have helped Mendel in the fields. The sound and smell of animals were comforting to me, and I had no desire to go to the town where my mother had died.

"And how will Shmulek get back and forth to the town, with his mother dead and you far away in Mszanka? Will he hitchhike on the roads, child that he is? Or do you expect Jaffa's parents to neglect the farm work in order to see to this matter?"

My father's eyes were black as he stared at her. His beard bulged as he tensed his jaw. Then, without saying a word, he pushed himself up from the table and strode out of the house. Grandmother brought me another piece of bread and smiled.

"Eat up, Shmulek. That's a good boy. You must grow up to be big and strong."

Turning away from me, she walked over to the cupboard and took down the sack of flour. I watched her prepare dough to make bread. The kitchen was quiet. A breeze came through the door my father had left open. Birds were singing in the trees outside.

Not until next day did I see my father again. He had evidently been on a journey of some sort and was very tired, but there was also a certain lightness to his step. Once more in the kitchen of the big house, he said, "I've made all the arrangements.

Everyone was at the table: Feigele, Moishe, uncles, grandparents and me. Isak looked at my father and waited for him to continue. In the light of the kerosene lamp, his face looked pale.

"Shmulek will live in Dukla with a man named Mr. Hershel. This man is partially blind. He has two sons who look after him, so the burden of his care will not be on Shmulek's shoulders. I have paid Mr. Hershel for Shmulek's lodging. Each day he will board in a different house."

Grandmother stared at him with hatred.

"Did you pay for his meals as well?"

"He will follow the tradition of *mitzvah.* Each day, a family will board him at minimum cost."

"Minimum cost! Charity, that's what I would call it," said grandmother. "Such a tradition is for the needy, not for the miser who wishes to save a few pennies. Did Jaffa rely on charity, too?"

"It is a good deed for which God will reward them, and besides they are getting paid. I have done what I can. I am Shmulek's father, and this is the way it will be."

Grandmother said no more. Moishe had been going to *cheder* all along, hitchhiking on the road. Feigele would be in Dukla as well, studying to be a nurse. At least, I would not be alone in the strange town.

The very next day my father hitched up the wagon and we were off. I sat huddled on the wagon seat. Watching the reins strike the horse's back, seeing the back quiver, I thought it would be a nice adventure to handle the horse, but this my father would not allow. My brother Moishe had driven the wagon when he was seven years old, but my father would not trust me with such a responsibility. That thought made me angry, and, in addition, I felt sick at leaving the farm.

Dukla was about twenty kilometers from Zyndranowa. The road was bumpy and I bounced around on the wagon seat. It wasn't very often that I got away from the farm, and traveling through the countryside was exciting. The relatively flat land of the valley was divided like a quilt into patches of woods and fields and acres of potatoes and grain. Set among clusters of trees were small farms. From the edge of the valley rose the foothills and high pastures. Up in these high pastures I could see cows and sheep. Sometimes there was the distant shape of a cowhand checking his herd. The farms in the foothills were usually located near the slope of the hill or some other kind of shelter. The winters in this part of Poland were very cold—so cold, in fact, that birds sometimes died in flight. The wind felt like the edge of a knife. The snowstorms came whistling down from the mountains and farmers took from the land what protection they could. Didn't grandfather Isak take special care to make sure plenty of wood was cut for the winter? I was very observant and knew a lot about these matters. I knew a lot more than my father gave me credit for.

Near Dukla, we started passing the homes of townspeople. Most of the houses had thatched roofs. The walls were made of mud and logs and attached to the houses were small, lean-to stables. Near some of the houses were wells, circled with stones and sometimes covered with thatching. Through the town of Dukla ran a river. The banks were muddy but the water reflected the sunlight. In the distance I could see a boy leading a couple of horses to drink. Along the edge of town, a little way upstream from this spot, some boys were swimming.

We drove on a dirt road leading into town. Once inside Dukla, we turned down a street paved with cobblestones.

People were everywhere. Carts were parked along the road and dogs ran about, barking and fighting over scraps of garbage. Some houses had tin roofs. Some of the poorer peasants actually slept with their animals. We passed one house that must have belonged to a very wealthy person because the stable was at a respectable distance from the house. It had a tin roof, just like the house, and was big enough for horses on one side and cows on the other. I wanted to ask my father if a house like that had running water, but he looked very quiet and I thought I'd better not bother him. We came to a crossroad and father held back the horse as a peasant got his cart out of the way; then we turned down another street set in cobblestones.

Presently we came to an old-looking house with wooden shutters and a crooked doorstep. My father pulled up the horse and hooked the reins over the wooden brake handle. He knocked on the door. We waited a while and he knocked again. A voice from the inside called, "Who's there?"

"Aron. Aron Oliner!"*

---

*Readers may wonder why my father's surname was Oliner instead of Polster: my father's mother was an Oliner who married my father's father who was a Polster. The wedding was a religious one, and since they did not bother to register

The door opened. Standing in the doorway was an old man with a grey beard whose shoulders were stooped. The cap he wore on his head looked ragged. In his hand he held a cane.

"I've brought my son, Shmulek, to lodge with you."

I watched the eyes which were turned downward and to the side. Shivers ran up my spine.

"Shmulek, this is Mr. Hershel. He will be your landlord. I'll come to Dukla every now and then to pay for your lodging and board, and also to see how you're doing in *cheder*. Listen to everything Mr. Hershel says, and do not disappoint your father."

I stood there, petrified, watching the eyes that couldn't see much. My father went to the wagon and returned with my few belongings; then he climbed up onto the wagon seat. With a wave of his hand he drove off.

"Come. Come, follow me," said Mr. Hershel, shuffling away from the door. I stepped inside. Tears were burning behind my eyelids, but I refused to cry. Mr. Hershel showed me where I was to sleep: a cot in the kitchen by the stove. The kitchen seemed empty and cold. The stove was made of iron and covered with soot. On a table by the wall was a solitary candle stub. Mr. Hershel shuffled off to his room.

I didn't know what to do next, so I just sat down on the cot. The place did not seem very homey to me without my grandmother. She may have been strict, but she always loved me. I missed the good Mendel and the black sheep Mordecai; I missed my brother and my beautiful sister. I even missed my father. How long I sat on the cot, I don't know. My thoughts were interrupted by Mr. Hershel's two sons who came home from their work. They were tired and didn't pay much attention to me, but they made dinner and I took Mr. Hershel's portion into his room. As I lay on the cot that night, I thought of the horses, cows, and chickens back home. There wasn't any part of the farm I didn't miss.

Just as the next day was beginning to dawn, a man came from

---

with the civil authorities, their offspring were considered to be illegitimate. Hence, my father took his mother's name.

house to house, knocking on the doors and calling out, "It's time to rise. All Jews get up and say your prayers."

Having lived on the farm, I was not used to this sort of thing. Mr. Hershel lived in the Jewish part of Dukla, and Jewish life was very different from that of the gentiles. Everyone seemed to know each other; everyone contributed to the welfare of the Jewish community. Mr. Hershel's sons were getting ready to go to work. We had a breakfast of bread and milk, and I put a piece of bread in my pocket for later. That evening I would start the system known as *taig,* the tradition of *mitzvah.* While I thought about this, wondering what kind of people I would have dinner with, the door opened and a small man with a wispy grey beard came into the house. He looked straight at me and squinted.

"Come on," he said. "The *melamed* (teacher) is waiting. School is to begin for another day."

Mr. Hershel's sons walked past this man and out onto the street. Mr. Hershel was in his room; and I was alone with this strange man, who came up to me and took my arm.

"Come on. Hurry! We'll be late!"

Feeling rather helpless, I followed him outside. Waiting on the street were other children, most of whom were much younger than I. One of the little boys took hold of the man's coat, crying, "Mamma ...." Some of the other children ran ahead but I stayed behind this man. The Jews we passed on the street wore strange clothing: fur hats and long black kapotas (coats). Some wore white stockings, and all were in a hurry to get somewhere. From a side street came a man with two water buckets suspended from a staff across his shoulders. One way to make a living for a poor man was to deliver water to homes in buckets. He shuffled to a stop and watched us pass.

The road twisted this way and that, along houses that seemed to squat next to one another. Blue smoke rose from their chimneys. How dismal city life appeared to me. The smells were those of garbage and smoke, and people were crammed together. Two mongrels fought over something in an alley, and a chicken that looked as if it had lost most of its feathers scooted across the road.

Finally, we arrived at a particular house and went inside.

The room we entered was partitioned with some kind of drab curtains. Chairs were set in rows. The doorway to the kitchen was open and a woman was bent over an oven. A man came from behind the partition. He had a stern look and carried a switch in his hand. This was to be *cheder*. In the next few hours, I learned some of the basic symbols of the Hebrew alphabet. The *melamed* made up riddles to help us learn the figures. One boy, about seven, was slow to learn and misbehaved. The *melamed* grew impatient. In front of the entire class the boy had to pull down his pants. Then the *melamed* hit him on the behind a couple of times with the switch he always carried in his hand. I was the oldest boy in class, and this alone was embarrassing. Most boys my age were learning to translate Hebrew into Yiddish. To receive punishment in front of the class would have been more than I could have borne. With this in mind I learned very quickly indeed.

After *cheder*, the man who had picked me up in the morning took me back "home." The other kids surged around him like a flock of baby chickens. Some children attending the *cheder* lived too far to walk, and their parents had to come to pick them up. Suddenly, I remembered my mother, her sweet voice and pleasant smell, and tears came to my eyes. Thinking of my father, a lump came to my throat. Somewhere in Dukla, Moishe was leaving his school and starting to hitchhike back to Zyndranowa. Grandmother was preparing dinner and Moishe would be there to eat it with her. I felt envious of him. I walked next to the man with the wispy beard. When we got to the house the man told me he would not be by to pick me up in the morning. Now that I knew the way, I was responsible for getting to *cheder* by myself. I watched him go off with the troupe of children who were all eager to go home. I hated them for their happiness. Feeling desperately lonely, I reached for the latch of Mr. Hershel's door. Then I remembered I was to have dinner with a Jewish family who lived down the street.

About a month had passed when one evening my uncle Mendel showed up with the horse and wagon. I was overjoyed to see him. He explained to Mr. Hershel that I would be staying for a while in

Zyndranowa. I thought I was to have a vacation; it seemed like hours before we were finally on the road.

A thousand questions rolled out of my mouth, and Mendel answered each one. It was simply a miracle to see his kind, smiling face. Every day I had prayed to be able to return to the farm; it was too good to be true.

As we neared Zyndranowa, I became excited. There it was! Darkness had long since fallen and kerosene lamps lighted up the windows of the farmhouse. The windows of the log cabin were dark and I was chilled by the sight of it, but the joy of being back on the farm quickly lifted my spirits again.

As soon as the wagon stopped in front of the barn, I jumped off and ran toward the house. The door was open and my grandmother was out on the porch. Behind her the lighted kitchen was warm and cozy, and I could see the tall shape of grandfather Isak.

"Grandmother! Grandfather!"

I hugged each in turn. The whole family was gathered in the kitchen. Even Mordecai was there and gave my head a rub. Feigele gave me a kiss. Moishe shook my hand, trying to act like an adult. Mendel came in from the barn and we all sat down to a dinner of stew. I had to relate all my adventures in Dukla, and grandmother was pleased to hear I was doing well in *cheder.* Even grandfather seemed proud. Underneath the joy of the occasion was a certain amount of tension and I began to think that maybe my grandparents had heard some disturbing news about me. Recalling some of the games I had played with peasant girls, panic flared through me. Was it possible that they had brought me home to punish me? Everyone seemed genuinely happy to see me, and no one mentioned any bad feelings. After dinner Feigele cleared the dishes from the table, while Mendel watched her every move. Moishe and I were excused for bed.

Burying my head in my very own pillow, a thrill filled me! Moishe was already sleeping, his breathing a steady sound in the darkness. I couldn't even close my eyes, let alone sleep. I wanted to run outside and say hello and goodnight to each and every animal, to the barn, the trees, and the good earth. My father was the only one absent. I knew he was in Mszanka with his father. Just to have him near would have made my happiness complete. I felt a great deal of pain when I thought about my father. I tried to divert my thoughts; it was then that I paid attention to the voices coming through the wall.

"I should think Isak's daughter would have made a match for a better man."

"A man does as he sees fit. It is the Lord who takes away.

"And Aron has seen fit to invest in a new marriage—to a divorced woman."

" It is a matter out of my control.

"Mendel, my son, please tell your father I haven't liked this Aron Oliner from the very start. That he should go to the marriage broker is perhaps his own business. That he should so soon leave the memory of the mother of his children is my concern and it grieves my heart. When she was alive, he paid her little enough attention, and I am grieved it has come to this."

"Hush, Mamma. The children will hear."

"The children have a father who runs after a woman with land and a *szenk* (bar). A pity it is they must learn the hard facts of life right in their own home."

I didn't hear what else was said. My mind was racing: father remarried! Such a possibility had never occurred to me. And what was I to call this other woman? How could I possibly call her Mamma? The Polish peasants often believed in ghosts. I wasn't sure I believed in them, but I wasn't sure I didn't believe in them either. And what would the ghost of my mother think when she learned that my father had remarried? I buried my face deep in the pillow. For some time I had not thought about my mother. Now, I wondered what she would think about this marriage. I also wondered if she was in heaven.

After a while I felt better. From my sorrow rose a bubble of excitement and I began to look at the situation in a new light. Still troubled at the thought of having a new mother, I was at the same time a little excited at having a new member of the family. As I went to sleep, I felt a mixture of despair and hope, and very strange dreams filled the night.

A few days later, my father showed up at the farm in Zyndranowa. He had come to fetch some things from the log cabin, and my grandparents greeted him coolly. I found out he lived in Bielanka, which was a few kilometers west of Mszanka, on some property his new wife happened to own. It was in Mszanka that Herman Polster, my grandfather on my father's side, lived, and I remembered it as a warm, friendly place, though I had only been there a couple of times. I began thinking that my mother and my father were first cousins. I wondered how they had met and if they were ever happy together.

Father asked if any of us children would like to meet our stepmother. What a strange feeling the word "stepmother" gave me! Right away, I was sure I would not like her. Father looked at Feigele. She, in turn, glanced at grandmother Reisel, then said she couldn't go because she was to begin nurses' training in Dukla. Then my father looked at Moishe. He hung his head and said he couldn't go either because the year was getting on toward fall and he had promised to help Mendel harvest the grain.

My father didn't say anything, but I could see a red coal of anger deep down inside him. His beard seemed more bristly than usual. It wasn't really Feigele or Moishe at whom he was angry. He shot a glance at Reisel that gave me the shivers. At last he looked at me.

His expression seemed to say, "O.K., you, too, can say you don't want to go." But quite to the contrary, I was anxious to visit this place Bielanka. Perhaps I would get a chance to visit Herman Polster. Or maybe I would get to see Gorlice, a big town not too far away from grandfather Herman's farm.

So I said, "Sure, I'll go with you."

Both Feigele and Moishe gave me startled glances. Even my father looked surprised. Grandmother said:

"What about *cheder?* How will you continue his education in Bielanka, a village smaller than Zyndranowa?"

My father said, "That's no problem. There is a *cheder* in Gorlice and I will make sure he goes every day. "

"Perhaps you will put him in a rooming house?"

"I will do as I see fit."

I packed my clothing and said goodbye to everyone. Feigele seemed very tense. Moishe stood off a ways. Grandmother cried a little and Isak shook my hand as if I were a man. That made me feel very proud. I climbed up on the wagon seat and looked back one last time to wave. They all stood in a group, and I was deeply aware of the fact that they were my family. The wind stirred the leaves of the trees that lined the house and I waved as the wagon started off. The family waved back and I was torn with love for them all.

My father held the reins quietly as the wagon bumped along the road. He wore a black hat and a dark coat. His black beard and white cheeks made him look like a large animal—a bear perhaps—snug in its fur. I couldn't wait until my beard would grow. I couldn't wait until the time I could just hitch up the horse and drive somewhere—when I would be a man. Then, I thought, my life would begin.

"How was *cheder?*"

"Very good, I learned the Hebrew letters quickly. They look like animals, you know, and I memorized them in no time.

"Hmmm. And how is Mr. Hershel, your landlord?"

"He stays in his room all the time. In the morning I have to take him breakfast and clean the house. Mr. Hershel's sons leave early in the morning for work and don't return until evening. Each night I have dinner in the home of a Jewish family, a different family each night. When I am at the home of Mr. Hershel I have the house pretty much to myself."

What I didn't tell him about was the loneliness—the awful loneliness—that caved in on me each night as I went to bed. In the mornings, I watched the Jewish mothers and fathers bring their children to *cheder*. In the afternoon, these parents returned to take their children back home. At school I had a reputation for fighting and it was these children with whom I got into fights most often. I wanted to hurt them in some way because they were happy; because they had mothers and fathers who picked them up.

My father said, "Do you like living with grandfather Isak?"

"Yes I do. They are very kind."

"But they never speak to each other. Doesn't that bother you?"

"They are very good to Feigele and Moishe and me."

"For twenty years they have not spoken to each other and not even I know the reason why. But Reisel's a very strange woman. Has she told you stories of me?"

"No. Why should she say anything about you?"

"What has she said that would make your sister and brother not want to visit their stepmother in Bielanka?"

"I don't know."

"Tell me. I am your father and should know these things!"

"I don't know what you're talking about. Grandmother and grandfather are always very friendly."

"But not where I am concerned. I can see that. I would only like to know what she says. I know she blames me for your mother's death, but that couldn't be helped. She blames me for not getting the best doctors to take care of her during her illness. Your mother had tuberculosis. There was nothing the doctors could do. It was just a matter of time, and your grandmother doesn't seem to realize it. She isn't always so smart and I would just like to know what she has to say when my back is turned."

Shaking all over, I huddled on the seat. My father got quiet again and gave the reins a flick. Gradually, I calmed down. From Zyndranowa to Bielanka we had to drive over forty kilometers and we arrived at my stepmother's farm late at night.

There was a corral and a small shed for animals. In one part of the house was the *szenk,* where peasants sometimes purchased and drank whiskey. The windows of the house were flooded with light. When my father opened the kitchen door, standing by the stove I saw the woman who was my stepmother. She had dark hair and dark eyes, like my dead mother. But she was younger than my mother had been and her kitchen didn't smell nearly as good as had my mother's. She smiled and came over to me, stooping with arms outstretched. The greeting was very warm and I thought perhaps I would like this strange woman after all.

Then, from the adjoining room walked the most frightening man I had ever seen. His face shook from side to side and his eyes rotated around in circles. "Hello, how are you?" he said to me, extending his hand and rolling his eyes. I hid behind the skirts of my stepmother. The man walked around her, bending over and extending his hand. "Hello, how are you?" he said, shaking his head. I started to cry.

"This is my brother," said the woman behind whose skirts I hid. "He is married and lives in Gorlice. From time to time he visits me. There is no reason to be afraid."

I noticed she gave me a strange look, as if she felt badly that I didn't like her brother. He tried to be friendly. I wanted to like him and please my stepmother, but it was no use; he was so frightening I couldn't bear to look at him, and the next day I asked my father to take me back to Zyndranowa. Of course, such a thing was positively out of the question. I was stuck in Bielanka for several months.

Once again the problem of *cheder* came up. I would have been perfectly happy not to attend at all. But social pressure was very strong and my father had an obligation to fulfill. Bielanka had no *cheder.* Nor did Mszanka where grandfather Herman lived. The nearest large town was about ten kilometers away. The name of this town was Gorlice and it was there that I attended *cheder.*

Happy was the day when I once more set eyes upon Zyndranowa. I was about eight years old and made the trip alone, hitchhiking on the road. I had quarreled with my father and was running away from home. Actually, I was running from one home to another. One did not have to stay with one's father, and I left a barely legible note for him saying I would be at grandfather Isak's.

The problem with my father was that he was not very open-minded. He was a good businessman and a hard worker: he had learned well what was offered in the *cheder*—the *Torah* and Jewish tradition—but beyond that, he didn't know too much. All I did was ask him why the Polish gentiles didn't believe in the *Torah.*

"Why do you want to know?" he said, writing some notes with a pencil on a piece of paper. Rarely did he pay much attention to me. I sometimes had the feeling I could die right in front of him and he wouldn't notice.

"I was just curious."

"Are you getting Christian notions in your head? Is it a goy I'm raising you to be?"

"No. I was just curious. Honest. It just seems strange that some Poles don't even know what the Torah is."

My father put down his pencil and glanced at me.

"Well, you just stick to your lessons. The Poles are not the chosen people of God. You leave them alone and maybe they'll leave you alone. And remember, it was curiosity that brought deceitfulness into the world."

After that I wouldn't speak to him. I didn't get along with my stepmother. She called me lazy when actually I did as much work as anyone. The argument with my father was the final straw that broke my willingness to stay at Bielanka.

When I saw the faces of Isak and Reisel again, my heart bounced. Feigele was home from Dukla and Moishe asked me a lot of questions about Bielanka. He decided he wanted to visit our stepmother. It seemed odd to see him go back to the place I had just left.

Grandfather Isak's farm was more or less the same. The harsh winter had passed and the trees were putting forth their new buds. Grandfather and Mendel spent all day working in the fields, plowing the earth and planting grain. I helped a little, but for the most part my time was free and I spent many days just soaking up the warm spring sun. The earth was warming all around me; cows were calving and birds were nesting in the grasses. During this time of restfulness, I began to pay more attention to uncle Mordecai.

For some reason this man intrigued me. He was the black sheep of the family. Even when he helped with the farmwork his efforts were never appreciated. My grandfather would say, "Look how hard Mendel works and how lazy you are." Grandfather Isak was never pleased with this wayward son. Consequently, Mordecai did only what he wanted to do. As he had no love for the soil, he generally ended up roaming the countryside. For hours, sometimes days, he would be gone from the farm. When I asked him what he did during these periods of time, he just grinned. The shepherds from the high pastures said he made love to peasant women.

The houses of most peasants consisted of two rooms, one of which was a bedroom where all the members of the family slept. Of course, I understood that if a peasant girl wanted to meet a man she had to do it in the woods or in high pastures during daytime. The town gossips referred to such meetings as lovemaking. I was about eight years old at the time and didn't quite understand what was meant by lovemaking, but the idea of Mordecai meeting a peasant girl in the fields filled me with excitement. My grandparents did not approve of these meetings, which made them all the more exciting for me. Several times I had seen the naked chest of my sister Feigele. I was sure "making love" had something to do with a woman's chest, and the thought of Mordecai doing this thing filled me with conflicting emotions. Very quickly I came to adore Mordecai. Why my grandparents would disapprove of his activities was beyond my comprehension. Fascinating man that he was, he could do no wrong, and the good Mendel began to seem like a dull person indeed beside this black sheep.

As I followed him around the farm and watched him I noticed that, like Mendel, he seemed to like Feigele very much. She was a nice girl—very kind to me—and I certainly could understand why someone would like her. With black hair, dark eyes, and lips like a ripe fruit, she was pleasant to look at. But I could not understand why Mendel would blush and get tongue-tied in her presence. Mordecai didn't blush; but he would get quick eyes; they would glance at her, then dart off somewhere else, back and forth. The difference between Mordecai and Mendel was that Mordecai usually avoided Feigele if he had any choice in the matter. If he saw her walking toward him, he might very well go off in another direction.

Apparently, he didn't avoid other women; the shepherds said he met with gypsies as well as peasants. There was a gypsy encampment just outside of Dukla. In a hollow on the side of a hill, they built their shantytown. One day I rode with Mendel to get farm supplies in Dukla. On the way home he whipped up the horse as we passed the gypsy camp. The frown on his face showed exactly how he felt and I didn't ask any dumb questions. Gypsy music and the smell of oil and cooking meat hung in the air. I looked back over my shoulder and there were their huts made of wood, sod, and canvas. A woman with dark hair tied back was tending a fire. Large silver earrings hung down her neck. Her eyes were dark, her mouth broad with thick lips. As she bent over the fire her blouse fell forward. I could see the flesh of her breasts, and in my imagination Mordecai was touching them. Gypsy smoke hung like magic in the air.

It just so happened that Mordecai was at the farm when we got there. He was sitting on the corral fence by the barn talking to Feigele. Mendel had the same frown as when we passed the gypsy camp. I jumped off the wagon. Mendel got down also and led the horses into the barn. Feigele walked to the house and I went over to the corral fence where Mordecai was sitting.

He looked at me, and grinning in a lopsided fashion said, "Hi."

From the ground I picked up a splinter of wood and twisted it in half. Then I looked at him. When our eyes met he looked off toward the horizon.

"We passed the gypsy camp outside Dukla."

Mordecai seemed amused. Unlike Mendel, Mordecai shaved his beard, and I could see his smooth jaw working.

"Say, I was wondering,..."I started.

"What's that?"

"Why don't the Poles like gypsies?"

"Well, if the gypsies see a chicken or something they like, they simply take it and cook it for dinner without asking the owner's permission."

"But don't they sometimes work for the Poles?"

"Who doesn't work for the Poles?"

"The gypsies!" I said.

"Sure. They get odd jobs and such. But just the same, the Poles don't treat them very well."

"Because the gypsies steal?"

"Who knows? Maybe. On the other hand, maybe the gypsies

steal from the Poles because the Poles don't treat them well. The rabbi seems to know everything, so maybe you should go ask him."

Mordecai wasn't very religious and his making fun didn't surprise me. But I was serious. There were many questions I had about the gypsies. Why did the gypsies cast such a spell over Mordecai? It certainly seemed such a strange life, to live in wagons and shantytowns and simply to pack up whenever one wanted to leave. Such a life I thought I'd like. No farm chores to do, no *cheder* to attend—what a way to live! The shepherds said Mordecai played games and laughed with the gypsy women, and this was the sort of thing I thought I'd like to do.

"Are the gypsy women beautiful?"

Mordecai looked at me shrewdly. "What do you know about 'beautiful'? Doesn't your grandmother want you to grow up to be like your good uncle Mendel? Or has she stopped speaking to you also?"

"Of course grandmother talks to me."

Mordecai laughed, sliding off the rail fence. Still laughing, he walked around the barn. He seemed in a hurry to get somewhere and I had to run a little to catch up. He stopped and waited for me.

He said, "Hey, you know what? Your grandparents are in the kitchen 'discussing' some important matters. Why don't you go and hear what they have to say?"

"But no one ever talks serious matters when I'm around.

"Well, go and spy on them," said Mordecai, bending over and whispering in my ear. "Do it for me, O.K.? Go listen to what they have to say and then tell me about it."

His eyes were dark and dancing and he had that lopsided grin. I had no idea why he would want me to spy on my grandparents, but the idea of doing something for Mordecai thrilled me, and I was determined to do a good job. Like a flash I ran out of the barn. Circling around the house, I crawled through some bushes up to the kitchen window, which was slightly open.

There were my grandparents, all right. My grandmother sat at one end of the table, my grandfather at the other. He didn't look at her and she didn't look at him. They were alone. For about five minutes I waited and not a single word was spoken. Finally, my grandmother said, "Isak should know I think it's about time for Shmulek to return to *cheder.* He did very well while he was in Dukla, but his education is not yet complete."

Grandfather said nothing. On the table in front of him was a clay mug. His back was very straight in the chair. Flies were crawling on my leg, but I held my breath for fear of giving myself away. I waited perhaps another five minutes, then Feigele walked into the kitchen.

"Tell your grandmother arrangements will be made. Tell her I have to go back to work now."

While Feigele relayed the message, I crawled out of the bushes along the house and ran to find Mordecai. Why would the subject of my going to *cheder* interest him? I had no idea, but he had asked me to spy, and I was anxious to please him.

First I checked the barn; the two horses were there in their stalls munching some oats and stirring the straw bedding with their feet. They looked at me with big, brown eyes and wrinkled up their noses, and I couldn't resist rubbing their necks. In another stall was the cow, its wet nose shiny. I patted the cow, too, then ran to the back of the barn where the hay was piled. Mordecai was the kind of person who could be anywhere.

I ran back outside, coming into the bright springtime sunlight. A sparrow flew up from the ground with string in its beak to make a nest. The air was cool, fresh and invigorating. I checked along the corral fence and out in back of the barn, scanning the fields and woods and the houses and barns of grandfather Isak's neighbors.

Dreadfully discouraged, feeling I had somehow been tricked by my uncle, I sat on the doorstep of the log cabin. Where he could possibly be was a complete mystery to me. Of course, he could be visiting a neighbor, he could have gone off on one of his hikes. But why then would he have asked me to spy on my grandparents? If his purpose had been to trick me, where could he have gone that he didn't want me to follow?

Then I thought of the cellar. Most Poles, and Jews as well, had cellars of brick, rock, or dried mud. Sometimes they were located under the house or sometimes they were dome-shaped structures dug into the ground somewhere away from the house. Certain things like butter and milk had to be kept cool during the summer; potatoes and other supplies had to be kept warm during the winter. Cellars kept an ideal temperature for these items and were therefore a necessity.

My grandparents' cellar was located under the house. I went around the honeysuckle-covered fence and approached the back of the house, where the cellar door was. The door was open a crack. In back of me was a large field and the edge of the woods. The village of Zyndranowa, and the farms and houses of neighbors were in plain sight. I stood by the trees next to the house and for a moment I stopped to look at the fresh new green of the leaves. A cool breeze moved through them and I quietly pushed open the cellar door. Some instinct warned me to be cautious, and I waited silently as my eyes adjusted to the darkness. What I then saw made my heart skip a beat and then it seemed to stop dead still.

There on the soft earth of the cellar floor was Natzcka, the most beautiful unmarried woman in all of Zyndranowa. Her skirt was up around her waist, making plainly visible the dark area between her legs. Her blouse was completely off, her chest exposed. All this I saw even before I realized that Mordecai was on top of her. In the next few minutes I got a lesson I would never forget. It had never occurred to me that men and women could possibly do such things.

At first, I thought Mordecai and this woman were strange, that they were doing something unnatural. After a while they laughed together. They seemed happy and I was puzzled by that.

As I felt it was very important that I should not be discovered, I slipped out of the cellar and pulled the door shut. Troubled as I was, I had seen something which made some of the gossip around Zyndranowa make more sense than it ever had before. I came to the realization that the practices Mordecai and Natzcka were engaged in were common. Mordecai wasn't the only one who made love in the woods! Furthermore, I had witnessed the love-making of animals and knew this was how animals were bred. What

Mordecai and Natzcka did was very similar to what I had seen animals do and it occurred to me it was this practice that made women have babies.

Thinking about what I had learned, I began to observe people in a new light. There was a learned man in Zyndranowa who had four very pretty daughters. They were too young to be married, yet each already had several suitors to choose from when the proper time would arrive. Then there was another man with four daughters long since past marriageable age. They were so ugly no man would look at them. The father was a sort of bully and chased after women. This family was known to sleep in the same bed and every one of the four daughters had a baby. Of course there was some gossip, but no one got too upset as illegitimacy among the peasants was common and quite acceptable.

Very soon I noticed the biggest and strongest men in the village were the ones who claimed the greatest number of women. Such a man would visit even a married woman at night. The husband knew about it, actually the whole village knew what was going on, but no one said a word. If someone said something the strong man didn't like, he would pay that person a visit. And no one wanted to get beat up or have his house wrecked.

Most of the time, the husband was afraid of the tough guy and did nothing about his wife's unfaithfulness, but not always. One day, I noticed the police at the farm next door to grandfather's property. The door of our neighbor's barn was open and lying on the ground inside was the body of a peasant who was a friend of Mordecai and known to be a very tough man. When he saw a woman he wanted he went right after her whether she was married or not. It was widely known that he was paying visits to our neighbor's wife. Now the man's head was in two pieces and a bloody axe lay near his body. This man was a friend of Mordecai, and the same kind of man as Mordecai. I thought of Mordecai lying there on the barn floor and the vision made me tremble with fear for the life of my uncle.

It seemed I was at grandfather Isak's farm barely long enough to shake off the dust of Bielanka when it was time to go to Dukla and resume *cheder*. By this time I was becoming used to change, living here, living there, visiting the homes of strangers and getting for myself what I needed. I could have hitchhiked back and forth to Dukla very easily, but once again I stayed at the home of Mr. Hershel. When my father came to Dukla to pay for my lodging, I generally avoided him.

During this time Feigele was also in Dukla studying to be a nurse, but seldom did I run into her. Mr. Hershel rarely came out of his room, and when I wasn't at *cheder* or having dinner at the home of some Jewish family, the house was mine to do what I pleased.

Dukla was where I happened to be when the Germans marched into Poland. The Polish radio blasted away: "We shall defend our land. We'll defeat the German armies. We will not give up even a button of our coat." Such words meant far more to me than the German threat. The Polish armies were passing through Dukla towards the Czechoslovakian border and I felt certain the country was secure. But soon there were sirens and gun blasts and bombardments and low-flying planes and retreating Polish armies. We had to stay in the darkness of our cellars. German planes machine-gunned Dukla and the retreating Polish units. From the city hall building Polish soldiers fired their handguns at the German flying machines. The firing of guns shook the ground. The cellar I was hiding in was packed with trembling people, and cries and sobbing filled the darkness. About two weeks after the war started the firing stopped. The streets of Dukla, built for the horse and cart, vibrated with the weight and roar of German army trucks and tanks.

Dukla was famous for the gap through the Carpathian Mountains which led to Czechoslovakia. I looked through the cellar window that faced the market place. The Germans were marching right through the Dukla Gap, and it seemed as if there were a hundred thousand of them. Poles were standing along the edge of the road waving to the passing cars, military trucks, and motorbikes, I climbed up out of the cellar when the German army came marching by like the links of a never-ending chain. From the marching column rose the odor of leather, cloth and oiled metal. This smell was so unlike any of the smells I was used to, I thought the Germans inhuman: they didn't smell like real people, they didn't walk like real people. Their faces were all the same—hard and expressionless—and I couldn't tell one German from another. A Nazi officer said something to a Pole who had evidently stepped too far out into the road. When Nazis spoke, the very breath that carried the word was a command. There was not the slightest doubt as to punishment for disobedience, and the Pole jumped back for dear life.

For two days the Germans marched through Dukla, and then a strange and frightful thing happened. The German army had required food and, quite naturally, a shortage developed. Someone began a rumor that the Jews were stockpiling food in their homes and shops. The Poles were going hungry; but, according to the rumor, the Jews had all they could possibly want to eat. A few of the bolder peasants began going around to Jewish houses, knocking on doors and saying, "Hey Jew, give us some bread. We need salt. Hey, give us potatoes and candles." The Jews kept their doors locked. They were all too familiar with tales about opening the door to robbery, rape and murder. The presence of a gentile defiled the home of a Jew, and no good was certain to come of it.

Then another rumor circulated: the Jews were having a big party at the other end of town, stuffing themselves with food while Polish peasant babies starved to death in the street. As if this rumor wasn't bad enough, someone added to it that the Jews had a Polish girl at this party and were raping her. It was apparently at this point that the Nazis authorized the clearing of all Jewish shops of their merchandise.

I had just finished dinner in the home of a Jewish family when the trouble started. The door was locked. We huddled together fearfully as it shook under the impact of some sort of battering ram. We knew of the rumors circulating among the Poles. For dinner, we'd had a very thin soup, but the Poles wouldn't have believed us had we been brave enough to tell them. They were convinced we were holding out on them. This was what they wanted to believe and nothing would change their minds. The door shuddered on its hinges and we looked at each other as if for the last time.

Then there were cries outside, shouts and screams. The pounding on the door stopped. After a few moments of fearful waiting, I ran to the window and looked out. Across the street the Poles had broken down the door of a Jewish home. Polish peasants I had met and often talked to were running out of the house with linen, food and cooking utensils. On their faces were mixed expressions of joy, horror, and frenzy that sent frightful chills down my back and through my belly. Never before had I seen such expressions; they seemed like total strangers to me.

The Poles, both peasant folk and a few townspeople, continued to loot Jewish homes and businesses, and to beat up the Jews they managed to get their hands on. After several hours the Nazis dispersed the mob. By the following day the Poles had lost their expression of frenzy. They greeted the Jews in a friendly manner, as if nothing at all had happened.

The enemy occupation of Dukla happened so fast it was like falling off a cart and waking up in a strange house. The town looked as if it had been hit by a hurricane. Roofs were missing from houses, windows were smashed, holes were all over the streets. Bodies lay for hours along the roads. Polish soldiers and snipers lay dead along with innocent peasants and peaceful Jewish merchants. As the enemy marched through the town some of the soldiers were making a house-to-house search for snipers. From a broken window I watched two Nazis coming down the street. They kicked doors open and stepped inside, pointing their rifles. I thought how terrible it would be to be a sniper and have those big, armed Nazis kick the door open. Never had I seen such a methodical search and I thought to myself that these Germans knew what they were looking for. I was chilled with fear.

The soldiers reached the house across the street from where I was hiding. The cobblestones of the street were torn up and scattered about, and one of the Nazis stood next to the door while the other kicked it open. In the front of the building was a large window which had somehow escaped damage, and through this window I saw them approach the occupant, a Jew with a long dark beard.

The man's jacket was also dark and his shoulders were slightly stooped. The hand he held at the corner of his mouth was trembling and the look he gave the Nazis was full of fear. One of the soldiers stepped up to the man and took hold of his beard. All the way across the street came the voice of the Nazi: "Swine! Jewish dog!" Still holding onto the man's beard the soldier hit him in the face with his pistol.

The blood on the Jew's face was clearly visible through the window. A woman rushed into sight from a back room of the building. She flung her stout body at the Nazi and I could hear her cries for mercy. The Nazi led the Jewish man about by the beard and dumped him on the floor. The second Nazi who had been watching and laughing all this time, stepped forward and grabbed the woman. She tried to stoop and tend to the fallen man, but the Nazi yanked her to her feet. Then he spun her around and with one jerk pulled off her clothes. I couldn't believe my eyes. From my post at the window I watched the Nazi throw the woman on top of the man on the floor. The soldiers were both laughing.

My grandmother came from Zyndranowa to fetch me. She had heard that many people were shot during the invasion. She came to Dukla in fear that some Nazi may not have liked my face.

BERGMANN THE DEFENDER

BEFORE I EVEN GOT OFF THE WAGON, Feigele came flying out of the farmhouse. She threw her arms around me and cried, hugging me and sobbing as if she hadn't seen me for ten years. Just before the war started, she had left Dukla. News of the German invasion had spread quickly and she thought I was lucky to be alive.

"Have you heard from Daddy?" she said.

"No. I guess he's in Bielanka with his new wife."

She frowned. Still sparkling in her eyes were the tears she shed when we had met.

She said, "Moishe is with him. Yes, they must be in Bielanka. But I wish they would visit us. The Germans are killing a lot of people and it seems they don't like Jews. I don't know what we have ever done to them, but they don't like us and I am afraid for Moishe. Oh Shmulek, I'm so glad to see you!" She threw her arms around me and cried some more. "I am afraid and don't know why. I wish Daddy were here."

Mendel came up behind us. He put his arm around Feigele and held her to his shoulder. "Everything is all right," he said. "We will take care of you. Shmulek is all right, as you can see. And so is Moishe and your father. If any Germans show their faces around here we'll chase them off.

Feigele dried her eyes and smiled weakly. Mordecai walked around the corner of the barn and Feigele looked in his direction. Mendel dropped his arm from her shoulder and got an expression on his face as if he were mad at something. Grandmother had gotten off the wagon and gone into the house. I waved to Mordecai and took off after her, hoping to find an extra piece of pie or buttered bread.

The German invasion of Dukla had certainly been a terrible thing. A town had been devastated, its people sent crawling into dark places. But the farm in Zyndranowa was isolated from all that. The house of my grandfather seemed far away from the Gestapo patrols, and farm work continued pretty much as usual.

Part of my job was caring for the horses and cattle. This I liked very much. There was no school, nothing to learn. Farm life was grand, with plenty of homemade food. My grandparents were wonderful to me. My uncles were very kind and both of them were great fun to be with. In short, it was paradise to be away from the Nazis, and away from Dukla, which had become a city of hunger and death. The mornings were sunny and bright, the air was filled with the rich wonderful smells of farm animals. The earth was free to walk on and I loved the people around me.

One morning a cloud blotted out the sun. The village of Zyndranowa was Ruthenian, and the Nazis asked the Ruthenians where the houses of Jews were located. The villagers were reluctant to give such useful information, and five Gestapo men pulled up in their car in front of my grandfather's house.

Everyone was in the house except Feigele. The Gestapo was known to tell young men to report to Gestapo headquarters, from where they would be sent to a work camp or a concentration camp; so my uncles cleared out of the house. They also had spontaneous roundups of people called *Lapanki.* Hurriedly we made sure everything was in order and that the dog was out of the way (they sometimes shot dogs that dared bark at them). I went out the back door of the house to chase the chickens away, for if the Germans saw a chicken they might demand its head be cut off. Sometimes they had chicken and other meat delivered to their headquarters.

As I rounded up the chickens and chased them into the orchard, I heard the car doors slam. My heart nearly burst through the skin of my chest. Peeking around the corner of the house, I saw that the driver had remained in the car. The others went to the door and my grandfather opened it. His face turned suddenly white. The soldier in front, who must have been the leader, said, "Are you a Jew?" My grandfather answered in Yiddish, his voice trembling, "Yes," and the four Nazis walked into the house as if they owned it.

The door shut. I felt my place was with my grandparents and I ran around the house and in through the back door of the kitchen. The Gestapo leader glanced at me and said, "Where is the rest of your family?" My grandparents stood together in front of the stove. "Where is the rest of your family! Can't you hear?"

I don't know," said grandmother.

The officer looked at her, his eyes hard and full of mischief. The other soldiers looked around the house, as if they were calculating the value of the curtains and furniture. Maybe they thought money was stuck under the chairs.

"Does the woman wear the tongue for her man?" said the officer. "That is not the way we Germans are. I can see very plainly why you Jews are such a weak and miserable race."

"I don't know where the rest of my family is," said my grandfather.

"Ahh, now the man has a tongue!" The Nazi walked over to my grandfather and pushed him gently back against the hot stove. Isak didn't dare resist. "Did you know there are three Jewish families living in this filthy village of Zyndranowa?"

"Of course," said my grandfather, his face white as wax.

"Respect! You will speak to me with respect!" The officer pushed against my grandfather's chest a little harder. The smell of singed cloth was filling the kitchen. "Are you also aware you are considered the wealthiest?"

"I am but a poor man," said my grandfather. "Each day I work hard and for very little more than the food for our bellies. "

"I want your gold."

My grandfather answered politely in Yiddish, "Sir, I have no gold or diamonds. I am but a poor man."

"I didn't ask for diamonds, did I? Where are they?"

The officer waited a second, then stepped back. One of the other soldiers stepped forward and knocked my grandfather down with a slap on the face. Then he turned to my grandmother and laughed fiendishly. Reisel turned her face toward the man on the floor and for the first time in my life I saw her look upon her husband with despair and pity.

The Gestapo brutality had been horrible to witness; but it was the look my grandmother gave her husband that struck horror in me. I tried to run out of the house, but one of the Gestapo men grabbed me around the waist and threw me in the opposite direction. My grandfather got up off the floor and Reisel steadied him by holding his arm. We backed into a corner. The officer unsnapped his holster and took out his pistol. The other soldiers leveled their rifles at us. With their thumbs they moved certain attachments of the rifles and the clicking noises raised the hair along the back of my neck. In that moment, when I was certain I was going to die, my mind played a trick on me. I remembered an incident involving a Polish boy.

The peasants were superstitious. They not only believed in ghosts, but also believed there were specific places haunted by ghosts and all kinds of frightful things. There was this one boy and some peasants decided to play a trick on him. They told him there was a haunted place and made a bet that he was afraid to spend the night there. He claimed that no one would do such a thing; so the other boys all stayed together in the haunted place overnight to prove they were brave. Thus the boy now had to show he wasn't a coward and stayed all alone overnight at the haunted place. During the night the other boys played a trick on him, and soon after everyone was horrified to find that his hair had turned white!

This is what I thought about as the officer raised his pistol and pointed it at my grandfather's face. I thought about my own hair and how white it must be at that moment.

"I will ask only once more for your valuables."

I started crying and my grandparents begged him to let us live. As I cried, my mind seemed detached from my body, as if it belonged to someone else. I thought how stupid it was to cry when the next minute I would be dead. Nothing seemed to matter. Certainly not tears. Yet I couldn't catch my breath; my body quivered and shook and there was a steady whining sound I recognized as my own. My grandfather was down on his knees begging for the lives of his grandchildren, his children, his wife. The Nazi officer just stood there, expressionless. his face strong and powerful and hard as a rock.

Suddenly a loud scream came from outside. The Gestapo officer dropped his arm and he and his men rushed out of the door. I staggered to the window. The Gestapo man who had driven the car was trying to kiss Feigele. She was pinned against the car by the man's fat arms and her face was twisted with terror. Her shoulders were bare and it looked like the German was biting her on the neck.

The officer shouted at the driver and he released her. She ran away from him, but one of the other men followed her and caught her against the side of the barn. He could have broken her in half as easily as if she were a twig, and he said something in her ear while holding her against the barn. My grandparents were next to me at the window. They were both on their knees praying to God in a loud voice. The man holding Feigele released her. Then the officer gave a signal and they all got into the car and drove off in a cloud of dust.

Feigele came into the house with red eyes and tears on her cheeks. Everyone sobbed together, even grandfather Isak. Reisel rested her hand on her head. Feigele said she had to report to the Gestapo station in Dukla. She didn't know why; no reason had been given, but no one refused a request by the Gestapo.

No one said much of anything. For a while we all sat around half dead; then my uncles came out from hiding. I guess they were outside someplace or in the attic. Feigele really should have been with them. As they had missed the horror, they tried to restore some semblance of normalcy to a day we all wished had never come. We tried to eat, but no one could get the food down. Someone told a funny joke. I didn't quite understand it, nor was I aware of who told it. But I did smile and it felt like a very strange thing on my face.

That night I slept fitfully. The blankets were wet with perspiration. Between cold sweats I had a dream: no longer was I a small boy. A weapon was in my hand and the Nazis were not so big and impervious anymore. They were mortal creatures with red blood like chickens and cattle. I dreamed I ordered these Nazis out of my country Poland, out of the house, and that their cruel faces melted, because they were just mortal men.

The days that followed were quiet and desperate. Everyone knew what the other person was thinking: Feigele might not return after reporting to the Gestapo, she might be sent to a concentration camp or harmed in some way. Mendel looked like he would burst into tears at any moment. In fact, this is what he often did, and everyone else as well. Mordecai was the most reserved of us. He came up with the suggestion that Feigele should not report to the Gestapo station. Instead, he thought she should go to Bielanka and stay with father. My grandfather didn't think this was such a good idea. Both he and Reisel obviously disliked my father. Also, they were afraid the Gestapo might come back to the farm. For disobedience the Gestapo might shoot us all and burn the house as well.

"It is only the life of my niece I am concerned about," said Mordecai.

Grandfather Isak looked at his black sheep son. He put his hand on Mordecai's shoulder. "I have not always treated you fairly, but your heart speaks for all of us. I also am concerned for Feigele, but I have other lives to think of also."

Mendel began to quiver. "And why should you worry about Feigele," he said to Mordecai. "Isn't it the other women of Zyndranowa you should be concerned about?"

"I merely suggest that Feigele not present herself to the Gestapo," muttered Mordecai, looking at her with sadness.

"Now is not the time to argue," said Isak.

Mendel's neck was red and he shouted: "You want to be a tough man like Bergmann, is that it? Well, I can tell you Feigele is not impressed. What is it that happened to Bergmann, hah,—isn't he dead? Yes, this big tough man was no match for German bullets and for all his bravery he is now dead. His very own family can no longer count on his protection and it is his mother and his sister the Germans visit. Oh yes, you think I haven't heard? They visit them by the carload!"

"That has nothing to do with Feigele. As for Bergmann, you

have no right to say such things of him. Who was it who made the Poles respect the Jews on market day? Bergmann. When the peasants got drunk on Jewish whiskey and then beat up the Jews who served it to them, Bergmann was there to make the peasants change their minds. Sure, Bergmann was tough. He was a good fighter. And when he was around, the peasants didn't drive through mud puddles in order to splash some Jew. He was certainly no coward. And when the peasants were raping his sister, he wasn't one to stand by and let it happen."

"He was a scoundrel. A woman-chaser. He slept with other men's wives."

"If you had only a little of his courage you wouldn't be saying such things."

The brothers glared at each other. In the brief silence I recalled this man Bergmann. One time he was on the road from Dukla to Zyndranowa and I asked him for a ride. As we jolted along on the cart, Bergmann spotted a peasant girl walking along the road and stopped the horse alongside her. He told me to climb into the back of the cart and the peasant girl took my seat. Immediately, he started to kiss her and squeeze and pinch her. He turned around and winked at me, as if to say I shouldn't look on. His look said: "Look, boy, you're too young. Just go to sleep in the hay."

There was another Jewish fighter-type, also, who was Bergmann's friend. As long as the two of them were around, the Jewish merchants weren't afraid of the Polish peasants or town dwellers on market day. They were the community's overseers, champions of justice and Jewish rights.

Oh…how we need Bergmann and his friend now! Why can't all Jews be like Bergmann—unafraid, tough, able to smash anti-Semitic heads? Why are the rabbis, the scholars, the Talmudists our heroes, I thought to myself? My stream of thoughts would not leave my hero Bergmann. I remembered one summer market day *(yereed)* in Dukla, where hundreds of peasants gathered once a week to trade, barter, and sell their crafts, cattle, sheep, horses, butter, fresh fruits, etc. The town's market place was crowded with people and animals. There were noises, haggling, and also incessant violence and abuses. Suddenly, as I sat at the north corner of the market place, the crowd stirred and loud noises and screams followed. Five drunken peasants were trying to steal some cloth from a Jewish pushcart peddler. Some fierce punches were directed at the peasants and soon all five of them were bleeding on the cobblestones. Shortly thereafter the Polish police arrived and, though usually anti-Semitic, they couldn't argue with Bergmann and his friend. The peasants were arrested by the Polish police and the proceedings on the market place continued until sundown.

This Samson of Dukla was looked down upon by the "proper" Jews, who felt that Bergmann and his friend were *apiskorsim* (non-observing Jews) who didn't keep the Sabbath and even rode horse and buggy through the town on the holy day. Yet this non-observing Jew defended the weak and the feebleminded. Polish anti-Semites used to enjoy taunting the town's idiots and the beggars, of whom there were plenty in the *shtetl* of Dukla. Bergmann and his friend made sure that the same ignorant Polish anti-Semites would not repeat this taunting. Oh, how I wished that we had a million Bergmanns now who would rid us of the German occupiers of our Polish soil. But it was an empty daydream and my attention focused back on the arguing brothers.

This argument between brothers I didn't like. I couldn't understand why Mendel was so angry at Mordecai. Mendel's cheeks were red and his clean-shaven face sparkled with perspiration. He glared at Mordecai and ground his teeth.

"You are not so tough as you…"

"Mendel!" said grandmother. "Enough! I will not have my sons fighting at a time like this. One is never too old to show respect in his father's house."

Mendel stormed from the house, slamming the door behind him. Mordecai sat down at the kitchen table. He covered his face with his hands. After a moment he made two fists and brought them down hard on the tabletop.

My grandparents decided that Feigele should report to the Gestapo as ordered. They also decided I should be the one to drive her because I looked like a gentile boy and it was less dangerous for me to be seen on the streets of Dukla than for either one of my uncles.

The following morning Mordecai hitched up the horse. He kept his eyes on the ground and said very little. Feigele and I climbed up onto the wagon seat and off we went. From Zyndranowa to Dukla was a distance of about twenty kilometers. Normally, having the reins in my hands would have made me feel so important I would have enjoyed every second of the journey. It was only men who drove the horses and seldom did I get the chance. On the few occasions I happened to be in the driver's seat, I felt I was doing a manly thing in spite of my father's lack of confidence in me.

Under these circumstances, however, it wasn't very exciting at all. I was afraid of what the Gestapo would do to Feigele and the kilometers seemed to pass all too quickly. Every now and then Feigele tried to say something funny, just to see me smile. The road was filled with ruts and deep holes. The terrain was rocky and below the road was a river.

Shortly after noontime we arrrived in Dukla. I left the horse and cart on a side street and we walked to the Gestapo headquarters, which was located in what had been the Polish mayor's residence before the war. As we approached the guard, Feigele's steps slowed down and her knees shook. The guard asked what we wanted. Feigele said she had been asked to report to a man named Finke. I was kind of surprised to hear the name spoken aloud. For some reason it had not occurred to me that the Gestapo men would have names like everyone else.

The guard told us to wait in the corridor of the huge building. Soon Herr Finke came out. He seemed both surprised and delighted we had come. Apparently he did not remember making the request. Feigele told him I was her younger brother.

Finke was a gigantic man with a red face and a clipped blond mustache that didn't move when he talked. The guard left us and we were shown into a reception room. It was a cold, white room with a picture of Hitler hanging on the wall. There was the aroma of cigar smoke. Finke closed the door behind us and then, surprisingly enough, spoke to me in a friendly manner. His words were Polish which I understood very well. Feigele was as white as a sheet.

Finke said I should not be afraid and offered me some sweets. I thought perhaps they were poisoned, but I did take them for I imagined he would kill me if didn't.

He asked how we had made the journey and I said by horse and cart. He seemed amused that we had come all the way from Zyndranowa. Then he called down the corridor. I thought, "Now the other four will come. All five of the men who came to the farm will be in this room and what will happen to us then?" The person who came was the guard who had seen us into the building. Finke told him to see me outside so that I could look after the horse and make certain it wasn't "stolen." I asked in Polish, "What about my sister?" He said she would come along after they had had a little talk. Feigele smiled, as if to say, "Everything will be O.K.," and the guard escorted me to the door.

While waiting with the horse, I imagined all the horrible things that could possibly happen to Feigele. What would I say to my grandparents if I couldn't take her back with me? What was love if I couldn't even take care of my sister? I felt pretty foolish, then, because the whole trip to Dukla had been unnecessary. Finke didn't remember telling Feigele to report to the station. We had all been worried sick and my grandparents were afraid of losing the farm. Mendel and Mordecai had nearly come to blows, and Feigele and I walked into the jaws of the lion, like two dumb rabbits.

Now we had every reason to be afraid. We were in Dukla with the Gestapo. I stayed with the horse for what must have been nearly an hour or so, shaking with fear. I started walking around in circles and jumping on the spot to keep warm. Then I decided to walk back to the Gestapo headquarters. Perhaps Feigele was on her way to meet me. It was only a ten minute walk from the horse and cart. The town clock struck three. I did not know what to do. Timidly, I walked sticking close to the buildings. Some Jewish men passed me with their shaven beards and sorrowful eyes. All Jews had to shave off their beards as soon as the Nazis occupied Poland. As I neared the Gestapo headquarters, Feigele came out of the building and walked down the steps to the sidewalk. My heart suddenly beat faster. She walked all right, I thought. She looked O.K. She didn't look beat up or anything: but she was crying and looked worried. I reached her, out of breath, and asked what the matter was and she answered in a tone that said she was going to cry harder: "Nothing!"

We started off for home, whipping the horse to a fast trot. Feigele looked upset and I asked her whether Finke had beat her. She said no. By the time we arrived in Zyndranowa it was late and very dark. As we approached the farm I could see a lantern light in the window and the whole family waiting. Grandmother came running out on the porch. "It's the children. It's the children. Thank God, the children are back."

Uncle Mordecai took care of the horse and we went into the house. Supper was waiting and I was cold and starving. Feigele couldn't eat. Grandfather asked her what the Gestapo wanted. "Nothing," she said bursting into tears and running from the kitchen. Reisel looked at me and asked me what had happened. I said I didn't know and she got up from the table and went after Feigele. After dinner I fell into bed and didn't move all night long.

The next day I overheard grandmother saying to Mordecai that Herr Finke and the others at the Gestapo station had made advances on Feigele and that she was very much afraid Feigele had been raped. Then I realized why Feigele had been so melancholy during the trip home from Dukla. At breakfast she ate little and after we finished I offered to help her with the dishes. I felt sorry for her and wanted to make her laugh. I tried to tell her something funny but it didn't work. She didn't talk much. Finally, I did manage to make her smile.

The weeks rolled by and then father came from Bielanka to see Feigele and me. Curiously enough, I was happy to see him. By horse and cart he came and I noticed he didn't look well. He looked skinny. Most shocking of all, his beard was shaved and his naked face looked weak and sickly. Breathlessly I asked, "Are you O.K.?"

We embraced and he said, "Yes, son." Never had I felt so close to him, this brute of a man whom the peasants left alone because he was big and strong; this good *soicher* (buisnessman), educated in the Torah and Jewish tradition, who knew nothing of the religion of his Christian neighbors; this man whom at times I hated because he treated me like a child. He smiled and I felt warm all over. The look he gave me was the look adults give someone they love. I liked it when he called me "son," because it made me feel like he cared about me.

"What happened to your beard?" His eyes were deep and tired and I thought at first no words would pass his lips on this matter. Then he spoke slowly looking over the top of my head at the fields and houses in back of grandfather Isak's farm.

"Long ago, the Jew was invited to this land by the Polish kings to help improve the land. It was a great honor, and to this day, certain Jews wear strange clothing. On high holidays they wear fur hats and long *kapotas* (coats) and white stockings which are copies of what the medieval nobility wore. "

He stopped talking and I waited with downcast eyes. He was merely telling me what every Jewish boy learned from the stories of the *melamed.* Yes, the Jew was invited to Poland and he prospered, as did the gentile Poles. So what my father said came as no surprise to me. What was touching was that he chose to speak at all to me, the son he had never seemed to trust. I waited, thinking perhaps he would say no more.

"There is much that has always belonged to the Jew. His way of living…."

Once more I waited and waiting was agony.

"In *a shtetl* not too far from here called Zmigrut, a man had a very lovely, long and well-cultivated beard. He was a rabbi, a widely known and very respected man. One day the Nazis drove through his *shtetl* on their jeeps, and most of the Jews ran to their houses and bolted the doors and hid. This rabbi refused to run. The Nazis could tell he was a Jew because of his beard. They jumped out of the jeep and grabbed him. They tied his beard to the bumper and drove back and forth across the marketplace until he died." As he finished speaking I could feel his eyes upon me. I was trembling and unable to meet his gaze. "I am no less of a Jew," he said, "because I choose not to wear a beard."

My grandfather came from the house and gave my father a

rather perfunctory greeting. I was shaking all over and glad Isak had stepped in. Never had I thought of my father as a Jew; he was always just my father. Feigele appeared while the two men were standing together exchanging what appeared to be grunts and nods. She ran to him, throwing out her arms: "I'm so glad to see you, Daddy!" He kissed her and they both went for a walk in the garden. Grandfather Isak shuffled off. His step was normally quite springy for an old man, but now he seemed heavy, as if he had left much unsaid while talking to my father.

When dinner was ready I went to find Feigele and my father and caught up with them just as they were passing through the far end of the vegetable garden gate. They seemed happy. Feigele was talking about the farm and father was telling her about Moishe and my stepmother and the new baby—our stepsister, Jaffa. Father took my hand in one of his and Feigele's in the other. "You sure have grown up, son," he said with a smile. Feigele said, "He should—he sure eats enough." As we walked along I pointed out to father the strip of grandfather's land. Of course, he already knew what grandfather owned; but in the quiet glow of good feeling that filled my body it was nice to be able to show him something as one man to another. Feigele asked when he would go home. He said, "Tomorrow. These days, I can't keep those at home wondering what's happening to me."

Suddenly, a strange yearning came over me. I hadn't seen my stepmother, Ester, in a long time. The thought of a new baby was exciting. The last time I had been in Bielanka was late in '37 or early '38, and I hadn't seen Moishe in a long time, either. The two days journey by horse and cart seemed like a great adventure. It would be a lot of fun, and I'd get the chance to live someplace else for a while.

As we neared the house, the smell of Reisel's cooking came to greet us. I said, "Dad, I want to go with you." Both he and Feigele looked at me in surprise. Feigele, in particular, was speechless. As glad as she was to see father, it would never occur to her that she might go with him to Bielanka. Father shook his head cautiously. "O.K., son, if you'd like to come. Your stepmother will be very pleased to see you. But I warn you, the journey will be very tough."

"I've done it before."

Darkness was quickly falling. Dinner was not quite ready. My grandparents accepted the news of my departure quietly as if they had anticipated it all along. My father sat in a corner chatting with my grandfather while Feigele and grandmother set the table. All of a sudden I didn't feel so good. No longer was I certain I wanted to leave this place. It was too late, I told myself, too late to change my mind. I walked outside for some air.

The barn door was open and the yellow light of the lantern spilled out onto the ground. Inside the barn the peasant girl my grandparents hired for certain chores was finishing milking the cows. I walked inside the barn to watch her. She was wiping off the teat of my favorite cow. A morbid thought came to me that maybe this was the last time I would see this cow give milk.

"I hear you're going with your father," said the milkmaid, smiling up at me with crooked teeth. The lantern light made her hair look thick and yellow like butter. Her skin looked soft, her eyes dark and friendly, as she waited for me to respond. And I thought, "Even she knows! How could she know when only a minute ago I told my grandparents?" I felt miserable, miserable! I had never experienced such a heaviness in my heart before. This would not be the first time I went to Bielanka with my father. Yet for some reason the decision seemed to be one whose consequences I would have to deal with for the rest of my life. Not knowing why I felt that way made me all the more miserable. The weight of the decision was a heavy burden on my shoulders and I became depressed. To the milkmaid I silently nodded.

Feigele came into the stable calling my name.

"Shmulek! Didn't you hear me calling you? Dinner is ready."

As we walked toward the house I felt a very strange sensation. It seemed I was as light as the wind and for some reason would be unable to enter the house; but rather I would blow right over it and out among the stars where there was only cold and loneliness forever.

"Shmulek, you're not paying attention to me. What's the matter? Don't you feel good?"

"No, I'm fine. Don't worry. I'm all right."

She said, "Tomorrow you're going with Daddy. I'm going to miss you, Fatty. You know it's just not going to be the same without you." I could say nothing; the words stuck like a ball of lead in my throat. We reached the veranda on the north side of the house. Feigele took me by the shoulder and held me back.

"Promise me," she said. "Please, you must promise you will never tell Daddy I went to see the Gestapo men in Dukla."

Looking at her sweet, gentle face, I almost broke out crying. Before my very eyes the face seemed to become that of a stranger. I wanted to throw my arms around her and squeeze and squeeze until something happened. Until what happened? I don't know. I was being silly, I told myself.

"Don't worry. I'll never tell him."

She gave me a squeeze and went into the house. I followed.

Everyone was sitting around the table and no one said a word. After dinner I went to bed. The night seemed to last forever. Every time I closed my eyes they seemed to pop back open. Finally, I got up and sat on the edge of the bed. There was my grandfather twisted in blankets. My grandmother was a soft mound under hers. Feigele lay with her head up, her face pale and beautiful. Mendel was snoring and Mordecai faced the wall. Each breath my father took seemed to shake the room.

As I looked at each of these people I felt as if a cold knife blade was stuck into me and twisted. I prayed to God to help me through the night. Then I sat on the edge of the bed until the rooster crowed.

The house was still dark as I tiptoed out to the barn to see father's horse. The barn was warm and smelled of hay and manure. The horse stomped his hoof and made a low whinny and I rubbed his velvet soft nose. The journey would be tough for this gentle animal. I scratched his forehead and rubbed his neck. Then I went back into the house and lit the fire and woke up Feigele. Silently I waited while she dressed, watching her every move as if I were never to see her again. "You couldn't sleep?" she whispered, as we walked out into the kitchen.

"No. I guess I'm just too excited about the trip."

She tousled my hair. "Shmulek, how strange you are."

She made breakfast and soon everyone was up and sitting around the table. Mendel made a joke or two, but no one laughed. I couldn't eat anything.

"Look at Shmulek," said Mendel. "He must be sick, not eating anything."

"He's just excited about the trip," said Feigele smiling at me.

Grandmother seemed more quiet than anyone else.

After breakfast I went out with the men to harness the horse and make sure everything was all right. My father said goodbye to my grandparents and uncles. There seemed to be an unusual warmth between them. Then he kissed Feigele. I thought they were both going to cry. "You know you remind me more and more of your mother," he said. She smiled weakly. He hugged her once more, then jumped up on the wagon seat.

My grandmother Reisel kissed me and started crying.

"Will I ever see you again?" she said.

"Of course," I said, feeling like I was dying inside. "Why do you ask such a question?"

She said, "Promise me you will be a good boy and try to go to school so you will not grow up to be a goy. "

I promised. I hugged her and kissed her and climbed up next to my father.

Feigele shouted to us: "Maybe I will come and see you soon!"

I smiled and nodded, waving, while tears ran down my cheeks. The morning was but a grey dawn and they stood all together in a group, first waving, then just standing watching us off; every now and then someone would lift a hand. It was when they were out of sight that I realized that we were on our way. I turned around and the wind bit my wet face. My father pulled the wagon to a stop along the road. "Here, why don't you take the reins?" Without a word I took the reins, thinking, "Is this what it's like to be a man?" With a flick of the reins I started up the horse. The wagon bounced along the rutted road. Father seemed to doze next to me on the seat. I looked to the horse, my friend.

We planned to spend the night at the house of my father's cousin who lived in Zmigrut. The horse was collapsing as we approached the town. He was a nice speedy animal compared with grandfather Isak's old klunks (see photo front cover). As a matter of fact, he had a tendency to run too fast; my father had told me that horses of this nature are known to work themselves to death. He knew a lot about horses as he used to be a horse trader before the war.

That night I slept very well at the home of my father's cousin, Wolmut. We had also a good breakfast: during the meal my father and Wolmut spoke of Nazi brutality in Zmigrut. This I did not particularly want to hear. We had a lot of traveling to do and it was difficult making good time with a horse and wagon. As soon as breakfast was over we left Zmigrut and this time my father drove. I had had my day behind the reins and I felt very good about it. My father turned onto a two-lane road that was relatively smooth. I felt sleepy and he suggested I go to the back of the wagon where there was a little hay and rest. This I was only too happy to do and the motion of the wagon rocked me to sleep.

The sound of a motorcar awakened me. I opened my eyes and was immediately blinded by the sun directly overhead. The hay made me sneeze. The sound of the motorcar got louder and I peeked over the side of the wagon. Coming down the road in a cloud of dust was a German car. My father quickly turned the horse to the side of the road, for the Germans always needed the whole road to themselves to speed through. The car was coming so quickly that my father didn't have time to quiet the horse. It reared up a little and he struggled with the reins.

The motorcar pulled to a stop in the middle of the road and dust drifted past the car. My heart was beating in my ears as I watched three Nazis get out of the car and walk over to my father.

One of them said, "Are you a Jew? Why isn't your *opaska* (star of David) clearly visible? Are you hiding something, Jew?"

Without waiting for an answer he turned to one of his comrades and said, "You see? They shave off their beards and then think they won't be recognized." He turned back to my father and his eyes were blue and cold as ice. "They think we are stupid."

"Yes, I am a Jew."

One of the Nazis looked over the wagon.

"Got anything in the cart?" he said.

"No. Nothing. I am just traveling to my home."

"I didn't ask where you were going. I said do you have anything in the cart. And that's all I said."

"No."

"You liar." The soldier stepped up to the wagon and slapped my father in the face. "Is the boy there 'nothing'? Maybe we will just shoot him then."

"Please, I want no trouble. Yes, I have my son in the wagon. Please do not hurt him."

The three men grinned and turned back to their car, laughing and barking to each other in German. The motorcar roared away and dust settled on the wagon. I crawled up to the wagon seat and asked my father if he was all right. He nodded, whipping up the horse.

"Did the slap hurt?"

"No. Go back and sleep in the hay."

"But I'm not tired."

"Do as I say."

Feeling hurt and rather foolish I crawled back to the hay. I lay down and closed my eyes. I kept thinking how unjust and humiliating it must be to be slapped for no reason. When I opened my eyes it was dark. The air was cool, the stars bright spots in the sky. The horse was standing still in the harness and father wasn't on the wagon seat. We were in Bielanka. My stepmother, Ester, came out of the house. With her was my brother Moishe. There was a lot of tension in the air and no one seemed too excited about my arrival. I asked about their baby but she was asleep. Early the next morning, Moishe hitchhiked to Zyndranowa. He didn't like to live in Bielanka and wanted to return to see Feigele, my grandfather Isak and grandmother Reisel.

As a boy of ten years of age, the seriousness of Hitler's plan for world conquest bothered me very little. Oh, I often heard my father say the Germans were killing innocent people. I myself had been with Feigele in Dukla. I had been threatened by the Gestapo men on the farm in Zyndranowa and had seen my father slapped in the face along the road to Bielanka.

One could still walk around Bielanka and not see Nazi uniforms or hear the imperative German speech. The noonday sun shone warm on my neck and the people I met on the village roads smiled and said hello. It was a village of peaceful Ruthenians, where neighbors were still friends; it was easy enough to forget that the Germans were occupying our country.

My relationship with Ester had started off on the wrong foot. Ever since the first time I met her and had been frightened by her epileptic brother, she had looked at me with suspicion. Suspicion of what, I didn't know. I tried to be friends with her but nothing I did seemed to turn out right. The first child she had had with my father was a boy named Shaia. He was two years old, and I spent a lot of time with him. We became like buddies and even this Ester seemed to hold against me. I wanted to hitchhike back to Zyndranowa but the Germans had required that all Jews wear on their arm an *opaska* (the yellow Star of David), a symbol of disgrace and subhuman status, and this worried my father. "It is a long way to Zyndranowa," said my father. "And I will not allow Shmulek to go. With the *opaska* on his arm the journey would be dangerous."

"Why doesn't he just not wear the Star?" said Ester. "He looks Aryan enough that no one will know the difference."

She looked at me and her eyes sent chills down my back. I wanted to shake her and say, "Why don't you like me?" But instead I felt cold and angry. I had very few good feelings toward her. My father looked at her and frowned.

"He is my son. He is a Jew. And he will not take such a dangerous journey."

I looked at my father with gratitude. He was a hard man and I was afraid of him. He had shaved from his face his own ethnic symbol; but it made no difference. In a Slavic country like Poland, anyone could tell he was Jewish. It was my stepmother who got my father to shave. He called her a Delilah for it, but at the same time was careful to keep his face smooth. Razor blades were becoming increasingly hard to find. It seemed many other Jews were also shaving their beards, and among Jews, razor blades were sometimes used as currency. One of my jobs was to get them for my father and to do this I traveled quite a bit in the immediate area around Bielanka.

Just before the war broke out, I drove with my father to Bobowa, a small *shtetl* which was about forty percent Jewish. This was a delightful town. The buildings were kind of ramshackle and set on crooked streets of dirt and cobblestone. The streets were filled with bearded Jews and children playing. Dogs ran barking after wagons and blue wood smoke hung about the rooftops. Bobowa was a quiet place, a community of Jews who knew each other by name and looked after the welfare of everyone. On market day my father and I, along with hundreds of peasants, drove to the marketplace and set up our booth of farm produce. There were booths selling everything imaginable: textiles, boots, tools, all kinds of wooden products made by the nearby village craftsmen, and all kinds of food that filled the air with rich, delightful aromas. There were horse traders with their horses, peasants who wanted to trade horses for cows, butchers who wanted to buy cattle for beef. Other livestock was also there to be sold. A peasant would come up to a booth and haggle over the price. When he thought he had a good deal he would take the item. Sometimes he thought he was cheated and this was when trouble was likely to start. The peasant might decide to get together with his friends and beat up the Jewish merchant. In Dukla men like Bergmann would make sure this didn't happen. Bobowa had its strong men as well and my father was one of them. When the peasants saw his big chest and powerful arms they didn't think it was a good idea to cause trouble.

All this was very exciting to me. For hours I would sit next to my father's booth or wander around the marketplace feeling glad to be alive. Sometimes my father would give me some money and I would buy ice cream and food and stuff myself. I liked to watch the pious Jews walk around in the company of a rabbi. They had strange-looking hats and kapotas. How slowly they walked! Their shoulders seemed bent with the weight of the world. Their brows were wrinkled with profound thoughts. The rabbi was the dispenser of justice, the chief judge and arbitrator, and his authority ranged from decisions as to whether the chicken was kosher to the problems concerning the coming of the Messiah. My family observed Jewish ritual and tradition and expected me to do the same. But I could more easily appreciate the cynicism of a man like my uncle Mordecai.

As time passed, a feeling of unrest crept up on me and my childish contentment seemed to grow more and more fragile. My father and stepmother were constantly on edge. The slightest thing would irritate them. The Jews I met on the street were no longer open and friendly. Haunted looks began to appear in their eyes. With tight lips and hunched shoulders they did their business, and market days lost their air of festivity.

A deliberate hatred of the Jews was being spread among the Polish people. This hatred was fostered by the "Master Race" and did not become serious until about 194 1. We, the only Jewish family in Bielanka, were suddenly isolated from the other members of the village in which my father had lived in peace for a number of years. Some Poles in the village had always been suspicious of the Jews and may very well have hated them. In turn, some Jews regarded the Poles with contempt and caution, but we had still been on good terms. My peasant friends came to my father's home and enjoyed the homemade cakes my stepmother made and we got along fairly well. After the "Master Race" started its campaign, my friends would still come over and enjoy Ester's baking, but they seldom talked. When they did, their tone was filled with resentment for the occupying Nazis. For Jews they had no love either. The poison and the anti-Jewish propaganda worked well.

One day a boy named Jacek said very suddenly: "Is it true that you Jews killed Christ our Lord?"

He was sitting in my father's house and his mouth was filled with my stepmother's cookies. At first I didn't know what he meant. But I soon found out that the new village teacher had told the schoolchildren that the Jewish race was the enemy of all people and that they had murdered Jesus Christ. Every day my father became more and more worried.

"Now the Nazis want young men to work in their labor camps," he said, pounding the table with his fist. "Where will it all end? It is not the Poles they want, either, but the Jewish men. First they beat us up. Stores are looted and girls raped. Then they say come and work in our labor camps. Where will it end?"

The knowledge of Feigele's experience in Dukla burned in my mind. I wondered how much father knew. When he said, "Some girls were raped," did he know that one of these girls was his own daughter? What would he do if he found out? He wouldn't hesitate to beat up a Pole, but I had never seen him so much as look defiantly at a Nazi. And would he stand up to the mighty Gestapo? Anyway, how would I tell him? How could I tell him fear had made us stupid and we had walked right into the Gestapo station and offered ourselves up? The memory of what had happened made me sick with shame. More than anything at the moment, I wanted to go to Zyndranowa to see Feigele. The faces of my grandparents, Isak and Reisel, beckoned to me, but here I was trapped in Bielanka.

Then my father, along with all other Polish citizens, received a new order from the Nazis: all horses and cattle had to be registered with the occupying authorities. Father planned to go to Mszanka and help his father, Herman, who lived there, register his animals.

"Why bother to do this?" said Ester. "Let's hide the animals, for certainly we need them."

"Do you want to have me dead? The penalty for all disobedience is the same. The penalty for lying is death."

When he returned, he reported that the city Jews were far worse off than those in villages. The German armies had used up all the available food. Rich Jews who lived in the cities had been reduced to beggars and poor Jews were starving in the streets. The Polish peasants were hungry, too, and blamed the Jews. Hardly a day passed without some Jew being beaten up, robbed or killed; for this reason most of the Jews lived in houses shuttered and bolted tightly. A black market was flourishing alongside the fear and violence.

About this time I decided to visit my grandfather Herman in Mszanka. My father didn't have any objection to this as Mszanka was only a short distance away—a few kilometers at the most. A Jew could still walk the village of Bielanka in relative safety, and I should have no trouble crossing the few rivers and ridges that separated Bielanka from Mszanka.

Over the past few years I had made the trip to Mszanka several times and knew the road very well. With great joy I reached Herman Polster's farm. He had a small house of mudplaster and wood, a barn, a woodshed and a chicken coop. Next to a garden was a cellar where he stored potatoes and milk. Ivy grew around the porch. Excitement surged like electricity in my hand as I reached for the door knob. Behind me I heard a cow moo. I paused and decided to savor the moment which was filled with peace and tranquility.

When I saw grandfather's face I was shocked at the lines of age on it. Of course, he was an old man. For over eighty years he had been on this earth. In this village, surrounded by mountains, he had tended his land, cattle, two horses, goats and chickens. He was a small landowner who struggled each year to see his family and livestock through the winter. All his children except my father had left for America in the beginning of the century.

It seemed that during the past few months he had aged at a faster rate. At one time he had been a robust man with blue eyes, set widely apart. Now those eyes were faded and watery. He suffered from asthma. His hair was white and feathery. In spite of this, however, his jaw was still firm. He still held onto the land.

My grandfather Herman's wife put her arms around me and kissed me fondly on the cheek. She was plain-looking and rather unintelligent, but I liked her very much. Herman had married her after his first wife died. My father was a young boy at the time. By this second wife Herman had another son Getzel. This boy, his mother's only son, was her pride and joy; hardly a day went by that she didn't take great pride in his accomplishments.

This kind woman had always something nice to say. In fact, she talked incessantly and this was probably why her husband was often annoyed with her. He sometimes verbally abused her. When I heard her cries I was sure to stay out of the way. On such occasions I was terrified. What a man did in his house was probably his own business. Unlike my grandparents in Zyndranowa, my grandparents in Mszanka at least spoke to each other and exchanged pleasantries.

On this particular trip to Mszanka I noticed right away the absence of Getzel. He was a lot like my uncle Mordecai.

"Where's Getzel?" I asked grandfather Herman. He looked at me in a strange way and his wife got red around the eyes and I knew right away I had said something wrong.

"He is in jail in Gorlice; he was arrested for his activities in the black market. You know what the black market is? That is how he helped support us during these trying days." Grandfather Herman squinted at me then raised his faded blue eyes toward the hills outside the window of the house. "The Nazis don't like the black market and even less do they like those who work with it. Getzel has become a criminal. In the eyes of the Nazis, his situation is even worse because he is a Jew."

"You mean they won't let him go?"

"Have you ever heard of a Jew being allowed to go free by the Gestapo?"

My step-grandmother was crying in the bedroom. Herman shuffled off and I was left feeling there was no place on earth free from the Nazi curse.

Sometime later my grandfather Herman asked me to go to the prison in Gorlice and take Getzel some food. My step-grandmother loaded boiled potatoes into a bucket. Underneath these potatoes she put some boiled chicken. It was strictly forbidden for the prisoners to have meat, so she hid the chicken well. Then off I went on the road to Gorlice.

Soon a cart came along with a peasant at the reins. He stopped and picked me up. We bounced and jolted along the rutted road in silence and I gripped the bucket between my legs as if it were a treasure. Before long we passed some beggars on the road. With sad Jewish eyes they looked at us. One man supported himself with a stick. His coat was dirty and ragged.

"Hah! Some trick those Nazis played on the Jewish dogs," said the peasant driving the cart. I looked at him with surprise thinking it strange he would talk like that to me, a Jewish boy.

Then I realized I had not worn my opaska. Without the yellow

Star of David on my arm there was no obvious way to tell I was a Jew and the driver had mistaken me for a Polish peasant boy .

"Before the Germans came those very Jews along the road were fat with Polish wealth. They had done very well for themselves at the expense of the true citizens of this country. Now," he threw back his head and laughed, "they would give their coats for the potatoes in your bucket."

Fiercely I gripped the bucket as if the peasant might take it away from me.

"I have heard that the Polish kings asked the Jews to live in Poland long, long ago."

The driver glared at me. "Who told you such nonsense? Say, are you a Jewish sympathizer?" He pulled up the horse. "Where are you taking those potatoes anyway?"

Fear closed like a fist on my throat. Most peasants in the country knew they could do nearly anything they wanted to a Jew and no punishment would be forthcoming. The Nazis enjoyed Jewish misery. Jews banded together for their own safety, and here I was, alone, in the clutches of an angry peasant.

"To Gorlice. To Gorlice!" I stammered. "My aunt lives there. She is ill and my mother sent me with some food."

The peasant continued to glare at me, looking me over from head to foot. Finally, he flicked the reins and the horse started down the road once more. The mood of the driver was sour and he did not say another word the entire way to Gorlice.

Inside the city I was only too glad to hop off the cart.

"Where does your aunt live?" growled the driver.

"Over there." I waved my hand in the general direction of the center of the city. Before the man could say anything else I took off, twisting through several streets until I was sure he could not possibly be following me. Pausing to catch my breath, I felt the potatoes. They were stone cold.

As I walked along the streets of Gorlice, I felt pretty good for having escaped from the peasant driver. After all, I had been in his clutches. He might very well have beaten me up. Not too long ago a Jewish boy in a similar situation had been maimed when a peasant drove over him with his wagon. Mulling over my good fortune, I didn't even realize I was walking right past the Gestapo station. For some reason I happened to look up—and there was a Nazi standing on the balcony looking right at me. He waved and told me to come inside.

My knees nearly buckled as I climbed the steps. Over and over again I cursed myself, thinking how stupid I had been not to watch where I was going. Inside the door of the headquarters the Nazi officer was waiting. Against his leg he beat a switch.

"When a boy walks past the station with a bucket of potatoes in his hand he is usually going to the prison," he said. "And those are potatoes, aren't they?"

"Yessir. "

"And it just so happens that most people in the prison are Jewish."

Humbly, I mumbled, "Yessir."

"And are you Jewish?"

He slapped me and the next thing I knew I was lying on the floor looking at his black shiny boots.

"Why don't you wear the yellow badge on your arm as required?"

"I'm sorry. Really I am. I had no idea it wasn't on my arm.

"So what are you carrying in the bucket?"

"Potatoes."

"I know that. What else do you have?"

"Nothing, sir. Nothing at all."

By now I was crying, choking with sobs. The German took the bucket and dumped it on me. Right there for all the world to see was the chicken.

"Nothing? Nothing else, you say? You know the rules, don't you? Take that! You filthy lying Jew! You know the prisoners aren't supposed to have meat. Take that! And that!" Again and again he kicked me. I rolled up into a ball and his boot struck my head, shoulder, belly, back and legs. "I'm sorry," I cried, "Please, oh please—I'm sorry—oh sorry—oh please!" He pulled my head back by the hair and kicked my face. Blood from my nose had spilled on the floor. There was blood and potatoes and chicken. "Where did you get the meat?" he shouted. "I don't know." He kicked me again.

"Where?" And again. "I don't know, I don't know!"

"Pick up this garbage," he said.

Blinded by tears and blood, I scraped up the potatoes and chicken and put them back in the bucket. The officer yanked the bucket from my hands and dumped it in a waste can. Then he threw the empty tin at my face. I ducked and he kicked me in the belly.

"If I ever catch you again without your armband, your *opaska,* I will kill you. Do you understand? If ever I catch you. And be certain I will keep my eyes open. Now get out of here. Get out!" He kicked me again and I stumbled out the door.

The next couple of days I spent in bed. When my body had healed I got a good scolding for getting caught by the Gestapo.

In spite of the tension of day-to-day living, my grandparents tried to make my stay in Mszanka relatively pleasant. One Saturday morning I was given a new suit. With Jews all around us reduced to poverty and begging in the streets, this was indeed a very nice gift. Actually, I should have gone to the *shul* in the next village of Moszczenica with my grandfather Herman, but I went instead out to the fields and ended up mildly taunting the cattle. Why I did such a thing, I don't know. Perhaps I just felt so good I was bursting at the seams; such a mood lent itself well to taunting those stupid, lovable creatures.

Much to my horror one of the angry bullocks started chasing me. I fell in the mud and the bullock gored me a little, tearing my new suit. Needless to say, I had to go back to the house and explain how the suit got muddy and torn. I would have much rather grown wings and flown away. With each word of explanation I sputtered, grandfather Herman seemed to grow in size and terrible might. He was a tornado, a hurricane, the end of the world! But all he did was scold me, to my pleasant surprise. As for the bullock, grandfather Herman sold it to some peasant and I never saw it again.

About this time the Nazis ordered that no Jew was to move from where he lived. German patrols went through Mszanka and the terror of the cities spread to the country villages as well. Rumors were spreading that the Nazis were preparing ghettos for the

Jews to live in. I had no idea what a ghetto was, but gone were the days when Hitler's plans meant little to me. The days of freedom through isolation were long past. I quite naturally assumed any plans the Germans had for the Jews couldn't be pleasant and that it would just be a matter of time until I found out what a ghetto was.

The Nazis were diabolical creatures. They seemed to know the very thoughts in your head. One day a Gestapo car drove up to the house of grandfather Herman. Five Nazis got out of the car. The leader did not look German. Rather, he seemed to have a touch of Slav-Ukrainian in him. He waited until Herman came out of the house. The other Nazis surrounded my grandfather, who obviously began to fear the worst.

"I hear, Jew, that you sold a cow."

The officer slapped Herman in the face.

"Is that true?"

"N-no. I w-would not do such a thing."

I stood there and watched my grandfather punched, kicked, and dragged in the mud. He cried and pleaded with them, saying he was an old man and stubbornly denying he had sold the bullock. The Nazis beat this eighty-year-old man. They pushed his face in barnyard dung and made him eat it. In spite of this, he refused to confess he'd sold the bullock. Whom he'd sold it to and where the money was hidden was a secret locked in his heart; when the Nazis finally left he was a breath away from death.

My step-grandmother nursed him night and day until he was strong enough to get out of bed. The farm was falling apart. Herman had known exactly what to do and when to do it. Without him something was always going wrong. The weeds choked the garden; the cows got into the grain; the horses refused to work. Night and day I prayed for his recovery; it was a happy and thankful day when he appeared in the fields once more.

But he wasn't quite the same as he'd been before. The spring was gone from his step and he spent long moments standing still just staring at the mountains, breathing heavily. When he did that it gave me the chills, for I was certain he was seeing something invisible to me. It wasn't long before he decided I should go back to

Bielanka. "Life is too short," he said. "A boy must spend time with his family." Before I left he asked lengthy questions concerning Feigele and Moishe and my grandparents in Zyndranowa. Thinking of these dear ones made me sad and I missed them terribly. I would much rather have gone to Zyndranowa than to Bielanka.

Returning to my father's home did give me the opportunity to get to know my stepsister better. She was named Jaffa, after my mother who had died of tuberculosis. Jaffa means "pretty" in Hebrew, and the child was appropriately named.

As it turned out, I was to have a short stay in Bielanka. In June of 1942, Hans Frank, the Nazi governor of occupied Poland, issued a proclamation that all people of the Jewish faith were to leave their homes and move to prescribed towns: anyone who did not comply with the order within seventy-two hours would be shot on the spot. The proclamation further stated that all personal property had to be left behind, except for bundles which could easily be carried. The town we were told to report to was Bobowa. This was to be our "ghetto" for two months.

My father and stepmother were deeply troubled. They walked around the house trying to figure out a way to carry along with us the most valuable articles and the most essential food, which was extremely scarce. With a feeling of powerlessness and depression, we climbed into a wagon provided by a kindly peasant neighbor. Each of us carried as much as we could. We took a final look at our home where there had been a relative happiness and security. It was a simple house, built after World War I. The roof was covered with tar paper like any number of Polish farmhouses; but it was ours, all ours. The harsh feelings my stepmother Ester and I had had toward each other now seemed like exchanges of love in a house full of life. I closed my eyes. Some Pole or Lemko would move into the ready-made comfort of our home, and live there free.

The horse was whipped a few times and started out quickly. As the house disappeared into the distance, Ester broke into sobs. She must have felt it was the last time she would see her village. My father tried to console her saying the leave was temporary and that they would soon return. And perhaps he convinced her we would, in fact, return. Certainly I was convinced: for who could possibly have guessed the truth?

The first thing I noticed about Bobowa was that it had a barbed wire fence around some parts of it. This fence was entirely new and it struck terror into my soul. With pity in his eyes, the kind peasant who had been my father's neighbor and who had let us use his wagon took leave from us. At the gate of Bobowa—a heavy gate of wood and barbed wire-—he let us off and said goodbye for the last time. On the dusty street that used to lead into a free and thriving *shtetl* before the war, my father stood holding in his arms all the bedding he could carry. Ester held the baby, Jaffa, and some food in a sack. I carried extra clothing and some more food; my young stepbrother, Shaya, had in his little hands a potato for our dinner. We were not alone. All around us stood other people who held in their arms their earthly belongings. Not everyone in the Bobowa *shtetl* had been Jewish. The Nazis had divided the town, and the Poles, who now lived either outside the barbed wire enclosure or in special sections of the ghetto, gathered outside their houses and looked at us with curiosity. My family who stood in confusion at the gate of the ghetto, was greeted by the Jewish police.

A greeting party of several individuals approached us from inside the ghetto. They walked with heavy steps, their eyes on the ground. One man detached himself from the rest and walked up to my father. He was beardless and rather skinny. I was shocked to see the emptiness in his eyes.

"I am a member of the *Judenrat,*" he said. 'The *Judenrat* is a council of Jewish elders, appointed by the Third Reich to take care of Jewish affairs here in Bobowa, as in other ghettos all over Poland. I will represent you on the *Judenrat* and pass on to you its instructions. Now I will show you to your new home."

No other words were spoken. I was bursting with questions but didn't really want to know the answers. Stumbling under the weight and bulk of our loads, we followed the member of the *Judenrat* down narrow streets and dingy alleys. The magic of Bobowa that I used to feel on market days before the war was now gone. The Germans had changed everything. The member of the *Judenrat* turned around and asked our name. Apparently, this was an important procedure. The Germans had listed the names of all the local Jews, and anyone not showing up at the ghetto within the four-day period set forth in the proclamation would be considered a fugitive.

After my father stated his name, the *Judenrat* member just stared at him in a rather stupefied fashion. He seemed to have a difficult time remembering what he was supposed to do. He looked sick. As I learned later, the Nazis had been very smart: they avoided direct contact with the Jews by appointing the *Judenrat* council to look after the ghetto.

This council was a mouthpiece for the Nazis, and the members of the council were sometimes rewarded for their cooperation with better living conditions.

But even the *Judenrat* was not exposed to the truth. They did as they were directed by the Nazis; but they, too, were Jews and lived in the same constant fear as everyone else. This man who was leading us to our new home stood in a state of confusion for a long time after my father said our name. Then, he led us in a direction opposite to the one we had been traveling. Sometime after we were situated in the ghetto I was to learn that this man had shot himself. By then, death was such a common part of everyday life that the news neither shocked me nor caused any great concern.

Our house consisted of one room about twenty by eighteen feet. We found that my grandfather Herman Polster and his wife were already living there, as did also another family.

My grandfather had been brought there by peasants from Mszanka. The only furniture was a wooden table and some old dirty straw mattresses thrown along the walls. The bathroom consisted of a smelly, wooden outhouse in back of the house which we shared with several other households. The room had no running water. The crowded conditions came as no surprise. In the Bobowa ghetto, literally hundreds of people were crowded into buildings that normally held about one-tenth that number. Each Jewish dwelling had a blue paint mark under its window so it could be distinguished from the gentile houses. Ester and my father piled our belongings on one of the mattresses. No one said anything.

My step-grandmother gave us a sad look, as if to say "I knew you would end up here. I was waiting."

"Where's Getzel?" I said, desperate to break up the tension in the room.

My step-grandmother burst into tears. Her eyes were red and swollen and I should have known that she had been crying and for what reason.

"The Germans have taken my son from me," she sobbed, looking at Ester as if asking for pity. "From the prison he was sent to a concentration camp. There he developed a certain sickness. Oh, if they would only have sent him home to me! But no—what the Germans do is line up all the fine Jewish boys and divide them into two groups: one to the right, one to the left. If one is sent to the right it means work in the munitions camp. To the left… Oh, my son, I think they sent my son to the left. My only son…" She was in a hysterical state—mumbling to herself.

Ester went to her and tried to comfort her. My father stood in the middle of the floor staring at his feet, his face white as a sheet, his lips pale. At the wooden table sat Herman Polster. Completely expressionless, he stared at his sobbing wife and looked like a dead man. My father walked to the table and sat down next to him. Neither one said a word nor acknowledged otherwise the presence of the other.

The night closed in and a cold grey darkness filled the room. Ester spread our bedding on one of the mattresses and we got ready for bed. Along the far wall the other family who occupied the room did the same. The day had been one of the longest and most painful of our lives, we were exhausted, but no one slept. As I lay next to my stepmother, the coldness of the room seemed to take the breath from my body.

The woman of the family along the far wall was weak and sickly-looking. She had not greeted us when we arrived. In the darkness of the night she was crying.

After what seemed like hours, Ester got up to see if the woman was in pain and I heard talk of a baby. The woman already had two children, about three and five years old, and I couldn't believe she was actually going to have another baby. I thought no man in his right mind would give his wife a baby at a time like this. Then I thought of my father and felt a twinge of guilt for such judgment, as my stepmother Ester was also pregnant for the third time.

My stepmother came over to our mattress and shook my father. He let her shake him a few times, then asked what she wanted. "A doctor, " she said. "You must get a doctor. "

"How am I to do that in the middle of the night? There might not be such a thing as a doctor in this place."

"You must go and see," said Ester urging him to do something. "Wake people up if you must. But hurry!"

My father got up and stomped out of the door. Ester then told me to wait outside. The children were asleep. Herman Polster seemed to have fallen into a coma. My step-grandmother was in pieces over the fate of her son, Getzel; but she rose from the mattress and went to help Ester. Stumbling about in the darkness, I left the room and stood shivering on the doorstep. The night was starless and damp. From off in the distance one could hear the lonely bark of a dog, and I thought to myself. "A baby is actually coming into the world!"

After about an hour of shivering and waiting for the doctor, I heard the high-pitched cry. In a little while my stepmother came to the door and said I could come in. I followed her back into the house and found the woman's husband lying on the floor crying. The woman was asleep. The doctor arrived and the baby soon died. The doctor left. The baby lay in a corner covered with a rough blanket of some grey material. Herman Polster was muttering prayers and the sky outside the room's only window was the color of dirty water. The woman was still sleeping. Her husband left the room to see about the burial. My stepmother prepared breakfast for us and the woman's two small sons; I felt sorry for them. Three weeks they had been in the ghetto. We ate some potatoes and a tiny piece of bread. Then my stepmother went to assist the other woman.

The baby's father returned with a crude wooden box. The baby had to be buried outside the ghetto. That day happened to be the one in which the Nazis made one of their demands upon the Jews trapped in the Bobowa ghetto: all jewelry and other valuables had to be turned in to the *Judenrat*. Lack of cooperation would be punished by death. At the barbed-wire ghetto gate, the Nazis examined the crude wooden coffin and its contents because there was a rumor that the Jews were burying their gold.

Initially, the Bobowa ghetto consisted of a cross-section of the Jewish population. The young and old, the healthy and sick were all thrown together. Garbage and human waste piled up faster than it could be disposed of. Lice infested everything. Children walked naked through the cold damp alleys. Typhoid was common, as were diarrhea and dysentery. Jews who had once owned property and small businesses now dressed in rags. Elderly people, sickly and weak, used the sides of the buildings for support as they shuffled down the streets.

The most prevalent sickness of all was fear. What would the Nazis do next? What was going to happen? We had heard terrifying stories about Nazi visits into the ghettos. At any moment the ghetto gate might swing open; German youths driving jeeps would careen down the narrow streets and alleys, purposely running down anyone in their path. For all their youth, these were soldiers in the German army. They seemed to be only teenagers, yet they carried rifles on their shoulders; and when they got tired of chasing down pedestrians with the jeeps, they would yank those rifles off their shoulders and for the fun of it shoot down anyone within range. Laughing like schoolchildren, they would shoot out glass windows, and the Jews, packed like cattle in their houses, had to take cover on the floor, with bullets and glass spraying over them.

There was no place to run from such abuse. When a Jew was caught outside the ghetto, the *szmalcownik* (blackmailer) who found him was handsomely rewarded. If the Polish policeman in the service of the Nazis so desired, he could abuse the Jew with impunity before turning him or her over to the Gestapo.

Inside the ghetto, members of the *Judenrat* scurried everywhere trying to calm the people. They said the Nazis were preparing a better life for us on the outside. They said the squalor of the ghetto was temporary, that some day we would be free.

The *Judenrat* said all young men were to report to the marketplace. The Nazis needed them for work in various camps. This was to be part of the new life. Any life seemed better than that in the ghetto, and the young men gladly walked to the marketplace, also known as the town's square, an area of cobblestones and trees, with buildings on four sides. The Nazis loaded them into military trucks and we never saw them again. We never heard from them again. The *Judenrat* said they were carving out a new life outside the ghetto and we believed because all we had was ignorance and hope.

Then the Nazis wanted all men expert in particular trades. Once more the *Judenrat* offered us hope. "You see? These men will be working at jobs that will provide money for their families. Soon they will call for their families." And of course we all wanted to believe this. The Nazis gave us a food ration, but it wasn't enough to keep us healthy. The old and sick died off and the Nazis cut back our rations, saying food should not be wasted on people not strong enough to survive anyway. Every spare piece of ground in the ghetto was used to grow vegetables. A couple of people even owned goats for milk to give their ailing infants. They had to watch the animals constantly because they feared they would be stolen and butchered for food. There were rumors of cases of cannibalism, but I never knew firsthand of such a thing. People with bloated bellies walked around in a daze. Others died of starvation. Even our dead we could not protect from Nazi defilement, and the coffins were searched for jewelry.

Little by little, men of health and strength were taken away. If ever the ghetto could have set up a fighting force that day was past and gone forever. A few relatively young men remained, like my father and the man of the family we shared the room with, but they were not inclined to fight. We didn't know what had happened to the men who had left the ghetto; they may very well have tried to contact their families. Any kind of resistance would most certainly have been futile and caused our own death when salvation could possibly be near.

For another thing, a Jew was taught from birth to wait upon

the rabbi, even as the rabbi waited upon the Lord. If there was a decision to be made of any importance at all, one had to consult the rabbi. He was a *hassid,* a pious man, and would intervene on behalf of his people. He knew what to do about everything, even Nazism, Hitler, and the persecution.

During the tragic moments in the Bobowa ghetto, the rabbis had one standard answer. All the rabbis I ever met or saw said the same thing: "Children, go and pray because the day will come when the Messiah will appear and he will protect us. The Lord knows what he is doing. He will help us." There wasn't one rabbi or other leader I know of who said to his people: "Children, let's take up arms. Let's train ourselves. Let's fight. Let's barricade ourselves and save our lives. Let's not obey the German laws any longer."

Life was torture, anxiety and all-pervasive danger. On Saturdays, the *Shabbat,* the day of rest and rejoicing, people were irritable and lonely. The Nazis took sport with our women. The heavy gate of wood and barbed wire swung open and the jeeps came through. One sight, in particular, filled me with horror. The Nazis trapped a young girl in an alley. They pointed their guns at her and told her to undress. Then they made her get into the jeep and drove to the marketplace. There she was forced to dance for them. When the Germans tired of this amusement they tied her down and when they finished they left her there for the Jews to untie.

With lowered heads and haunted eyes the members of the *Judenrat* passed on the news: the Germans wanted all women between the ages of fifteen and twenty-nine. Once more, the German military trucks came to the marketplace. When they left, the heart of the Jewish people in the ghetto went with them. All that was left was a shell: the sick, the cripples, older folks and children. Old men muttered to themselves as they shuffled along the sides of buildings.

Young mothers had remained in the ghetto with their babies, and the babies, weak and sickly as they were, sucked the life from their mother's bodies. Garbage lay everywhere. We were surrounded by sickness and death. The buildings were still overcrowded, but now the wind roamed streets that seemed empty. People who happened to meet seldom spoke to each other. Long and hard they looked at each other and then moved on as if they had not seen.

The hollowness of these stares I couldn't stand. The spectre of death I saw everywhere made me want to scream, and I sought escape. I found there were places in the barbed wire fence surrounding the ghetto through which I could squeeze. For the first time in my life I appreciated the fact that I looked like a peasant boy. My blond hair blended in with that of the gentile Poles and I roamed the countryside freely. At every opportunity I stole food and clothing, razor blades and candles. With these items I returned to the ghetto and my family was much better off than most of the other families. They had extra food and clothing. By the light of candles my father and grandfather Herman read the scriptures. Each day I risked my life to make things a little easier for them, and all I wanted in return was a little appreciation, a kind word or a gentle look.

However, this was denied to me. My father rarely said anything and when Ester looked at me her eyes seemed dark and accusing. I thought she hated me for some reason. Everyone left in the ghetto lived in a state of fear and irritation and I was no exception. When I crawled through a hole in the barbed wire fence, I left the ghetto behind, but I carried the fear with me. I carried with me the feeling I was hated by my stepmother. To a word one can respond, but how can one respond to a look? With bitterness I conjured her face in my imagination and stared back at her with hatred. With his silence my father abandoned me and I hated him for it, too. The one thought that gave me hope was that somewhere away from Bobowa was my grandfather Isak, my grandmother Reisel, the beautiful Feigele, and Moishe, the only true brother I had. This thought I clung to. The proclamation said all Jews had to report to ghettos and I had no reason to believe Isak and Reisel and my sister and brother had escaped this fate. But they were in a different part of Poland and had not reported to Bobowa. Since they weren't in Bobowa I didn't have proof of their imprisonment. I could believe what I wanted to and this was that they were free people waiting for me to be reunited with them. I simply would not believe they were suffering the same ignominy as my father and stepmother. To believe this would have deprived me of any hope whatsoever.

One day, while I was outside the ghetto, I met a Polish boy. He greeted me and I stopped dead in my tracks with fear. We were on the road leading out of Bobowa and a peasant drove his cart past us. The boy looked me up and down. He said, "Hey, who are you? I've never seen you before."

My heart was pounding so hard I thought I would choke. But I had to be brave!

"Oh yeah? Well, I've never seen you before either."

"You talk a little funny. I'll bet you're a Jew."

"You talk funny, too. You're the one who's a Jew and maybe I'll turn you in to the Gestapo."

Just then a Gestapo car appeared down the road. I thought: 'Oh, no! Now I've done it! Now this stupid Polish kid will give me away and I'll be shot by the Gestapo.' The car drove on past us and the boy didn't make a motion to stop it. With great relief I watched the cloud of dust kicking up behind the shiny black car. The Polish boy looked me up and down again. I almost cried with joy when I realized all he wanted to do was fight. He squinted after the Gestapo car.

"You see those Nazis? They have smiles on their faces. I'll bet they just came from some Jewish girl."

I realized a fight could probably be avoided if I showed this boy a lot of respect. But he didn't know anything I didn't know about women. If worse came to worse I was sure I could punch his stupid face in. Also, what he said about the Jewish girl made me both steaming mad and curious.

"What do you mean? All the Jewish girls are in the ghetto!"

"Goes to show what you know," said the boy, spitting in the dust. "The Jews are so dumb they do whatever the Germans want them to. First they send out all their men. Then all their money. Then all their girls. They're sure dumb. All the Nazis have to do is ask and the Jews obey."

My knees felt weak. What did he know about the Nazis "requests"? He had never been in the ghetto and had no idea what it meant to be offered a life outside the barbed wire. He had no idea what it was like for me to walk around the countryside like a free Pole, and then have to return to the barbed-wire ghetto pen because that was where my family was kept like animals. For me to be caught outside the ghetto would mean instant death, and what did he know of endless fear?

I said hoarsely: "And what happened to these men who were taken out of the ghetto?"

Nonchalantly he shrugged. "Oh, I don't know. But I do know what happened to the girls." He sniggered. "Every single one of them are whores for the German army. That's right! They do something to them so they can't have babies, then they send them to the fields. If they don't do a good job they get cremated. Three reports it takes and then a girl is turned to ashes. Ha-haw—"

In the middle of the third "ha" I hit him right in the mouth. I never had so much fun in all my life as beating the stuffing out of that stupid kid. From my mouth came a hideous, insane noise; when I finished with him this noise turned to sobbing. The boy staggered to his feet and limped away. I screamed: "I am a Jew, you scum, you cow dung, you stupid—" Picking up stones, I ran after him hurling them at him and he ran shrieking down the road.

Then I stopped still and regained my composure. Fearing the boy would return with the Gestapo I worked my way back to the ghetto. My mind burned in agony, not for myself so much as for my father and Ester. Grandfather Herman was a man with one foot in the grave. He would accept rather stoically whatever was to happen. But my father still prayed every day for freedom. He said, "God will save us." He talked to the rabbis and believed the words of the *Judenrat.* And Ester, my stepmother, had two children to raise. Each day she prayed for their future giving no thought to herself. What would they say if they knew that our women between fifteen and twenty-nine had been released from the ghetto only to be field whores for the German armies? What kind of hope could they find in knowing that? How could I possibly tell them?

The day was Thursday. Distressed as I was, I remembered to take back with me the rabbit I had stolen from a Polish farm and I put it in a burlap sack. When I once more saw the faces of my family, my heart sweated tears. My feeling of hatred for them had been the luxury of a hurt child. Actually I loved them much more than I could have thought, and even for Ester I suffered the pain of knowing that her hope might very well be in vain.

Of course, I had to tell them what I had found out. A realistic appraisal of our situation had to be made. But how? How was I to tell them? I said, "Dad, maybe we should stop listening to the *Judenrat*. They say stay home and pray. But maybe we should fight back and escape." He gave me a scathing look. "The Lord has brought us this far and now will you turn your back on Him? You think the rabbis and our other leaders are fools? Go to bed and I don't want to hear such dangerous talk again." So I went to bed feeling sorrowful, hurt, denied; bottled up with so many feelings I thought I would explode. The following day was the infamous Friday of the Nazis' "final solution" of the Bobowa ghetto. All Jews that remained in the ghetto were loaded up into trucks and taken away. The *Judenrat* ran around trying to calm people, saying: "It's only another ghetto we're moving to. A better one with lots of room and more food. It's all right. Everything is all right. We are only being resettled in the East." The members of the *Judenrat* were Jews just like everyone else and they, too, got into the German military trucks. My stepmother Ester had given me a parting gift, a jewel of sentiment no Nazi could have extracted from her. "Shmulek, I love you"...the words echoed in my head. For all I knew, I was the only Jew in the Bobowa ghetto who did not get onto those military trucks. Desperately, I hoped I had company. Some dear face I longed to see: a relative, a friend, anyone at all.

How long does it take a sob from the belly to reach the throat? When is memory put to rest? A tear is a diamond, each drop a piece of soul: and this is the wealth of the Jewish people.

I survived the final solution. But at what cost? When would I ever see my family again? The whole of Poland stretched before me filled with a number of unfriendly gentile Poles and Nazis. Where to go—I didn't know; the road to anywhere at all was precarious indeed.

JUSEK THE PENKNIFE STEALER

IF A CROW FLEW from Bielanka to Gorlice it would pass over the villages of Biesnik and Mszanka along the way. A village was often just a collection of farms and houses at a secluded spot in the countryside, and several villages might be very close together. The villages had thatched roofs, outhouses, and no electricity, running water or paved roads. Bystra was a village near Mszanka and this was where the good peasant woman Balwina lived with her family.

One evening there was a knock at her door. The year was 1942. Poland was in the vise of Nazi occupation. The land was cloaked with fear and one was cautious to answer a knock on one's door. Behind the hand that knocked could be a Gestapo man, a beggar insane with hunger, or worse yet—a Jew. A person got money for turning in a Jew to the Gestapo—in fact, some murderous peasants made a business out of bounty hunting for Jewish fugitives. One of these murderers was a peasant called Krupa. If one wasn't careful one could also get marked with suspicion, and it was better to avoid the fugitives altogether. Just a few days before this particular evening the Bobowa ghetto had been evacuated. The Germans had called this operation the "final solution" of the Bobowa ghetto. Many Polish peasants applauded the operation. Some, however, at the risk of their own lives, were righteous, altruistic heroes. They helped the unfortunate victims.

The knock once more sounded at Balwina's door and her husband raised up his voice:

"Who's there?"

"Shmulek. It is Shmulek Oliner."

"Who?"

"Shmulek. Aron's son."

Balwina opened the door. Caught between the lighted kitchen and the darkness of the night she hovered uncertainly. Then she saw it was indeed Shmulek.

"For heaven's sake, what are you doing here? It's very dangerous. Where did you come from? Hurry, come on in."

The kitchen of this peasant farmhouse had whitewashed walls. There was a shrine in the corner. A cross made of two sticks tied together was on the whitewashed board above the doorway leading to another room. Heat from the oven made the smell of Shmulek's clothing rise dank and foul. Balwina was a big woman with a fleshy face and ample bosom. In the manner of a person used to thinking quickly she bolted the door and pulled the shutters over the kitchen window. "What's happened to you?" she said, in mid-stride. "Where're your parents?" Her husband was watching me carefully. He was a thin man with large ears; he was sitting at the table and smoking a pipe.

"The trucks came to the ghetto and took them away. I don't know where they are or what happened to them. A farmer I met said they were taken to Garbacz. All the Jews were taken to Garbacz and shot!"

"Oh, Shmulek, you dear boy! Whatever has happened to you? You look like you have spent a week hiding in ditches. Come. Did you hear that?" She turned to her husband who was idly puffing on his pipe. "Shmulek ran away from the Bobowa ghetto."

"What did they do to your parents?" he said.

Balwina turned on him. "Oh, you stupid goat. He just said they were shot and now look—you've made him cry! Shmulek, Shmulek..." The good peasant woman also cried, reaching out her soft warm arms. "Don't cry, my child. Don't cry. The Lord Jesus will help you. The Lord will help you."

"I had to come here. You were the only person I knew. I had to go somewhere and I was so afraid. I don't believe it. I just don't believe it. They couldn't have killed my parents. I'm sure my parents are somewhere. I have to go look for them. I have..."

"No, my child. You stay here. You realize I am endangering my life keeping you here and I'm telling you this because I want you out of sight. I want you to stay in the attic. Go up in the attic and stay there until I find out what happened to your parents and what the story is about this thing. Under no circumstances should you show your face outside this house because the neighbors may be spying on me. They know I was the friend of Herman Polster and his son Aron. They might suspect me of being friendly to the Jews and if they saw you here they might turn you in. I don't want Krupa to recognize you because he will deliver you to the Gestapo for sure, and you know what would happen then. That's right, they would shoot us all and maybe even burn down the house.

"Yes, I'll stay up in the attic and hide."

"Now, you must be hungry."

"Yes, I am. All the way from Bobowa I walked and it took me two days. A farmer gave me something to eat and that's all I've had."

The good woman placed some bread and butter and milk on the table. "Here you are, child, and don't be afraid to eat all you want."

"Thank you very much."

"Those wretched Nazis. Those merciless, brutal Nazis. How can they do such a thing to innocent people?" she muttered as she put dishes in a pile to be washed. She brought some more bread to the table. "Here's more food. Don't be afraid to eat. The war may be longer than any of us think and who knows when we'll be able to fill our bellies."

"I heard on the road that the Germans will be defeated in seven weeks. America has entered the war and the Nazis will be crushed."

"Don't be so quick to believe it," said Balwina. "The Nazis are diabolical geniuses. They spread misinformation among the peasants and no one knows what is happening. I'll bet you didn't know there were ghettos all over Poland? Yes, there were. All over Poland there were ghettos just like Bobowa. Tomorrow I will find out this thing about your parents. Now don't start crying again. There, there. I only want you to be strong and not be quick to believe the war will be easy. Before the English and Americans beat the Germans there will be a long hard fight and a lot of good people will die. This is what I think. The only thing for sure in the war is that if you do something the Nazis don't like you get shot, so keep your head inside the house. Now finish your bread. That's it—one more piece."

"Good. Now I want you to go up to the attic. There is a bed up there in which my son, Staszek, sleeps." Balwina looked at me, paused for a second and said to me, "Do you know that my Staszek looks like you? We will take care of him somewhere else tonight. Now go on up and take off your clothes before getting into bed. You are dirty and smell very bad and I will see to it that you have clean clothes in the morning. Good night, now."

The attic was a cold dark place where mice scurried in the corners. The bed was a mattress of straw plied high with blankets and quilts, and underneath this bedding was a little bit of paradise for a desperately cold and tired body.

In spite of the comfortable bedding, I couldn't sleep. My mind kept wondering about what the future would hold for me. The next morning bleak grey light came through the cracks between the boards on the wall.

"Shmulek. Hey, Shmulek, come down for breakfast."

The light that came through the cracks in the wall gave little information about what time of day it was. At the foot of the bed was a pile of clean clothes.

"Good morning."

"Good morning, Shmulek. It's about time you came down out of the attic. Did you sleep well?"

"Yes, thank you. How did those clothes get on the bed?"

Balwina laughed. "You were so sound asleep that a herd of cattle could have walked through the room and you wouldn't have known it." She spoke very lightly, but her eyes were red and swollen. "Sit down at the table."

She broke an egg into the frying pan on the stove.

"My husband was out checking around this morning. He talked to the villagers and it's true: the Nazis did shoot all the ghetto people. They made them take off their clothes and walk out onto planks and then the machine guns mowed them down. Twenty-one or twenty-two escaped off the military trucks, and the Gestapo are making house-to-house searches for them. It's only about eighteen kilometers from Garbacz to here, Shmulek, and I'm worried for you. You ought to try…you know what I suggest to you? You do not look Jewish. You don't have a beard yet and you speak Polish very well, just like a Polish peasant boy. You look just like one of our Polish Christian boys, and I suggest you change your name right now and pretend to be a peasant. Find yourself a job helping out on a farm or tending cows. That's what you should do." She was crying. The egg was burning.

"What happened to my grandparents living in Zyndranowa? Could I go to see them? Could I go stay with Feigele and Moishe?"

"Now Shmulek, you are crying just like me. How am I ever going to tell you what happened if you are already crying? I'm sorry the egg is burned. I liked your father, Aron, very much. Herman Polster, you know, helped me out when I was in trouble; he gave me livestock, too. In fact, just before the Germans took his farm away from him he sold me a very fine bullock at a fair price, and he also gave me his horse. Those two were very fine men and I feel toward you like a mother. I wish I didn't have such bad news to give you.

"What? What is it you are saying?"

"Ah, the Germans are such brutes. There were ghettos all around the country, you know, and each one had its 'final solution' decided by the Germans. Yes, it is a day that the good Lord wept at man's inhumanity to man. One at a time the ghettos were evacuated and the Jews were shot. No one knew what was going on, except the Nazis. On Thursday a ghetto called Biecz was evacuated and no one passed the word along. No one knew. On Friday the Germans went to Bobowa and no one knew what was happening. I keep saying 'evacuated' and it is because I cannot bring myself to say the word of horrible truth."

"But my grandparents—what happened to Feigele and Moishe?"

"Must I tell you? Can't you see the tears running down my cheeks and guess the truth? There is not a Jew in Poland who is not a fugitive from death itself. You and the Polsters went to the Bobowa ghetto. Feigele and Moishe and your family from Zyndranowa went to a ghetto in Dukla. It is all the same. The Nazis went from ghetto to ghetto doing what they do so well and now everyone is dead, also your family. Everyone that I know of is dead and the only Jews left alive are fugitives or Jews in concentration camps like Auschwitz, Maidanek, Treblinka, Sobibor, Chelmno and others. That's it, put your head in your arm and cry."

She put the burned egg on a plate and set it on the table.

"In the cities there are bands of Jews fighting underground. There are fugitives hiding in the country. You are too young to fight underground and would probably get killed very quickly. Everywhere there are some peasants who keep their eyes out for Jews, because the Gestapo will reward those who capture fugitives with boots and money and things like that. But you do as I tell you and you will live. Only by living will you honor your family and I will help you. If you do what I tell you and change your name and become a Polish boy, no one will know you are a Jew and someday when the war is over you will be a grown man: then you will be able to do things to remember your family and tell the world what has happened to your people."

"What type of name…who will I…what shall I take?"

"How about Jusek…Jusek…Polewski?"

"O.K. If you think…"

"Do you know Polish *pacierz* (prayers)? Daily catechism?"

"No, I don't."

"Do you know how to read?"

"No. Polish I cannot read."

"Then I tell you what I will do. I will teach you, and you will memorize as much as possible. Then you will go around to the villages near here and look for a job. With what you will have learned, you will be just like a Polish Christian boy. So you just took around for a job and tell everyone who asks that your name is Jusek Polewski.

"And remember—be careful when you undress so that no one will see that you are Jewish. Your circumcision could give you away and you know what will happen if someone sees it and realizes you are Jewish.

"I will watch myself. I am so grateful to you for doing all this for me—helping me. I don't know what I would have done without you. I'm scared, though, really scared. Maybe someone will recognize me. I have been in many of the villages around here and it's possible that someone will recognize my true identity."

"Don't be afraid. You will act like a Polish gentile boy and if you see anyone you know then avoid that person and watch yourself. Be careful. Now have breakfast."

Realizing that the egg was burned, she made another one and put it on the table. Her husband came in from outside. He was much younger than Balwina, uneducated and rather simple. Balwina wore the proverbial pants in the family, and whatever she said was the law. The man walked through the kitchen and into the other room. A boy about eleven years old came into the kitchen followed by a younger girl.

"Staszek," said Balwina, "Sit at the table by Jusek. I might need you to help me. Yes, that's right. Of course, I mean Shmulek."

"Now, Jusek, for that will be your name, let me try to teach you the catechism. O. K., repeat after me: 'Our Father, who art in Heaven, hallow'd be Thy name.' Now remember, repeat after me. Memorize what I say. After you get a job, try to go to church every Sunday."

"Our Father, who art in Heaven, hallow'd be Thy name...."

The days passed, and early one morning Balwina climbed the stairs to the attic. She was still in her nightshirt. The roosters had not yet crowed; and she gently shook the shoulder of Jusek Polewski.

"Wake up, Jusek. Wake up. Remember now, your name is no longer Shmulek Oliner. Jusek, it will be dawn in just a short while and if you hurry no one will be able to recognize you. I want you to go. Leave this village now. Go to some other village and look for a job. Go from house to house and ask if anyone needs a *pastuch* (cowhand or stable boy)." She began to cry. "I will miss you. Be careful. If you ever…if it's safe—but only if it's safe—try to come back some night and visit and tell me where you are. Now be very careful because you know what that means for us."

"Of course. I know what would happen if anyone found out and I will be very careful. I am grateful to you for letting me stay. I am very, very grateful. And someday, if I ever survive this, I will never forget you."

A boy of twelve has lots of imagination. But reality was quick and sharp to cut these fantasies in half. Tears are a funny thing. You imagine things and the horror makes you cry until you think there are no tears left. Then you find out the truth and there are plenty of tears all over again. Balwina told me of the execution at the forest of Garbacz where my family and my people were stripped of their clothing that cold, cold day and told to walk the wooden planks. And for days, it seemed, I cried. A thought or a word—anything at all—sparked the feeling of agony. Balwina was always there, moving about like the mother I didn't have. Two mothers I had had and both were dead. Life seemed unbearably cruel. Balwina said Jewish fugitives were doing whatever they could just to stay alive, and as quickly as I could, I had learned the Christian catechism.

The agony never went away, but the tears stopped and rarely after that did I cry again. Just to survive each day took supreme effort and there was no time for tears. The Germans were everywhere and Balwina was afraid I would be found out if I stayed with her. She said: "Change your name. Learn the catechism. Pretend to be a peasant boy and go to church every Sunday." I felt, partly, that she expected properties my grandfather had owned. Already she had his horse and other presents. Also, she was very religious and quite likely sought the religious reward of converting an infidel. For the most part, however, she was a humanitarian woman with a great, kindly heart. In order to help save another person's life, she was risking her own and her family's during the entire period I stayed with her.

Walking barefoot on the road leading away from Bystra, the village where Balwina lived, I was certainly not an unusual sight. Since the Germans had entered Poland, a lot of homes had been broken up. Orphaned children were frequently seen on the roads and the Poles generally treated them well. I hitchhiked along the road and the peasants picked me up in their old wooden carts. They shared with me their black-crusted bread and joked in a friendly manner.

In spite of their kindness, I lived in constant fear of being found out. I imagined how glad these poor friendly Poles would be for a pair of boots or a few hundred zlotys. Some Poles as Krupa, for example, sometimes crippled a captive just for fun before delivering him to the Gestapo, and I vividly imagined this done to myself.

The premature death of my mother had saved her much sorrow and I wondered if she was watching over me. It began to occur to me that death was, indeed, forever. In fact, it seemed death was the only certainty there was. And if death was forever, then there had to be some meaning to the shortness of life—there must be some hope in living. I tried to remember what my mother looked like, but there was just an impression, the smell of *Shabbat* bakings. Even the face of Ester, my stepmother, was sliding away, sliding into the sound of a harsh voice, the look of fear, the touch of last-minute tenderness. Also sliding away was Shmulek Oliner. He was a thing of the past, buried in the memories of people now dead.

A friendly peasant had given me a ride and in the village of Ropa I hopped off the cart. Away he went, sitting up there on the wagon seat behind the plodding horse. From house to house I went, asking if anyone needed a pastuch, a cowhand. No luck. I picked apples that still clung to the trees at this late season and ate them for my lunch. From the fields I pulled carrots. Night descended quickly and I crawled into a peasant's barn and hid in the hay. Sometimes a snoopy dog would discover my presence in the barn and bark without letting up. When that happened I had to move on and find a more friendly barn.

Sometimes in those barns, in the middle of the night, I woke up covered with sweat. I had dreamed that the Gestapo was chasing me and had finally trapped me in Balwina's house. My father was there and I turned to him for help. He told me to leave him alone and I screamed: I hate you!" Then my heart broke because even more than I hated him—I loved him. This I tried to tell him but my efforts were futile. No amount of entreaty seemed to have an effect on him. Then I realized he was dead.

The rich warm smell of animal manure reminded me I was not at Balwina's house but sleeping in a peasant's barn in the village of Ropa. For a moment I let myself think my life might be a dream within a dream, and that I might wake up in England or America or some other safe place. But such thoughts were luxuries hardly to be afforded, and I stopped thinking them right away.

The next morning I got up before dawn. The farmhouse windows were yellow with light. Across some low hills I made my way and finally ended up in a village called Biesnik. By now the sun had risen and at the first farm I came to the farmer was just letting his cows out of their stables and driving them to the nearby pastures.

"Do you know who needs a *pastuch?*"

He leaned on the wooden side of the stable and squinted at me. Cold air was coming through the open barn door, and the manure in the stable was steaming.

"Yes, I know of such a place. You go up about ten houses. There is a large house there that used to belong to a Jew. A man named Padworski lives there now; he and his wife. You'll find he's a nice man and I just happen to know he needs a *pastuch.* You tell him that I, Woitek, sent you and he will talk to you."

"Thank you very much."

"Good luck."

At a brisk pace I set off down the dirt road counting the houses as I went. Each number I had to repeat several times in my mind because the houses were far apart and I didn't want to lose count. Wild bleak grass grew along the side of the dirt road. There were no wires for electricity as there had been in Dukla. The houses didn't have modern plumbing. There were no German motorcars roaring down the dirt road; and the morning rested peacefully in the stillness of the earth. For a moment, I stopped and stood as still as a blade of grass that glistened in the rising sun. These quiet moments I began to collect and appreciate for I didn't know how many of them I would ever have.

The tenth house from where Woitek lived turned out to be a snug farm. There was the house, a barn, and a small cherry and apple orchard. Under a large shade tree next to the house was the entrance to a cellar dug into the ground. Even if Woitek hadn't told me that the Padworskis lived on a Jewish farm, I would have known. The wooden fence surrounding the lawn reminded me of my grandparent's farm in Zyndranowa. A small dog ran limping on one foot out of the barn and barked as I approached.

The door of the house was open and I took my cap off and stuck my head inside. A man was sitting at the table in the kitchen. Through the window next to the table sunlight shone on the newspaper he was reading. The air outside was cool but warming with the sun.

"Mr. Padworski? Are you Mr. Padworski? Woitek from down the road sent me to you because he, I mean, he told me you might be needing a *pastuch.* I have experience with animals and I can tell you I will work very hard."

The man put down the newspaper and turned toward me. The hair and sideburn on one side of his head were illuminated by the sun and his eyes were blue and looked very cool. Shrinking back a little I thought: 'I can't go through with this. The Jew who used to own this farm is dead and if this gentile Pole finds out I am Jewish, I too, will end up dead.'

"Yes, son. As a matter of fact we are looking for a *pastuch.* How old are you?

"Thirteen, sir."

"Thirteen? My, you don't look thirteen. What's your name?"

"My name is Jusek Polewski."

"Hmmmm. Never heard of you, Jusek. Where do you live?"

"Im from Lużna."

"Lużna. That's very strange. Where is that? What are you doing so far away from home?"

"Oh, I…I came looking for work from village to village."

"Where are your parents?"

"My father is dead. My mother lives in Lużna with my brother.

She is very poor and there is not enough food for everyone in the house and she told me to look for work. So I was going from village to village. I've just been to Ropa and there was nothing there for me to do so I thought I would try here."

The door opened and a woman walked into the kitchen. She looked rather young, with a broad face and blonde hair tied with a handkerchief.

"You know, honey, this boy wants to be our *pastuch. I* think we need one, don't you agree?"

The woman looked at me and smiled.

"Hello, son."

"Hello, Mrs. Padworski."

She turned to the man sitting at the table.

"Oh yes, definitely. We could use a *pastuch.* He looks like a strong boy."

"Thank you. I will work very hard. I can harness horses and drive carts and plow fields and milk cows. I can clean horses and take them to the fields for grazing. There are a lot of things I know how to do. And I can keep the stable clean."

"Yes, but you're so young and I don't know how much you would be wanting for work like that," said Mr. Padworski.

"Oh, I don't want much."

"Tell you what," said Mr. Padworski. "You can start working now, but in a few weeks I want you to go back to Lużna and bring to me your mother so that we can negotiate."

"Sure, I'll do that. If you want to talk to her, I'll bring her to you and then you can do these negotiations."

Mrs. Padworski squeezed her hands together and smiled at me.

"I'm so glad!" she said. "I think you will like it here with us. We have no children of our own. And as long as you do your work well and obey and respect my husband, I'm sure we will all get on very well."

"Thank you very much, Mrs. Padworski. "I took her hand and kissed it gratefully. She smiled a little nervously and said, "Well, let me…let me show you where you are going to sleep. We don't have any room in the house. Let me take you to the stable. There is a bed in the corner of the stable and you can sleep there. I don't have any blankets but there's lots of hay and soft straw."

"Thank you very much. That will be just fine. Many times I have slept on straw and it is a very good thing."

She showed me the stable and then I had the rest of the day to wander about the farm getting used to it. That night, as I lay in the stable, I thought of the Padworskis and what I had previously learned about them from Woitek. They had an aristocratic background. While they were not Nazi sympathizers, they certainly showed no love for the Jews. In fact, Mr. Padworski was an engineer and had had some litigations with Jewish businesses. The farm had belonged to a Mr. Herman Schiff who was also driven out to the Bobowa ghetto at the same time as my family, and who also died at Garbacz. The Padworskis rented it from the occupying German government. Mr. Padworski was not actually a farmer by trade, but a city dweller. In addition to his engineering work he had paper work of some kind to do, and as his *pastuch,* much of the farm work would rest on my shoulders. The stable had a pleasant smell and was very warm with animal heat. Lying on a bed made of a few wooden planks covered with straw, I prayed that no one would find out that I was Jewish.

The next morning I woke up early. Mrs. Padworski came out to the barn and milked the cows. She sang a little as she squirted milk in the bucket and flashed a smile at me when I said good morning. Then she set the bucket aside and winked at me as she walked to the back of the barn. She squatted out of sight in a particular stall and I wondered what she could possibly be doing, because the stall was empty. Presently, she came out of the stall. Gently she put her hand on my shoulder and led me out to the field where the cows were grazing. After pointing out where the cows were not allowed to go, she walked back to the farm. There was no fence separating the pasture from the field of grain and I spent the morning making sure the cows stayed in the grass.

At noontime I drove the cows as far away from the grain as possible and returned to the farm for lunch. As I neared the house I saw a shiny black Gestapo car leaving the driveway. My heart seemed to skip a beat and sweat stood out on my forehead. With weak knees I entered the house; my mouth felt as if it were filled with dust. Mr. and Mrs. Padworski were sitting at the table staring down at the table top. They seemed very tense and neither looked up at me. Mr. Padworski turned his cold blue eyes on me and my stomach seemed to pour down into my legs. I stammered:

"The cows, the cows, they are—"

"Jusek, I have something to ask you.

"Uhhh…"

"Jusek, do you have a knife?"

"N-no, sir."

Mrs. Padworski spoke up: "Well, have you got a penknife on you?"

"No, ma'm. I don't have a penknife on me. I don't own a knife."

"Did you own a knife before?"

"Yes. Once I had one, but not now. I must have lost the one I had a long time ago."

"We just wondered. We thought you might have a knife with you." Silently I bowed my head and ate my bread and butter with a bowl of soup. Mrs. Padworski continued:

"How do you like our cows? Aren't they nice fat Jewish cows?"

"What do you mean they're Jewish?"

"Oh, they were left here when Herman Schiff was sent to the ghetto and we got the farm. We are renting the farm from the government."

"Oh, is that right? I didn't know," I lied. "I thought you owned the farm."

"Not at all. This was a Jewish farm."

Mr. Padworski said, "The Jews have caused me much trouble in the past, but now I feel sorry for what has happened to them."

"The house is very nice," I said.

"Yes," said Mrs. Padworski. "It is the nicest house here. It is well kept, not like some of the other houses in the village. Did you know that some of the other houses around here are like stables? Some of the farmers keep cows and horses right in the same room where they sleep."

"I know that, yes, because in my village some farmers do the same thing. I've seen goats, for instance, and sheep in the same room with people."

"What village did you say you were from?"

"I'm from Lużna."

"Lużna. Oh yes, now I remember, I've heard of it. It's not far from Bobowa, isn't that right?"

"Yes, that's right."

"Don't you miss your mother?"

"I guess I do miss her, but I'll get used to it. I like it here. This is a very nice house and you are very good to me. I've never seen a nice house like this before."

As quickly as possible I finished eating and took up my cap. Outside I breathed more easily but I was so scared that I could hardly think straight. Briefly, I considered running away. But then came the realization that if the Padworskis knew I was a Jew I was done for. They would spread the word and every Pole in the vicinity would be looking for a Jewish boy who looked just like me. Then I would not find work as a *pastuch*. Most likely a Gestapo bullet would finish me off. I decided that the best thing I could do was to hold on to the identity already established and try to convince the Padworskis of it.

In the evening I took the cows back to the stable. Mrs. Padworski milked them and not once did she smile at me. When I went into the house Mr. Padworski greeted me very coldly. If the Gestapo had been in the next room, I would not have been surprised. After dinner I excused myself and went out to the barn.

The next morning I noticed the same cold feelings in the Padworskis' behavior toward me. If they suspected I was Jewish, I couldn't figure out what they were waiting for. A word to the Gestapo was all that was needed to end the affair. I wondered, 'Is it possible that they are very cruel people after all and that they want to keep me on edge?' Mrs. Padworski acted as if I had done her a personal injury. At breakfast I was so nervous I could hardly eat. Mr. Padworski lifted his eyes from the newspaper he was reading and gave me an "I know all about you" look; when I pushed open the kitchen door to go and drive the cows out to the field, the perspiration on the palm of my hand left a print on the door.

For a long time I considered not going back to the farm at noon, although I had already decided not to run away. If I didn't return to the farm for lunch the suspicions concerning me might very well be increased. So I did, in fact, go back, but I was so scared that I didn't see how I could possibly keep any food in my stomach.

Mrs. Padworski was waiting for me in the stable.

"You know something Jusek? I have a very unusual story to tell you."

An instant sweat came over me. Right then and there I wanted to beg her not to turn me over to the Gestapo, but my tongue was stuck to the roof of my mouth and wouldn't make a sound. She said:

"Do you remember that yesterday we kept asking you about a penknife and you said you didn't have one? Well, my husband had a very beautiful penknife which had sentimental value, and it was stolen by Jusek."

"Which Jusek?"

"Jusek Szlachta."

"Oh, is that right? I didn't know that."

"He was here yesterday morning. He came to ask for something and he was inside the house, saw it on the mantelpiece and took it—this beautiful knife. Then, would you believe it, last night I had a dream that it was he who took the knife, and I went over to his house this morning and said: 'Jusek, can I have my husband's penknife back?' His mother took it out of his pocket and gave it to me. Jusek Polewski, we thought it was you who took the knife and you know what we were planning to do with you?"

"No. What would you have done?"

"We were planning to fire you, to tell you to go, because we thought you were a thief."

"Oh, I'm sorry you had to think that. I never stole anything in my life!"

"I know, dear, and I'm ashamed we suspected you. I'm sorry we thought you might be a thief. Can you ever forgive us? I know you are a hard-working *pastuch*."

"Thank you. I'll try and work hard for you. I know you won't be sorry for hiring me."

She left the stable and went into the house. So great was my relief I started trembling. For several minutes I just sat on the straw in the stable and trembled. Finally, I got hold of myself and walked into the house for lunch. Mr. Padworski smiled broadly at me and patted my back.

"You're all right, son. Just keep up the good work."

One thing still bothered me very much.

"Was that the Gestapo I saw here yesterday at noon?"

Mr. Padworski laughed. For the past day everything had, been tense; now he was trying to make up with me, and in a sense, everything was funny.

"Oh, yes. That was just the Gestapo looking for some Jews. Some Jews escaped from the ghetto, you know, and the Gestapo was hunting them down."

I swallowed a mouthful of soup and felt it travel all the way down my throat. From the corner of my eye I looked at him. "Maybe they should hire dogs for that," he continued, "To hunt for Jews like they hunt for rabbits and foxes." He was goading me, trying to make me laugh. Only the coldness of his eyes disconcerted me. And I could never be quite certain he did not, in fact, suspect I was Jewish.

Mrs. Padworski said, "Do you know that the Germans are advancing into Russia? They claim they're going to defeat Russia completely in another three to four weeks."

I thought: "God, what will that mean for me? What will that mean for Jews all over the world if the Germans win the war?"

Mr. Padworski leaned back in his chair and smoked a homemade cigarette. I finished my lunch and returned to the fields.

Photo c. 1936
My grandfather—Isak (Hycko) Polster with his horse in Zyndranowa.
In the circle is me.

NEVER TO FORGET

ONE FRIDAY AFTERNOON I was tending the cows on the rugged mountain pasture above the Padworski farm. The pasture land was divided into patches of grass and grain and potatoes; and as I watched the cows to make sure they stayed in the grass, I thought how clever animals can be. Each cow seemed to have a mind of its own, and edged closer to the grain to get a mouthful on the sly. Sometimes the cows would go in different directions, so that while one was stealing mouthfuls from one forbidden patch, attracting my attention, another would steal something from another forbidden patch.

With me was Jusek Szlachta, who had stolen Mr. Padworski's penknife. He often played with me while I watched the cows and, although I didn't trust him, I liked his company. He always seemed curious about my origins and I had to be careful not to betray myself (a thousand times, at least, I had to repeat I was from Lużna). I often worried: if someone who now lived in Biesnik came originally from Lużna, he could tell the Padworskis that there was no Polewski family living in Lużna. Also, I had to be careful about my circumcision. This was sometimes difficult, as Jusek was fond of taking off his clothes and exposing himself to the sun. Our conversations usually centered on girls and sex.

Jusek offered me a cigarette he had made out of clover and scraps of newspaper, and I accepted it.

"Have you heard of the Jews who escaped from jail? The Gestapo is looking for them."

"Oh yeah," I said. "That happened a long time ago. Mr. Padworski told me all about it."

"Well, I hope they find them and round them all up. Then we'll have a Jew-free Poland." He watched my face for a reaction. "My father said that before the war all the wealth was in Jewish hands. The priest... Hey, you're not paying attention! Yeah, the priest said the Jews killed Jesus Christ. Did you know that?"

"Of course," I said. "Everyone knows that."

I wondered, how long would I survive if he knew I was a Jew? I anticipated each step he would take to finish me off. First, he would go to his dirty house and announce the discovery to his father. Then he would go to the Gestapo station in Gorlice, report me and get the reward. A Gestapo officer would come to Biesnik in his big black car, get hold of me and tell me to take off my pants. The circumcision would confirm that I was a Jew and I would be taken to Gestapo headquarters, tortured and asked where other Jews were hiding. After the Gestapo was through with me, I would be taken to a Jewish cemetery and told to dig my own grave, as I had heard a number of other Jews had been forced to do. Then I would be told to lie down, facing the bottom of the grave and they would shoot me…I shook my head in order to recover from this dismal fantasy. Fortunately, I was still on the hillside and not in the Jewish cemetery.

As I watched the cows grazing and noticed that they were moving closer to a large patch of grain, I thought: 'It would not be bad to live the life of a cow.'

"What are you thinking about?" asked Jusek.

"Oh, nothing in particular. I was thinking how nice it would be if the Germans were driven out of Poland and Poland were free again."

"My father says that the Germans will be defeated pretty soon by the English and the Americans."

"I certainly hope so because the Germans are really occupying our land."

"Do you hate the Nazis?"

"I sure do," I said. "They're occupying our land."

"Yeah, I hate the Nazis, too. But they've done a good thing for us. They've cleaned out the Jews."

"Yeah, I guess that's the best thing they could have done for us."

"Did you know they killed a lot of Jews at Garbacz?"

"Sure. Who doesn't know that?"

"They were shooting all day long. I have a cousin who heard the machine guns going for a very long time. Imagine killing that many people in one grave?! Do you know that it took the farmers of that area two months just to dig the hole for all those Jews?"

"Those Nazis took care of everything. They have such fine, fast machine guns." I looked around in search of a way to change the subject. It was a little warmer. Clouds appeared in the distance along the horizon and Jusek commented on them:

"I bet it's going to storm tonight." Then he said, "Are you going to church this Sunday?"

"To church? Oh yes, sure. I go to church every now and then."

"I go to church every Sunday," he said giving me a sly look. "I'm a real good Catholic. Are you a Catholic, too?"

"Of course I'm a Catholic."

As I was trying to change the subject again I saw a man walking toward me. As he got nearer I started shaking from fright because his face was familiar. It was the face of a Jew. He used to live right next to us in the Bobowa ghetto and knew me very well. In fact, he was our landlord. Upon seeing me, he stood still for a moment.

"Shmul…Shm…"

Waving my hand at him, I quickly turned my back and said to Jusek, "Jusek, please do me a favor, will you get that cow out of the oats? See, she's eating up the oats!"

Jusek did as I asked him and ran to chase the cow. I walked over to the Jew I had recognized and said, "Simcha, please, please leave me alone. Nobody knows I am Jewish here. Don't give me away. I'll tell you what: you run into the woods and hide there. At night I'll bring you some food."

"O.K. I'll see you tonight behind the hill."

Jusek drove the cow out of the oats. Then he came running back looking after the man who was walking away.

"Who was that man?"

"I don't know. He said he was lost and asked for directions."

"Was he Jewish? He looked like he could have been Jewish."

"I don't know. Why don't you run after him and ask?"

"This is no joking matter. A Jew is worth a lot of money."

"Sometimes you are really stupid, Jusek. Why would a Jew walk around in broad daylight?"

"Oh—yeah." He scuffed the ground with his foot. "I guess you're right. No Jew would be that dumb."

We sat down on the grass and watched the cows. Nonchalantly they grazed tearing loose the grass with their strong, square teeth. They didn't care that I was a Jew, neither did they care that Jusek was a Jew-hater. Had I died right before their eyes, they probably would not have stopped grazing. How maddening it sometimes was being human! Jusek and I were each caught in our private thoughts and I worried about what his might be. After what seemed an eternity, he brought up the topic of girls.

That night I sneaked away from the farm and went to the woods. I met Simcha behind the little hill to which he had pointed that afternoon. He ate eagerly the potatoes and bread I had brought. I knew he was starving. So few of my people did I see, that I felt for him as I would toward a brother and steadied his shoulder with my hand.

"How did you run away? How did you escape from the Nazis?"

"I climbed through the fence before the shooting," he said.

"Do you know what happened to my parents?"

"No, Shmulek, I don't. All I know is that the Jews were loaded into trucks and transported to Garbacz and shot there. I think your parents were, too."

"What will happen, Simcha…what will happen to us?"

"I don't know. Maybe the Nazis will be defeated soon. In the meantime, just try to hold out."

He had eaten everything I had brought. The night was very dark, but I could see his face clearly. He was staring at the moon and the whites of his eyes glistened.

"Listen," he said, "I will tell you a story. I met another Jew on the road. His beard was tangled and filled with spittle. His eyes were wide expressing unspeakable horror and he cried out with fear at his own fantasies. At first I thought he was one of those afflicted from birth, that the war has separated from their families.

Then, between outbursts, he told me his story.

"From what I could piece together from his garbled sentences, he was one of those Jews taken to Garbacz. It was a big hole waiting there for all those Jews. The busy hands that dug it must have worked a long, long time. The Nazi butchers couldn't shoot the Jews and bury them fast enough. Our people lay in that hole dead or wounded: some had just fainted from shock. The Nazis couldn't bury them fast enough, so over these people, many of them not even dead, the butchers poured a chemical."

Like the eyes of a wild animal, Simcha's eyes reflected the moon.

"But this particular Jew who was now a madman happened to be near the top. The Nazi guards had more important things to do than hang around and listen to the moans of dying people, so this Jew escaped by climbing out of the hole and running into the woods. In that hole filled with bleeding bodies, he left his sanity. I tried to do something for him, but he was beyond help. It was only a matter of time until somebody would turn him over to the Gestapo for a pair of boots. I thought that the best thing I could do for him was to catch a few of the butchers and do to them the same as they had done to countless Jews who had never done anything to hurt them. At dawn I will leave this area for Gorlice, where I hope to find the Jewish underground."

He turned his glowing eyes upon me.

"I tell you this for a reason. You are lucky. You have a good cover here on this Polish farm. And you must remember: if you survive the war you must not forget your people. You must tell the tales of horror. We must avenge the innocent. Our leaders and rabbis gave us bad advice about the Nazis. They should have told us to arm ourselves and fight against them. But the rabbis were holy men and they have died with their people. The leaders of the *Judenrat* did what they could for us in their own way, and they, too, have paid the price for being Jewish.

"You must remember what the Nazis have done to us. We must never forget the dead are watching us. The world must be told about Nazi bestiality. But first of all you must live. You are very young…and perhaps that is to your advantage. Good luck."

"Simcha, you must know I have a different name. I'm called Jusek Polewski. If you ever have to come to me for food, do come. But make sure no one else is around. Talk to me secretly and I'll bring you food at night. Good luck."

"Good luck to you, Jusek Polewski."

As I walked back toward the farm I noticed the lantern in the barn was lit. The last hundred yards I sprinted. Inside the barn, Mr. Padworski was in the stall with one of the cows. Mrs. Padworski was holding the lantern, and they both looked at me accusingly.

"Where have you been?" shouted Mr. Padworski. Rarely did he raise his voice and I was scared to death.

"Here we are, in the middle of the night, and you are out running around. Is there something going on I should know about? Or maybe you can explain why the cow is calving and you are not here to help?"

Without waiting for a reply from me, he turned his attention to the cow. Numbly, I helped. A short time later, he smiled proudly at the slimy wet calf that lay on the straw.

"I'm sorry, Jusek," he said, ruffling my hair. "I didn't mean to be so angry a little while ago. It was just that the cow was having trouble and I was concerned and needed help and you were nowhere to be found." He laughed with relief, then mused quietly, "I don't think I'll report this calf to the Germans. Why should a good calf feed some Nazi belly?"

"By the way, Jusek, where were you tonight?"

I broke out with perspiration, unable to think of any excuse that would sound even remotely reasonable. Not knowing what else to do, I walked to the calf and stroked its head which was still wet and very silky. Mrs. Padworski brought the lantern close to the calf and crooned softly laying her hand on my shoulder. My heart was pounding and I wrestled desperately with a possible explanation should Mr. Padworski ask his question again. But his mind seemed to be on other things; he said something to Mrs. Padworski and they left the barn and walked to the house.

Not until the kitchen door closed did I sigh with relief, but this sigh was a very short one. I was afraid that the following day would hold new dangers for me, and I kept groping for an explanation for my absence from the barn.

Fortunately, the next day Mr. Padworski seemed to forget all about the incident and the farm work continued as usual. I had to clean the stables, feed the cattle, and help with the harvesting. When the new calf learned to walk, it followed me around everywhere and before long we were good friends.

The Poles were not allowed to slaughter cattle. Rabbits, however, were an allowable source of meat and one of my duties on the farm was to kill rabbits for the Padworskis. To do this, I would pick the animal up by a hind leg and hit it with a stick right behind the ears. Then I would drop it behind me and assume it was dead.

One time, I had to kill four rabbits for a special meal. When I turned around, I found that one was missing. Apparently, I hadn't hit it hard enough, and it had wobbled to a bunch of hay and hid. I felt the rabbit was hurt enough so that it would probably die in pain. Searching through the hay I finally found it screaming as if to beg for mercy. The situation was very moving, so I left it alone and strangely enough it recovered.

Feeling elated that I had helped preserve a life, I went to find my friend the calf. Between us a special relationship existed and I talked to the calf and told it secrets as if it could understand. Nowhere was my friend to be found. I searched again in the barn, then in the back of the house. Usually, when I called the calf's name it came running to me. Now only the plaintiveness of my voice returned to me.

With a heavy heart I went to the farmhouse for my evening meal. Not only had I lost a friend, but the calf had belonged to Mr. Padworski; how would I explain to him the loss of such a valuable animal? Mr. Padworski and I sat at the table waiting for Mrs. Padworski to bring the food. As usual, he was reading his newspaper, the *Krakauer Zeitung* (Kracow News), a German language propaganda newspaper. Over the top of the newspaper he peered at me.

"Jusek, did you know the Gestapo is looking for a Jew reported to be in this area? On the road to Gorlice they captured a Jew from the Bobowa ghetto. They did some terrible things to him, and before they ended his misery, he reported having had contact with another Jewish fugitive. Do you think he would have held up under Gestapo torture?"

"I don't know."

"Not at all. The Nazis are very good at extracting any information they want." Mrs. Padworski set a platter of steaming meat on the table. She cast a look at me and walked quickly away. He continued, "And in our very midst—our geographic area, that is—we have a fugitive. I am not interested in any Gestapo reward. On the other hand, it would not be good for me to have a Jew discovered on our property, and I want you to keep your eyes open. "Very quickly I realized he wasn't talking about me. I was staring at the platter of meat on the table. "This Jew is reportedly a madman and, —Jusek...Jusek?"

He noticed my focus of attention. He put his paper down and cleared his throat. His wife came to the table and sat quietly with her head bowed. My forehead burned hot and a rush of tears came to my eyes and I was choked with emotion.

"Jusek, I thought perhaps you would take this well. We're in a war you know. People are dying everywhere. The Germans make us register our cattle and take our surplus beef. We who are alive must eat to stay alive and for a long time we've had nothing but a bland diet."

My eyes filled with tears.

"The calf wasn't registered you know."

"Jusek, eat," said Mrs. Padworski. "It's for your health."

The blood that had burned up into my forehead seemed to leave my body altogether and I felt faint. Numbly, I excused myself and left the table. As the cool evening air hit my face, I got myself under control, but my ears still roared loudly and I was in a state of confusion. Behind a bush, I vomited. I could not eat the calf who had been my friend. As I walked to the barn, I bitterly murmured the name, "Simcha." For a moment, I thought I would tell everyone I was a Jew just to shake them up. Of course, such a move would be fatal. As my strength waned, I remembered the words Simcha had spoken to me and I felt some comfort.

As if the sadness for the slaughtered calf were not enough, the Padworskis received an order from the German army to deliver one of their two cows to Bobowa for slaughter. The German army had all the cattle in Poland registered so that they knew at a glance how much meat was available. Mr. Padworski had no choice but to pick one cow and deliver it to Bobowa as ordered. Suddenly it occurred to me that he may want to send me on the two-day walking trip to Bobowa. Sweat came over me as I thought: 'What if someone recognizes me there, or what if Mr. Padworski wants to accompany me along the journey?' Quickly, another horrible thought crossed my mind: Lużna, the village that I purportedly came from, lay on the very road to Bobowa. What if Mr. Padworski wanted to stop in my village and meet my mother and talk with her about me? As I feared, Mr. Padworski announced that we would take the old cow (which I considered the smarter one) and we would both go to Bobowa to deliver it and get the proper receipts from the German authorities. He added, "That way we will pass through your village Lużna and we can see your mother."

I looked at him pretending that I was pleased with his suggestions.

Early Thursday morning we took sandwiches, put a rope on the cow's neck and were ready to walk in the direction of Bobowa. The cow refused to move. I pulled her by the rope and Mr. Padworski beat her with a stick. Reluctantly, she started slowly up a ridge. I felt she had a cow's premonition that this was the end for her, too. My confused mind kept worrying about what to do with my own predicament. What excuses would I offer to Mr. Padworski this time about my lies if he should discover them?

The cow didn't want to move quickly. The walk towards Bobowa proceeded very slowly until, with a sudden jerk, the cow got loose and began to gallop back towards Biesnik. I ran after her, but Mr. Padworski couldn't because he had angina pectoris. I caught the cow and we marched on.

Night crept up on us and it was decided that we would spend the night by the creek, still about 10 kilometers away from Lużna and about 20 kilometers from Bobowa. The cow grazed, Mr. Padworski slept, and I kept thinking of a way out of the imminent discovery.

The next morning, we woke, ate our stale sandwiches and marched on. We had to hurry because the orders stated that we had to deliver the cow in Bobowa by nightfall on Friday. We arrived at Lużna. Mr. Padworski asked: "Where is your mother's house?" I pointed in some direction six kilometers away from where we were and said, "My house is in that forest."

He quickly said, "That's quite far. We can't stop now because of the pressure of time."

A load was lifted off my chest.

We arrived at Bobowa: fortunately it was beginning to get dark and cloudy. 'Good,' I thought to myself, 'The darkness will hide me and we will get out of Bobowa under the cover of night.' We delivered the reluctant and tired old cow. She mooed and kicked and looked in our direction. I felt badly inside my heart. Mr. Padworski said, "Goodbye, you poor old Zosia" (that was her nickname), "you have served us well." He, too, was capable of grief, I noticed.

"Now we go back to Lużna," he said. My anxiety was renewed, and as I glanced at Bobowa, memories of misery raced before my eyes. It was only two years since I escaped from this hell hole. Now it appeared that life had returned there. Only now it had no Jews, and gentiles had taken over the Jewish houses. The ghetto was no more, and fences that enclosed the Jews were also largely dismantled. Mr. Padworski was tired and coughed a lot as we walked back in the direction of Lużna. He suggested that we rest and spend the night under the nearby orchard trees.

Next morning we got up early, and noticed heavy clouds covering the sky. Mr. Padworski said, "You know, Jusek, let's move on and save time. You won't mind if we don't stop at your mother's place?"

I was overjoyed with his statement, though I tried not to show it. I added, "That seems like a good idea. We would have to go about 10 kilometers out of our way, and my mother is probably at work in the field at one of the rich peasant's farm." 'My God' I thought to myself, 'What a narrow escape!' We arrived tired and sad at Biesnik thinking of poor Zosia's fate.

SOME FOUGHT BACK

"JUSEK, YOU KNOW it's time for you to go get your mother so we can negotiate. Then we'll know exactly what we'll have to pay you for working here."

"Oh, there's no hurry. My mother will...there's no rush—uh—I think maybe we ought to wait 'til—oh, when I make a trip home around Christmas time. Don't you think that would be a good idea? We have much work to do here on the farm and really I should stay here. Until Christmas I could work for room and board."

"Don't you miss your mother, boy?" asked Mrs. Padworski, looking at me with a mixture of pity and fondness. I liked her very much. She acted as if she had accepted me as a son, but seemed to have other feelings for me as well, which sometimes made me nervous. For instance, instead of using the outhouse, which was very cold, she would often come out to the barn. After a while, I learned not to pay attention, but I was disturbed nonetheless.

"Sure I miss my mother," I said, avoiding her probing eyes. "But my family is very poor and they rely on me. Now I have responsibilities here, too. Somehow, my mother will get the money she needs and I will get my work done, too. Without me to feed, she will be all right. When we get the negotiations straightened out she will get all that money; and it will be a happy day."

"All right," said Mr. Padworski. "If that's the way you want it. You can work for your room and board for the time being. And when I meet your mother we'll decide."

There was a long silence while he read the newspaper. I was sitting in the corner by the stove. His wife was also reading the paper.

"Yah," said Mr. Padworski. "It looks as if the Germans are having some trouble in Stalingrad. That's what it says here, anyway, and you know very well that if the Germans admit to having trouble they must be having it indeed."

"I hope so," said his wife. "I hope they're having good trouble, good and plenty. You know, there's an article here about how some Jews escaped from the Gestapo. Imagine, from the Gestapo itself!"

"Fantastic! How could the Jews have done that—to escape from the Nazis?"

"Well, it says here they were betrayed by a…some girl. I'm not sure who this girl was; maybe the lover of one of the men? You know the Nazis are very good at getting someone to talk. Anyway, these Jews were taken to the Gestapo headquarters where they were undressed and they were just about to be taken to the cemetery when they escaped in their underwear. Tell me, do they—the Nazis I mean—take Jews who are still alive to the cemetery?"

"Never mind," said Mr. Padworski. "Not now. What else happened?"

"One of the Jews hit a guard—a Nazi guard."

"Good for the Jew. At least when they hang up his hide he'll have that against the Nazis. Do we know him? Do we know any of those Jews?"

"Apparently they are local. The sons of a man named Schiff." She looked at her husband a bit quizzically. "I wonder if they could be… Tell me, did the Schiff who owned this farm have any sons?"

Her husband seemed preoccupied and didn't answer. Perhaps the question had occurred to him and he was trying to answer it for himself. One thing these Poles who lived in Jewish farms and houses had not yet had to face was the problem of the rightful Jewish owners on the loose.

She finally broke the silence: "I wonder what the rest of the world will say about Germany, how the rest of the world will express feelings toward Germany, in view of the fact they've destroyed the Jews and gypsies so mercilessly and butchered so many millions of other innocent people?"

"Oh, I don't know. If the Germans ever lose the war I think the

American Jews will really try to make them repay all the damages. Yeah, the American Jews and those in England, too, will not like the Germans very much. Did you know there are five million Jews in America? And most of them are wealthy!"

From the corner where I was sitting I spoke up. "Is that really true? I didn't know that." My hands were held out to the hot iron of the stove and my clothing facing the stove felt nice and warm.

He turned around and included me in the conversation for the first time. "Well, I'm sure there's a lot you don't know," he said with a frown, as if he thought that my tone had questioned his statement. For a moment, I was afraid I had placed myself in a position of danger for showing so much concern. I had not stopped to think he might suspect me; his statement had merely drawn from me genuine interest.

"What I said is true, every word. While I'm educating you, I'll tell you something else: the Jews have always caused us a lot of trouble. Do you know that most of the shops and factories in Poland were owned by Jews?" He turned abruptly to his wife. "Did you know that, honey?"

She said, "No, I didn't know that. I knew they had a lot of shops...but...well, I can tell you I didn't know they owned all those factories. I thought that most of the large factories were in gentile hands."

"It does not seem to be so. Many of the largest textile factories were owned by Jews. All this time Jews complained of being poor. Well, let me tell you, they were richer than most gentiles, and didn't even know how to appreciate it. That's right. And it's all at our expense. That's right. Here we are, renting a Jewish farm from the German government, and it's what we deserve for ourselves. We should be owning this farm, not renting it. And maybe after this war things will be put right, now that the Jews are gone."

This sort of talk I had not expected from Mr. Padworski. He seemed nervous and I figured he was upset that Mr. Schiff's sons were on the loose. My mind drifted and I thought of the Mr. Hershel I had stayed with while attending *cheder* in Dukla. I don't know why I thought of these two men in relation to each other; perhaps because the one thing they had in common was that they were both dead.

Mr. Padworski worried me and I shot him a glance. He acted mostly like a kindly father to me, and I didn't want to anger him. My life was very precariously balanced on the fine blade of a lie, and should he ever discover me, I had little doubt as to the outcome.

The following day the order came through from the Nazis: find the escaped Jews. The *sołtys,* or mayor, set up posses for house-to-house searches and required one male from each household in Biesnik for that. The Padworskis sent me: and I, a Jew, ended up searching for other Jews who were no more fugitives than myself.

In groups of two and four we searched houses, sheds, and cellars for the escapees. Constantly I prayed that none would be found. I thought up a plan whereby I might save any I happened to see. At the same time I joked nervously with my fellow searchers, solidifying my identity as a mere peasant by appearing eager to participate in the search.

Much to my relief the fugitives were not found. I returned to the Padworski farm late one night and was a little surprised to see the lantern lit in the kitchen. Eager to see who was waiting (and thinking it was probably Mrs. Padworski—her husband was always eager to get a good night's sleep), I burst through the kitchen door. Mr. Padworski was sitting at the table, his wife sitting across from him; both looked frightened. As the door slammed shut behind me, an arm encircled my throat and snapped tight. I was thrown against the table, and with a cry Mrs. Padworski caught me and held me to her.

"Well, well," said a voice in Polish with a Yiddish accent. I turned around. Two men, both carrying sticks, stood by the kitchen door. I assumed they were the sons of Mr. Schiff: as a matter of fact I recognized them as men I'd seen in the marketplace before the war.

"Isn't this Aron's son?" said one man to the other, this time in Yiddish. The man spoken to looked me up and down, hitting his club on his hand. "Oh, it can't be."

"Yes, I think it is!"

The Padworskis didn't understand Yiddish. But at any moment the brothers might direct a question to me and I panicked, winking desperately.

(In my mind raced the following scenario: 'Why did they speak to you?' asked Mr. Padworski.

'I don't know why they would do such a thing. I don't know what they want.'

'Why did they seem to assume you would understand their language?')

"Wait," said one of the brothers. In Polish he continued:

"We are going outside to look for the guns we have buried. The boy we will take with us. If you make a move to resist, we will kill him."

Mrs. Padworski released me and I went outside with the two Jews.

"Are you Aron's son?"

"Yes. Please don't give me away. They think I am a peasant boy."

The brothers laughed as if they thought it was a great joke against the Poles.

"Then I am not so upset some *goy* got my father's farm," said one of them. "They trick a Jew and a Jew tricks them."

"Laugh all you want," said his brother, "but we are still fugitives."

"That's right." The man turned to me. "Will you help us escape? We have to get our guns from the house. Then we will go and not give you away."

"Sure. I will do what I can."

At different spots around the barn they uncovered tin cans containing money which they had hidden before they were driven out of their home. Then we all went back to the house. They shoved me inside. The Padworskis were still at the table. Mrs. Padworski clutched me once more and I looked appropriately upset at the treatment I had received at the hands of the Jews. The brothers pried loose a board along the ceiling and removed two revolvers. Then they pointed the guns at us and laughed at the Padworskis' terror.

"Take good care of our farm; we will want it back when the Nazis are destroyed," muttered one of the brothers. They demanded food, which I offered to get while they made the Padworskis remain seated at the table. Leading them onto the back porch, I gave them all the potatoes I could find.

They thanked me, I wished them well, then they took off. Mr. Padworski lamented that I had given them everything, instead of just the food that was readily visible, but Mrs. Padworski came to my defense. The night had been so frightening to both of them that they were only too glad to be safe and to forget about the potatoes.

As Christmas approached, Mr. Padworski reminded me that he wanted to see my mother to work out with her the arrangements regarding my employment. For, several months I had been working for room and board. As I had portrayed my mother as a very poor person, Mr. Padworski naturally assumed she would be interested in some money. Of course, this presented a problem for me: how was I to present a mother I didn't have?

Mr. Padworski said, "Jusek, it's time for you to go and get your mother and bring her here to the house so we can negotiate. Remember, we said we would do this at Christmas time?"

He had been hinting for months that he would like to see my mother. Although I didn't know what I could do about it, I was afraid that if I stalled much longer his suspicion would be aroused.

"O.K.," I said. "I'll go get her."

"I'll tell you what. You can spend Christmas Eve with us and share with us the Eucharist. The next morning you can go to mass if you want, then you can pack your clothes. We will give you some presents to take to your mother and after Christmas you can bring her here and we can decide on the amount of the salary you will receive for your work. We are very satisfied with you. You are doing a good job and you can tell your mother that we think you are a good boy."

Laughing, I said, "Thank you."

Mrs. Padworski said, "Does your mother bake *paska* (Christmas cake)?"

"No. Not this year. She…I don't think she will have enough flour and sugar to make *paska.*"

"All right then, we'll give you some to take home to her. By the way, I forgot to ask: do you have any brothers or sisters?"

"Oh yes, sure," I said, having to think fast. "I have a sister called Sofia and, uh, a brother called, uh, called . . . Staszek. "

"How old are they?"

"Oh, my sister is older and my brother is younger.

"How old is your sister?"

"Oh, she is now about fifteen, I guess, and my brother is ten.

"What does your sister do?"

"She's employed as a housemaid at a wealthy farmer's inn in Lużna."

"How about your brother?"

"He stays with my mother."

"Uh-huh."

In private moments behind the barn or out in the field, I was almost frantic over the meaning of the 'Uh-huh.' Every word the Padworskis said, I had to analyze for any possible threat and that particular response to the explanations concerning my family did not fit comfortably in the categories I marked as safe. What if the Padworskis knew someone in Lużna who could report on the existence of a family named Polewski? What if someone said, "I have never met this Jusek Polewski or Sofia or Staszek. This Jusek must be fooling you." My fear of Gestapo brutality was stronger than ever and I began to wish I had run away from the Padworski farm a long time ago. I made funny remarks to Mr. Padworski and joked with him just to see if he felt friendly towards me.

On Christmas Eve, Eucharist was placed on the table. This I had never seen before and I was therefore ignorant of the religious meaning. I was used to sitting in various parts of the kitchen for breakfast, lunch, and dinner, but now it was a special occasion and the Padworskis sat beside me. Mr. Padworski handed me the Eucharist and said something over it. Not knowing what to do, I tried to copy him. He looked at me and said, "Don't you know what that is?"

"Sure. It looks like a cookie."

"Didn't you have Eucharist before in your home?"

"Yes, of course we did. But it looked different. I didn't recognize it."

Taking a I piece, I ate it with them.

"Are you going to mass tomorrow?"

"Yes."

"Fine, then. You only go if you want to, you don't have to go. I don't go to church very often, you know, but you better go. We wouldn't want your mother to think we were trying to make a Jew out of you by not letting you go to church."

"Oh, O.K., I'll go to church tomorrow. I like to go to church. My friend Jusek…"

"That kid who stole my knife is your friend?"

"Well, he does seem like a nice boy," I said. "When I am on the pasture with the cows he often comes out with me and we play and talk a little."

Mr. Padworski said, "I hope you don't play too much and let the cows get into the oats and barley instead of staying in the pasture."

"I watch the cows very carefully, and by now I have them trained. All I do is call out a name and that cow immediately knows I want it to turn around and go in another direction."

He seemed to think this very funny. After he stopped laughing he said, "So you're going to church with Jusek the knife stealer?" He winked and I felt a little more confident.

"Sure I am."

"Fine."

As we walked into church the next day I was petrified. Not having the slightest idea what to do in a church, I copied every move of Jusek, the knife stealer. When he made the sign of the cross and kneeled, I did the same. When he went over to a particular section of the church and prayed for a long time, so did I. Every now and then, I cast glances over my shoulder. No one seemed to notice that I didn't know what to do. I felt as conspicuous as someone with a big sign 'Jew' on his back, but no one seemed to be aware of my presence. When I finally walked out of the church and into the bright sunshine, a sigh of relief escaped my lips.

"What's the matter?" demanded my friend Jusek.

"Churches make me nervous," I blurted out. Then, as an afterthought, I added: "I have a lot of sins on my conscience, you know, and it takes a long time to get it off my chest."

"Yeah," said Jusek, with a slight smirk. He swaggered a little. I know what you mean."

When I got back to the house, Mrs. Padworski had soup on the table. As I sat down to eat, my mind was spinning wildly with ideas. I thought of Balwina. For some reason I had used the name of her son as my brother and maybe she could help me out. I didn't want to place her in danger; but I had to do something and it seemed I had no one else to turn to.

Suddenly, Mr. Padworski's voice cut through my thoughts.

"Jusek, you didn't tell me you were a Jew!"

My heart flew up into my throat and nearly strangled me.

"What—?"

He said, "You have your hat on your head and the only people I know who wear hats on their heads in a house while they eat are Jews. So you must be a Jew!"

Panic raced through my body. I forced myself to look at him as casually as possible and noticed that he was grinning, as if he'd made a joke. Slowly, my body relaxed. My eyelid twitched a little. "Of course, I'm no Jew," I mumbled. Then I said, "You scared me. I thought a real Jew was in the house. You shouldn't joke around like that and call someone a Jew."

"No," he acknowledged. "That's nothing to laugh about."

He was still grinning as I lowered my eyes to the soup bowl. Some lice were swimming in it. During the war, soap was hard to find and people therefore didn't wash very often. Lice infested everything and when I took off my cap some must have fallen out of my hair.

My clothes were packed in an old leather satchel. The Padworskis stood on the porch together as they waved goodbye and I waved back. Mr. Padworski had said I could use his horse for the journey and as I sat on the hard wooden seat holding the reins, the cold wind made my face numb. I had on a ragged but very thick coat and around my neck was a scarf of Mrs. Padworski. The ruts in the road were frozen solid and the cart skidded along like a sled.

For the rest of the afternoon, I traveled in the direction of Lużna. Not until darkness fell and I was sure that no one would see me did I turn back.

When I arrived at the home of Balwina, the good peasant woman who lived in Bystra, it was very late. I knocked on the door. After a while it opened a crack, then it flung open.

"What are you doing here?" said Balwina. "It's so nice to see you."

She embraced me, smiling warmly.

"I'm glad to see you, too."

"Well, here," she said. "Don't stand out in the cold. Come on in. "She led me to a chair. Then she turned up the lamp she had evidently lit when she had risen from bed. "Who is it?" asked a man's voice through the open door of the bedroom.

"It's nothing. No one in particular. Go back to sleep," said Balwina.

"You know," I said. "I'm working as a *pastuch* for the Padworskis in Biesnik. They live at the old Schiff farm and they treat me very well."

"Oh, I'm so glad. Do you have a different name? Oh yes, that's right, you do. The name we gave you here, 'Jusek Polewski'."

"That's right. Jusek."

"And let me look at you. You've gained weight!"

"Yes, I guess I have. Mrs. Padworski is a very good cook."

"But what are you doing here?"

"Well, I told them I had a mother and they told me to go and get her so that money negotiations could be made. You know, negotiations about how much I am to be paid and all that. So I thought I'd just come here and spend the night, if you will let me please, and then tomorrow morning return and tell them my mother's sick and can't come to Biesnik and, you know, make up some sort of excuse."

"O.K., that sounds like a good idea," said Balwina. "You're welcome to stay, but things are very dangerous around here as you know. There is my neighbor, Bujak, whom I don't trust. Then there is that traitor Krupa, the *Szmalcownik,* who lives not far away. You see his house in the distance," and she pointed to a nearby valley.

"He told me just the other day that he had caught a Jew and delivered him to the Gestapo, for which he received a pair of boots and three thousand zlotys."

"Is that right? I didn't know a Jew was caught around here."

"Yes. Krupa is a real traitor to his fellow human beings. In fact, I'm surprised you didn't hear of the Jew he caught. It seems he was the son of a man named Schiff, who I think is the one that owned the farm you are working on. I think it is the same Schiff. There were two brothers, weren't there?"

I was stunned. After a long silence, I said quietly, "Yes."

"Well, it's the same Schiff then. Because this Jew that Krupa caught had a brother. This Krupa is a very mean person: he has been known to rape young Jewish girls, and to have broken the legs of old women and dragged them to the Gestapo. He must have done some things to that Jewish man, because he learned he had a brother who was a lover to some local girl. For some extra money, he told this to the Nazis.

"This girl was a peasant named Polka who lives just down the road. The Nazis found this Jewish lover in her house and shot him right there in front of her. The house had a dirt floor and she was forced to dig a hole right there and bury him. She pleaded to be allowed to bury him somewhere else, but the Nazis said he was her lover, and since she liked Jews so much she might as well bury him there so he would always be with her and she wouldn't forget him."

"How do you know all this?" I whispered, thinking of the night I had helped the Schiff brothers by giving them all the potatoes I could find.

"This Krupa was sure to tell me the whole story. Maybe he heard it from some German friend, or maybe he was with the Nazis at the time. It's all the same. He's pretty dumb, and he can't stop bragging about it, you know. Let me tell you, someday the war's going to end and he better hope the Germans win, because if they don't, someone's for sure going to take care of him. Take care of him, good."

"Well, I hope so. Why does he do such things? Doesn't he have any feelings for human beings?"

"I guess he doesn't."

We went to bed. My place was in the attic where I had stayed the last time I was in Balwina's house. In the morning she insisted that I take Staszek back to Biesnik with me (the two villages were not very far apart and it would be a simple matter for him to return). So I went back to the Padworskis and told them that my mother was very sick and couldn't come to see them. Then I introduced Staszek to them. It just so happened that Staszek and I looked very much alike, and the Padworskis believed he was my brother. I had coached him well and he supported my identity. When it was time for him to leave, Mr. Padworski offered to drive him to Lużna by horse and cart, but Staszek insisted he wanted to hitchhike. As if on cue, the cold weather broke and there was a day of warm breezes. Staszek left the Padworski farm and hitchhiked "home," and I was thankful to God for the warm weather because I hated to think what would have happened if the cold weather had held and Mr. Padworski had thought it was too dangerous for an eleven year-old boy to be hitchhiking in such temperatures.

Mr. Padworski seemed satisfied to have met my pretended brother. Negotiations with my mother were put off. Staszek's visit gave me some peace of mind in that my made-up identity was reinforced; but as it turned out, my euphoria was to be short-lived. The very day Staszek left the farm, the horse I was working with was a little skittery and kicked me in the thigh. Things would not have been so bad had not Mrs. Padworski insisted on seeing the wound. We were in the barn where the accident happened, and *Gospodyni* (mistress of the house), as I sometimes called her, pushed me gently against the side of the stall insisting to take a look. If she pulled down my pants to see the wound, my circumcision would be in plain sight. In desperation I turned my head toward the barn door. "Someone's coming!" I hissed. Mrs. Padworski quickly ran to see who it was. "Oh," she said, turning around and facing me. "There's no one coming. You're just shy!" I admitted this was true and she believed me so I got out of the dangerous situation.

During the next few months I worked very hard. Mr. Padworski still wanted to negotiate with my mother and I managed to put things off. As spring turned into summer, Staszek showed up at the farm every now and then to tell that my 'mother' was still sick and report on her progress. Sometimes he would say she wanted to see me and in this way I managed to get away from the farm and spend some time playing with Staszek in the fields and woods. Mrs. Padworski would sometimes ask Staszek how my mother was doing. I had coached him very well; he mostly spoke only when spoken to.

One of the things that Staszek and I used to do when we got away from the Padworski farm, purportedly on the way to see my non-existent mother, was to look up some peasant girls that Staszek knew in the remote corner of Bystra, a mountainous village. We both had certain sexual feelings, and we would invite the girls from their thatched-roof log cabins into the nearby forests and attempt to feel their naked pubic areas under their long skirts. Often the girls protested this forward act on our part, and they would run away in a flirtatious manner. We would catch up with them, wrestle them to the ground, and lie on top of them for a fleeting moment while we planted kisses on their lips and cheeks.

I was still too young to have sexual intercourse; but during those few months of games in the forests and fields I was able to forget about the war.

One night I had a dream. My mother appeared and warned me that I would be betrayed by Balwina. There was some logic to this dream, for the peasant woman could very easily have gone to the Gestapo and told them about me. She could have been forced, or she could have done it for three thousand zlotys. Also, Staszek or Sofia could have had a slip of the tongue.

All of a sudden I realized how vulnerable I was in relation to Balwina and became very frightened. The Germans required a daily milk delivery from the peasants with cows and it was one of my duties at the farm to take this milk to the adjacent village of Ropa. It just so happened that Staszek made milk deliveries from Bystra, and while I was in Ropa we met. "Do me a favor," I said, "tell your mother I am leaving the village of Biesnik."

Two days later I was in Ropa with another milk delivery. I tried to look out for Staszek so I could avoid him; but as I happened to turn around one time, there he was, around the corner of a building, waving for me to join him. Reluctantly, I walked to where he was standing. "It's too dangerous anywhere else," he said, urgently. "You are already settled here. You have been here over a year and it's safe for you. Mother says you must not go away. You mustn't run away from here."

What he said was true. Anywhere else my life would be in more danger than it was now; and if she had wanted to, Balwina could have caused me harm a long time ago. She had, in fact, done much to help me and I decided to remain with the Padworskis in Biesnik. I was doubly careful not to expose myself, never to bathe in public or go into the river with the other kids. Even when I played certain games with the peasant girls I was very careful. I pretended to be anti-Semitic and the big lie helped me survive. I had prepared all kinds of statements for various occasions that I felt would reinforce my position as a true gentile.

Life went on somehow in Poland, but the war had brought on many changes. Among other things, the government was in German hands and therefore reflected the interests and concerns of the Third Reich. Many Polish aspects of the government suffered from this and the mail system, for one, was unreliable.

One morning I was in the Padworskis' kitchen having soup for breakfast. Mrs. Padworski was reading a letter written by a friend of hers living in Warsaw. Tears ran down her cheeks.

"What is the matter?" asked her husband, looking at her over the top of his newspaper.

"It's what my friend here has to say about the Warsaw ghetto." She stopped, unable to continue, and leaned her forehead against her hand.

"What's the matter?" I said. "I would like to know about the Warsaw ghetto. They had lots of…Jews…there, didn't they?"

Mr. Padworski smiled at me. Over the past few months I had begun to think of his eyes as less cold. Behind all his Polish aristocratic bluster and anti-Semitic utterances, he was a kind, humanitarian person. I would not go so far as to reveal to him that I was

Jewish, but I was no longer certain that he would be hostile if he knew.

It was he who kept me informed of the state of the German army. His various newspapers provided a steady stream of information. He seemed able to read between the lines and frequently chuckled at Germany's "minor setbacks."

His wife was evidently still thinking about the letter. In a gentle voice Mr. Padworski gave me a brief history of the Warsaw ghetto.

"In 1940 the Nazis turned part of Warsaw into an area reserved for Jews. Around this area they put barbed wire, solid walls, and watchtowers. Jews are used to living close together, but in their cruelty the Nazis went so far as to pile them up literally one on top of another. In 1942, late July I believe, this Jewish area was evacuated. That is, about three hundred thousand people were sent to death camps and about seventy thousand ended up as forced labor in the war factories."

"How do you know all this?"

"I read a lot. I talk to people. There are ways of finding out." He sighed." "Do you want to hear the rest?"

I nodded, trying not to look as upset as I felt. Visions of my previous life—the one I had spent as Shmulek Oliner—were surging and reeling through my mind. No, I did not want to hear the rest, but I was afraid to reveal my weakness.

"On April 19, 1943, the Nazis undertook the final solution of the small number of people remaining in the ghetto. General J. Stroop, commander of the ghetto operations, was there. The Jews were slaughtered like sheep."

"However, the Nazis found out something they didn't expect: not all of the Jews were sheep. They took up arms and it took the Germans three weeks to break the resistance. A few Jews escaped through the sewers, tunnels, and rat-infested canals, and fugitives were shot down all over Warsaw. I'm afraid some Polish hostages were killed as well. The Nazis have a rule, you know: for every German killed here, one hundred Polish people must die. It usually doesn't matter whether it's a Jew or a peasant that killed the German."

He might have continued, but his wife gave a little sob.

She smiled and brushed the tears from her cheek. "Would you like to read the letter out loud?" said her husband. Her chin trembled a little at the suggestion, but she picked up the letter.

She read: "'Here I stand on the balcony and the entire Jewish ghetto is aflame. Dive bombers are attacking it, cannon are blasting, and tanks are moving into the ghetto. Poor devils, they haven't got the slightest chance to survive. All you see is flames and the smell of human flesh which comes from that part of the city.'" She paused and looked at her husband. "The vision of it all, why…it just makes me feel so sorry for those poor people. They were just people, you know, with their hatreds and loves…their children just like us. They do fight very bravely," she said.

"In removing the Jews and making Poland *Judenrein,* Germany did us a great favor," said Mr. Padworski. I felt horrible, as if I were about to burst into a million pieces. 'Why did he have to say that—especially now?' I thought.

"Do you really believe that?" asked his wife.

After a long pause he spoke. His head was bowed. "No. No, I guess I don't. Some feelings are better left unsaid."

Mrs. Padworski seemed satisfied with that answer. I didn't. Yet, I felt proud that the helpless, defenseless Jews of the Warsaw ghetto had taken up arms and had fought back. They cannot be thought of by ignorant men as spineless sheep any more. After all, they were the very first people to start an armed conflict against the mighty Nazi machine in all of Europe. They killed many German soldiers in the battle of the Warsaw ghetto. To quell the uprising it took S.S. General Jurgen Stroop, a 48-year-old veteran of campaigns in Poland and Russia, an armored battalion, a cavalry battalion, a German police battalion, Ukrainian and Polish police squads, Latvian and Lithuanian police units, artillery, engineers and demolition squads—in all, a 9,000-man force.

Against that might, the Jews had far less than a thousand young, inexperienced men, women and children armed with only a few hundred revolvers, a few rifles and a few grenades: but one thing they had, an enormous amount of courage.

RETRIBUTION BEGINS

THE HEAVY GUNS of the Soviet army began to roar about forty-six kilometers away. It sounded as though the Russians were in the next village. From pulpits all over the country the "good news" was announced. The air seemed brighter, sharp and fresh, like the thaw after a long winter ice. On Sunday, the peasants flocked to their village churches filling the buildings with happy voices. And it was on Sunday that the sheriff came back from the county seat of a city called Szalowa with the order given him by the Nazis to get one man out of every house to go and dig trenches in the Strurzna area. The Germans were preparing for retreat and building lines of defense every one hundred kilometers or so.

Naturally, the Padworskis sent me. I would be living in Strurzna until the project was completed. As I was leaving the farm, *Gospodyni* gave me some sandwiches and I joined the rest of the Biesnik men and boys for the long march.

It was autumn and snow began to fall. The snow collected on the soles of my wooden shoes and I felt as if I were walking with a giant tree stump on each foot. My feet hurt. But wooden shoes were better than no shoes at all.

All day we walked and finally drew near the Strurzna area. An old familiar feeling came over me and I was reminded of the time I went to Dukla with my sister Feigele and of the time I rode in the wagon with my family to Bobowa...I was delivering myself into the hands of the Nazis, but strangely enough—I wasn't afraid. One possible reason was that by this time I had become a veteran of trickery. Perhaps I was a bit smug in this, for as a boy of fourteen I thought I had fooled the German Army.

The Germans viewed all Jews as one creature, to be shot as one and put in one grave. According to this reasoning, when they killed one Jew they killed us all. Likewise, for me to achieve a victory over a few Nazis was to outsmart the entire master race. This master race wasn't as infallible as it had wished to seem. Lines of retreat were being formed and I reveled in the power of the Western Allies. My dreams of England, America, and Russia coming to the rescue, once dashed when Balwina confirmed the death of my family, were renewed. I looked on the Germans as vicious dogs who had had their teeth pulled out. Inasmuch as the Allies were winning the war, I myself was victorious, and I swaggered just a little on that last stretch of road before Strurzna.

As we walked in single file through the gates, we were told to stand at attention while our names were called out. This was to determine whether anyone had run away. I heard my name called, "Jusek Polewski," and said, "Here!" The officer gave me a look, finished reading the list and showed us to the barracks, which were small wooden huts built with one-inch boards.

I was separated from my Biesnik neighbors and put with a group of boys my own age, one of whom I immediately distrusted. He reminded me of the "knife stealer." The guard pointed to a spot on the floor and told me that was where I had to sleep. It had been the "bunk" of a boy who had run away from the barracks during an air raid. On this spot I spread the coarse blanket Mrs. Padworski had given me. A whistle sounded and I took my tin cup to the mess area for some soup. After the cold walk to Strurzna I was more than happy to drink something warm. After that I went back to the barracks to get some sleep.

The other boys in the barracks looked tired and rather vicious. They said they had worked there four days and that the German detail boss was a real devil. He would come around by jeep every hour of the day and beat those who didn't work hard enough. If any of the peasants would say anything, the German answered, "Die you devil." In fact, the peasants had nicknamed him, *Zdechipieronie,* or "Die You Devil."

That night I didn't sleep very well. Most of the time I lay waiting for dawn. Then we got up and received soup and a piece of dry army bread.

All too soon the work started. The fields marked off for trenches had been sown with winter corn. A truck appeared with spades and picks and each of us took a tool and started to work. The only clothing I had on was a pair of pants, a homespun shirt and an old jacket Mr. Padworski had given me. Of course, I had no underwear, and the wind made matters even worse. We dug in the frozen ground until twelve o'clock and then a whistle blew for a half-hour lunch break. I had saved the sandwich Mrs. Padworski had given me. It was dry and hard but I was so hungry it tasted absolutely delicious.

At six-thirty in the evening we went back to the barracks. I was dead tired and slept soundly in spite of the cold. The next day went by just as the first. We dug in the frozen ground all morning and had a short break for lunch. At six-thirty the whistle blew for us to stop work.

Strurzna was an important railroad junction and some German military trains stopped there. Some of the cars were unloaded into open wagons, others were filled up with food for the German Army. We were marching by the railway station on the way back to the barracks one day, when two "sisters"—small Russian planes that harassed the German military lines—appeared very swiftly and machine-gunned the Strurzna station. We all jumped into the trenches we had dug the previous day. More planes arrived and then the real fire opened up. Bullets hit so close we could hear them whistle by our heads. The roar of the diving planes was deafening. The train started out quickly and the two sister planes followed it, diving and machine-gunning the box cars. Pretty soon whistles blew and we climbed out of the trenches and resumed the march back to the barracks.

After dinner, which was more soup and bread, I returned to the barracks with the other boys. There was not much light inside the building. In the light of a candle everyone knelt down to say prayers. Everyone spoke loud enough for his neighbor to hear and I did the same. It just so happened that the boy who reminded me of the "knife stealer" was beside me on the floor and apparently my prayer was not to his liking.

He said, "Hey, everybody knows how to pray. Only Jews don't know how to pray to Jesus Christ."

He seemed to be talking to me, so I said, "Sure, that's right."

"Are you a Jew?"

I grew pale from the sudden shock. Very quickly I said, "Yeah. You're a Jew too, aren't you?"

"No, I'm not. Hey fellas, we got us a Jew boy."

He laughed and waited to see what I would do.

"Oh yeah, fellas," I said. "We got two Jews among us. Don't you see? Doesn't he look like a Jew?"

The boy walked over and pushed me. I pushed him back. Then he hit me and I hit him in the eye as hard as I could and just then the guard walked by the window and saw the scuffle. He opened the door and said, "What's going on here?"

"Here is a Jew, that's what. I caught him right here in the barracks."

The guard glanced at me: he seemed irritated at all the commotion.

"Here is a Jew," the boy repeated his accusation, pointing his finger at me.

Right there in front of me I saw death, and the guard said:

"It's too dark in here now. Tomorrow I'll take a look at him."

After the guard left the boy was surly. He said, "Don't tell me, Jusek, your mother never taught you the *paczierz* (the prayer)?" Then he kidded: "Maybe you are a Jew. I heard last week a Jew escaped and maybe you are that guy.

"Oh sure. Sure, I'm that guy."

My heart was beating so hard I thought that everyone was able to hear it. At any moment I could be delivered into Nazi hands. I pretended to laugh at the other boy and he got up and walked toward the door, apparently to go to the bathroom.

"Gee," he said, "I better leave here. I don't want to share these barracks with a Jew."

That night I lay on the hard floor with the rough blanket on my shoulder and sleep seemed as far away as the Free World. If the guard inspected me in the morning he would plainly see that I was a Jew. I really didn't want to fall asleep because that would only make the morning come faster. I was very upset and prayed to God over and over again, trying to think of what to do.

Then I remembered a conversation I had overheard the previous day. Two peasant men were planning to run away. They had commented that the Germans didn't keep very good track of the workers; the records were not kept up to date and the only thing a person had to be concerned about was the danger of getting shot in the actual moment of escape. In my own case, I had answered the roll call and I was sure that if some German guard noticed I was missing he would think I had been transferred to another work team or something. Until nearly daylight I made plans and all kinds of fantasies filled my head, including torture and death in case I failed.

Toward dawn I dozed off, and in a dream my mother appeared to me. Very clearly, she sat by the bed and whispered in my ear, telling me to take a certain route of escape down by the river that flowed near the place where we were digging trenches. In the dream I ran and ran, crossing a river and running on, my mother following me. Then, suddenly, we were standing on a nice lawn: the sun was shining and there was a pleasant smell in the air.

When the whistle blew for us to wake up and everyone crawled grumbling out of bed, I decided I better do something about my prayer. There were about six words I knew and I got on my knees and said each word very loudly. The Polish boys turned and looked at me and one of them said, "He's no Jew. See? He knows the prayer well enough."

When I had recited the prayer twice to make sure everyone had a chance to hear, I went over to the boy I had fought with the night before and apologized. "I'm sorry we had that fight," I said. "We should not be arguing and fighting. We have a hard day of work ahead of us." He turned so I could plainly see his black swollen eye, then he walked away without speaking to me.

All this time I was aware that the guard could come into the barracks without a moment's warning and have me take my pants down. It would be all over then. Every time the barracks' door rattled on its hinges—as it did quite often because of the wind that had started blowing during the night—I would hold my breath. After living in a state of fear for years, I thought that I was conditioned by now to any kind of strain. Instead, I was simply terrified as the likelihood of losing my life seemed so great and the very next minute might very well be my last. All the pain and trickery of the past seemed to have been in vain. I might as well have died with my family; why was I allowed to hope and dream and fight for the impossible? The end of the war was near. Russian bombers flew regular missions across Nazi territory. Why was I allowed to survive the worst, only to perish when the Allies were knocking at the door?

Then the bombing started. The barracks shook and sawdust fell from the cracks in the ceiling. There was mass confusion and the workers flopped on the floor, some whimpering and others just very quiet. I was lying next to the "knife stealer" and for the moment we were comrades, both gripped by fear, forgetting the differences between us.

Suddenly, the bombing stopped and the roar of the planes vanished into the distance. What a difference between this profound stillness and the explosion of crashing bombs! The boys got up from the floor chattering and trying to tell jokes. Those who had cried, now laughed nervously trying to pass it off. I was wiping sawdust from my pants, feeling a great relief that the bombing was over, when the door opened and the German guard walked in.

I snapped erect and the blood left my head so quickly I nearly fainted. He looked straight at me and I wished I had died in the bombing raid. "Everyone out!" he said. "Out in formation!" My knees were weak and I felt sick in my stomach. I thought, 'He is just playing with me. Maybe I should start running and get shot running.' While we marched in formation, he looked at me again. His face was cold and ugly, hard as metal, and I was sure he was playing with me, waiting perhaps to see me die of fright. The wooden shoes had made large blisters on my feet and I limped a little. I wished it were yesterday all over again; or tomorrow; or a year from now.

As we passed the Strurzna junction the guards ordered us to look straight ahead. The bombing raid had left masses of bodies, shattered arms and legs, and blood all over the place. The guards ordered us not to look to the left or right, but to keep our eyes straight ahead as we marched past the station. The moans were sickening and I felt a devilish joy that the master race was so human after all. Not only were the Nazis losing the war, they were lying dead at my feet. They died with pleas for mercy on their lips. With calls to God they passed into death and I felt somehow Zyndranowa and Bielanka and countless Jews were getting their revenge.

We were digging in the trenches when the second bombing raid occurred. The planes came one after another, dropping bombs, and the ground shook and quivered. From the direction of the train, ghastly human screams split the air only to be cut off in the explosions. The station was a shambles. One of the airplanes spun around in the air and came over so low above the trenches that I could see the grim expression on the pilot's face. 'This is the end,' I thought. 'Now I will be machine-gunned by a Russian plane.' The deafening roar of the engine seemed to draw from me a long and hideous sound and I lay shaking in the icy bottom of the trench.

After about twenty minutes of bombing the planes flew away. Silence descended over the trenches. The cries and moans of wounded men, mostly Germans, sounded far away and a little unreal. Smoke filled the air and fire licked and hissed among the ruins of the Strurzna station. It seemed impossible that I was still alive. Like a phantom I rose from the ground and was appalled at the death and destruction strewn everywhere. Deep inside me was a satisfaction that it was the Germans who had suffered most in this ordeal. Secretly I applauded because the Germans were finally getting what they deserved.

A whistle blew and we were ordered to resume working. Some of the work force had been killed and other members had to carry the bodies off a little ways to the edge of the woods. It started to rain. What clothes I had on were wet through and through. The Germans walked about in shiny black slickers, bending over with water dripping from their helmets and taking care of their dead and wounded comrades. My wooden shoes were filled with water. The ground became icy mud and my shoes stuck in the mud and came off. From time to time I fell. The trenches were filling with water and we had to dig and splash with the pick in the muddy slosh. The German guard seemed to keep his eye on me. I was sure he knew I was a Jew and that he would want to take a look at me back at the barracks; or maybe at the end of the cold miserable day he would shoot me and let me die in this muddy water.

The rain came down even more heavily and we ran to the woods for shelter. The guards kept a close eye on everyone. The two peasants I had overheard planning to escape took their break for freedom, running hunched low through the trees and wiry underbrush. One of the guards sounded the alarm and another guard several meters farther in the woods shot five times and both peasants were killed in their tracks. From where I was taking shelter under a stubby evergreen tree I could see the bodies washed by the rain.

Escape seemed impossible. The rain let up a little and Russian bombers made another pass at the Strurzna station. The Germans were trying to move their men out of the Russian front, but the Russians bombed the lines of communications again and again. As fast as the German Army could lay railroad tracks the Russians blew them apart again.

The guards ran through the woods shouting at us to get back to the trenches. Some of the workers did as they were told and ran as quickly as they could through the rain. The roar of airplane engines was deafening and the guards were firing their rifles into the air. The planes flew so low I thought I could reach out and touch them. The German soldiers were clearly as frightened as we were. The workers were milling about, some heading for the trenches, others just running around in circles with their hands over their ears. A peasant right in front of me spun around on his heels and collapsed on his knees. His mouth was open and I knew he was screaming, but his voice was lost in the din of the plane engines. The bombs fell, whistling first, then hitting the ground and exploding. In the confusion I scrambled on my hands and knees in the direction opposite to the trenches, tearing the underbrush with my hands, rolling and crawling and shoving my way through the woods. In the deafening noise I couldn't tell whether I was being shot at, nor did it seem to matter. With the wings of fear I skidded through the sodden tree leaves and rolled down a bank while the rain was hitting every part of my body. When I came to a river, I plunged right in and crossed to the other side. The bombing back at the station continued, but now the explosions didn't quite drown out everything else. I realized that I was some distance away from the station and this thought was comforting. I could hear the hiss of rain falling upon the surface of the river. I imagined that back at the station the hiss was that of fire. Even at this distance I could hear an occasional bloodcurdling scream. In the dream in which my mother had appeared, there was a river like the one at my feet. The river was behind me now and, as in the dream, I knew I was safe.

One of my shoes was gone and I threw the other one into the river and watched it float away. My feet were so blistered that the freedom felt good in spite of the cold. I was weak from lack of food, but I started to walk anyway. Toward nightfall I knocked at a peasant's door and asked if he would put me up for the night; I told him I had visited a little village past Strurzna and was on my way home. He looked me up and down and a strange sight I must have been! The rain had washed the mud from my clothing; my hands were scratched and my feet were torn and blistered and bleeding; the skin of my face burned and I knew that it must have been scratched as well.

Finally the peasant said, "All right, you can sleep in the stable."

He gave me some bread and milk which I took to the barn. The peasant let me find out for myself that I was not alone in the stable. Also sleeping there was some kind of deformed, crippled child. When I sat down in the straw to eat the bread and drink the milk, the youngster made strange noises. In Poland it was customary that deformed children born to peasants were kept at home and often in some isolated place such as a stable, attic or spare room; they were fed and left alone until they died.

When I finally succeeded in returning to Biesnik, the Padworskis greeted me warmly. Many persons from the village had escaped from the labor camps as I had done. The Padworskis were concerned that the Germans might try to hunt down the fugitives, but for now they were just happy to see me alive.

During the short period of rest and relative peace that followed, I spent long hours thinking about the events of the past few years of my life. Everything that was dear to me had been crushed. My family was dead; because of my heritage I was considered a criminal, but my will to survive had saved me so far. If the Germans caught up with me now I would be shot, not as a Jew, but as a fugitive from the Strurzna work camp.

For some reason I recalled an incident that had happened only a week after I came to live with the Padworskis. I had found a Jewish prayerbook which I hid under my pillow in the barn and used each night to help me pray. One day Mrs. Padworski found it. She said, "What is this? Where did you get it?" I said, "I just found it. I don't know what it is. I found it in a little cloth sack along the road outside of town. What is it?" She said, "Well, you better burn it because it is a Jewish book and if anyone finds it on you they will think you are a Jew."

So I said, "Oh sure." And I burned it.

Not long after my escape from Strurzna I began to notice a change in the German soldiers who were passing through Biesnik. Their hard, cruel masks were disintegrating. Little by little they were forced to realize that the arm of the Third Reich had lost its muscle. They even began to smile, sometimes, in the nervous, ingratiating manner of defeat, and to help out the villagers. One German soldier lent his hand to the changing of a broken cart wheel. Another helped build a chicken coop and refused to accept payment for his work. On the village streets some German soldiers greeted pleasantly the passersby and tried to engage them in conversation, doing what they could to prove they weren't so mean after all.

The air was crisp and filled with rumors that the German Army was retreating. The three-year-long dream was coming true: the Germans were taking a beating; they were being shot down like dogs by the Polish partisans. Small groups of Jewish partisans also operated in the area. Germans feared the darkness and no longer dared come out of town at night.

Polish traitors who had mistreated Jewish men, women and children got diminishing support from the master race and were understandably less brave. I knew of a man named Lega who had turned many Jews over to the Gestapo; a Jewish partisan group operating out of a forest just outside Gorlice paid this Lega several visits and after these he was left severely beaten and bleeding.

For the next few weeks the guns of the Russian liberators blasted at the enemy from Jaslo, a city about seventy kilometers away. The German Army was withdrawing under the pressure. Partisans sabotaged the lines of retreat: bridges were blown up, trees chopped down and thrown across the escape routes of the demoralized army. Russian planes strafed the roads during the day, so the Germans were forced to flee by night.

It seemed only a matter of days—perhaps even hours—before the enemy would be kicked out forever from the Gorlice-Biesnik district. The future was bright and mysterious and I awakened each day with a feeling of excitement. Fear no longer seemed justified and my chest swelled with fresh and powerful hope. With freedom so close I tried to recall the prewar days. It seemed too good to be true that I would no longer have to fear being a Jew. Once more I would be able to walk the streets openly and speak Yiddish to my people. Yet some vague notion kept my happiness from being complete. After the war was over I vaguely expected my life to return to the idealistic simplicity of my youth. Life had robbed me of my family so quickly I couldn't completely comprehend their disappearance. I guess that, actually, some small part of me held tenaciously to the hope that they were somewhere safe and sound, waiting for me—perhaps in England or America, countries which were only names to me but certainly symbolized heaven. Some elusive but nevertheless ominous cloud threatened my shining sun, and I thought this uneasiness was due to the fact that in spite of their losses the German armies were still occupying my country—Poland.

The Germans kept saying they would push the Russians—the sweet liberators—all the way back to Russia. I could not imagine the nightmare of losing the war at this point. Not after all the hope and dreams. During those four weeks I prayed to God that the Russians would come quickly. When the shooting was very near, with shells exploding above the roofs of Biesnik, I said the longest prayer I could remember from Hebrew school.

The shells were exploding right outside Biesnik and bullets were flying everywhere. Sleep was impossible and I huddled with the Padworskis in the kitchen of their house. We sat in darkness. Not a sound did anyone make, yet we knew what each one was thinking. 'What is happening? Will we make it? What does this all mean?' Life was extremely uncertain. By dawn the next day we could all be gone and there was no telling whether it would be a German or a Russian action that would cause our death. Mrs. Padworski clutched me and her husband held onto both of us. One morning at three o'clock someone came pounding at the door and Mr. Padworski got up to open it.

Standing out on the porch was one of their neighbors. Exploding shells illuminated him and he burst into the house and took Mr. Padworski by the arm.

"The Germans are taking horses with them," he shouted. "The Russians are pushing the Germans back and they're blowing up bridges and supplies as they retreat and they're taking horses!"

The man dashed out into the night once again and Mr. Padworski took his wife and headed toward the cellar, shouting at me to save the horse.

Out in the cold blue night lit by flashes like lightning, the snow was deep and frozen hard. As usual I had little to wear and I felt the cold right down into my bones. I took the horse out of the stable, but he was jumpy and I had to fight him in the barnyard while rockets exploded overhead lighting up the snow on the ground. The noise made the horse buck, but I kicked my heels into his ribs and succeeded in driving him in the direction of the woods.

Just when I thought I had controlled the animal and we were finally safe, a low-hanging branch of a tree knocked me off the horse's back. Strange sounds trickled through my head as my body felt dull and soggy. Strangely enough I felt no pain; the coldness of the night seemed far, far away and I came to the logical conclusion that I was dead. I thought: 'I have outsmarted the Germans as I vowed to do so long ago only to lose my life to a tree while on the back of a dumb animal.'

Then the pain started creeping up on me and there was soon no doubt that I was very much alive. My body seemed broken into a million pieces and each piece ached. Coughing and groaning aloud I got to my feet and stumbled after the horse. In the terrible light shed by rockets I found him and we waited out the night huddled together. As dawn made the sky pink I headed back toward the farm, my aching body stiff and numb from the cold. The horse was calm now and I lay on his back. Only the hope of a Russian victory had kept me alive.

That morning was the morning of mornings. On such a cold and miserable night as the one I had spent in the woods, a person might have wished for death. I was lucky to be now back at the farm, where Mrs. Padworski fed me bread and hot tea and insisted that I sleep in her own bed. The tea spread a wonderful sense of warmth into my body. As I headed toward the bedroom I just happened to glance out of the kitchen window and what I saw made all the pain and fatigue instantly leave my body. Marching across the field in back of the barn were five men in white snow uniforms. They came from the east. I fell to my knees and recited a silent prayer in Yiddish.

My rescuers, from left to right: Staszek, Balwina, Voitek, and Zosia in the village Bystra.

Photo 1994
Dedication ceremony for the opening of Zalman's regional museum. From left to right: Staszek (my rescuer), myself, and Mr Teodor Gocz in Zyndranowa.

THE LIBERATORS

IN THAT MONTH OF MARCH, 1945, the Germans were pushed out of Biesnik. The Russians marched into the Padworski house and set up a radio in the bedroom. Mr. Padworski became seriously ill and his wife made a bed for him in the stable. He suffered from angina pectoris, I was told. The Russians were constantly drunk on the vodka they carried in their canteens. They had no food supplies or extra clothes with them. They were known to live off the land, and Mrs. Padrowski fed them from the larder.

My bed was also in the stable, as it had been all along. *Gospodyni* continued to sleep in the house, although she made frequent visits to the warm stable in order to attend to her husband.

"The war is nearly over," sighed Mr. Padworski, looking pleased but very tired. His bed was made up in an empty horse stall where he could have some privacy. From my own bed I couldn't see him, but frequently he called me over for conversation.

"For us the war is already ended," I said. "Isn't it? The Germans are being pushed out of Poland. Biesnik already is saved by the liberators."

"The liberators..."

Mr. Padworski lay on his bed and stared at the ceiling. He seemed very pale. Throughout the war his friends, whom you might call members of the intelligentsia, had come to the farm on periodic visits. On these occasions reports on the progress of the war were followed by philosophical discussions about war in general. Mr. Padworski felt no love toward the Germans but neither did he seem particularly fond of the Russians. His interest lay exclusively with the Polish people, and it was only opportunism that ever made it seem otherwise.

"Yes, the Germans have been pushed back," he said. "The Germans are gone and I am thankful. When the Russians will leave, too—then I will say the war has ended and we Poles will be truly free."

I sat on a wooden crate at the end of the stall. The barn door was open and I could see a Russian officer standing on the porch of the house, smoking a cigarette. Wood smoke was coming from the chimney of the house and every now and then someone moved past the kitchen window. Soon spring would break the grip of winter and the vine alongside the house would bloom. The earth would be ready for planting. A new season would come and then go.

"It's ironic," continued Mr. Padworski. "It's ironic…when the war came to Poland I left the city and moved to the country. I was an engineer with a good business. But you know, I left the city because it is a bad place to be in time of war. I brought my young wife here to this Jewish farm because a farm is much safer than the city. Here, I thought, we could be safe. We could sit out the war and be sheltered and await the brighter days of the new future."

He was staring at the ceiling, speaking aloud the thoughts that ran through his head. I felt uneasy.

"My wife is fifteen years younger than myself. She is good to me and a very hard worker, but we have been unable to have children of our own. I sometimes fear she is lonely."

Nervously, I coughed and got up from the wooden crate. Just then his wife walked into the stable carrying food for his lunch. Her eyes looked tired and the war had aged her so that now she looked as old as her husband. She sat on the wooden crate I had just left and smoothed a place in the hay so she could set down the plate of biscuits.

With hushed voice she said: "Some German soldiers who apparently were stragglers have been captured!"

I glanced at the porch of the house and noticed that the Russian officer was no longer there. Mrs. Padworski fed her husband some soup from a bowl she had carried on the plate of biscuits.

"While I was in the kitchen these two Germans were brought in. They were dirty and unshaven and looked very frightened. They looked at me pleadingly, as if for help, and Lord knows I couldn't help them. Not that I wouldn't if I could, even though they are the enemy."

Mr. Padworski murmured: "The tides of war have changed."

"And then while I was standing right there…well, the Russian who brought the prisoners in asked what should be done with them. I thought they would be locked up in the barn or something, maybe tied up. But the Russian officer just glanced at the prisoners and said, 'You know what to do with Germans.' Simple as that. And the Russian who had brought the prisoners in pushed them back out of the door."

"Where are they now?" I said.

"Behind the barn someplace, I think. I am afraid of what's going to happen. In spite of their cruelty, the Germans are still people. The Russian officer didn't seem to see this."

Filled with morbid curiosity, I ran outside the barn and looked around. The glare of the sun on the snow momentarily blinded me. The snow was trampled and muddy between the house and the barn; there was no one in sight. I ran around the barn and stopped short.

Two Germans were on their knees in the snow at the Russian soldier's feet. With tears running down their stubbly cheeks the Germans choked: "Please, please. We have wives. We have children." With the barrel of his machine gun the Russian motioned them to their feet. "Walk on," he said in German. Desperately, the Germans glanced at each other. Once more they turned to beg and again the Russian motioned them to their feet.

Trembling, the Germans rose to their feet. Their coats had been taken away and they wore only coarse army shirts. Snow clung to their pants all the way up to the knees. Resolutely they turned around and walked away from the Russian. One of them stopped and turned back and the other waited for him. "Please..." The Russian said, "Walk on." As the Germans resumed their walk, the Russian very suddenly opened fire with his machine gun and the Germans were flung face down in the snow. They struggled feebly. The snow was red with their blood and I vomited against the side of the barn. The Russian turned around and saw me. "You shouldn't have seen this," he said, his face expressionless. "Go to the house. My captain wants to see you."

Gospodyni was in the kitchen when I walked through the door. I avoided her eyes. A pair of Russian army boots were against the wall by the door. Several white snow uniforms hung on nails newly pounded into the wall. Steam rose from a large pot of stew on the stove and from the bedroom came the sound of voices speaking Russian and the static of a radio. Throughout the war Mr. Padworski had saved his newspapers, stacking them in a corner of the kitchen. Now they were gone. Thick was the smell of gun grease and the odor of unwashed bodies. The Russian officer was seated at the table.

The Russians had demanded *Forshpun,* which simply meant they required any type of transportation Mr. Padworski had to offer. The Russian officer looked directly at me. "You will go to the neighboring farm, get a horse and hitch it to the wagon along with the horse that is in the barn."

I glanced at Mrs. Padworski and our eyes met. She was usually a very expressive person and I was shocked by the lack of feeling in her gaze. In this house taken over by soldiers she evidently kept her emotions carefully guarded. Someone would have to drive the horses to the Russian front. The Russians couldn't spare soldiers for this purpose and I feared I would be ordered to do it. For several moments my eyes were riveted to those of *Gospodyni.* Then she turned her attention to the stew that was cooking on the stove.

When I returned from the neighboring farm with the horse, I found several Russian soldiers I had not seen before standing in the barnyard smoking cigarettes. Every once in a while they took drinks from their canteens and I could tell they were drunk. I took the Padworskis' horse out of the barn and hitched the two horses to the wagon. One of the Russians shouted at me to put straw in the wagon bed. This I did, and some of the soldiers piled in. The officer came out on the porch of the house. He told me to drive the wagon to the front lines where it was needed for supplies and transportation.

As I whipped up the horses and drove out of the driveway I couldn't help but glance toward the back of the barn. There in the snow lay the two Germans, face down and stripped to their underwear.

The soldiers in the back of the wagon were wild and boisterous. Every now and then they had me drive into a farm that was close to the road and they would get off the wagon and knock on the door of the house and ask for women. All the young women were taken to the various outbuildings, and I could hear them pleading and screaming and sometimes crying. The Russians would say, "I have liberated you. Now let me have you."

Sometimes the farmers knew what the Russians were after and when they saw the wagon coming they hid their women. It was on one of these farms that a particular Russian's appetite turned from women to beef. He paid the farmer for his cow (the farmer had little choice), then took an axe from the back of the wagon and went into the barn. The cow was in its stall. The Russian led the cow out of the stall and tied it to a wooden post in the middle of the barn. Then he hit it between the eyes with the axe. The head of the axe flew off the handle and the cow fell to its knees with a terrible bellow. The cow just stayed there on its knees while the Russian searched the hay for the axe head. He finally found it and hit the cow again, and so there was food in the evening for the soldiers. The meat was cooked in a huge cauldron.

As spring finally came, the weather changed quickly. The snow turned soft and very wet. In some spots roads were covered with mud so deep as to reach the axle. I had to whip the horses constantly to keep them going. The fighting seemed to attract dark clouds which filled the sky and rain fell steadily turning the road into a quagmire of running water. The noise from cannon and machine-gun fire filled the air and bullets whistled close overhead. In addition to myself, there were other drivers—boys my own age from other farms—along this treacherous front. One of these drivers was killed by a stray bullet and there was no way of telling whether it was a German or a Russian who fired the shot.

The war was moving over territory previously occupied by the Germans. In the fields were the hollow shells and crumbling remains of farmhouses, and in spite of the ever present danger, my mind kept wandering: I thought of my family, of Isak and Reisel, of my two mothers and of my father. Desperately I clung to the hope that someone else had survived somewhere, for the burden of their memory seemed too much to bear alone. The thought that I was all that was left made me feel desperately lonely and unhappy.

Driving near the front I witnessed many acts of cruelty: dead German soldiers dismembered, decapitated, hung in grotesque display. I was appalled, yet also morbidly gratified. The souls of murdered Jews numbered in tens of thousands. The more I found out from stories here and there, the more I was convinced that millions of my people had perished. At this point I learned of the existence of gas chambers all over liberated Poland and Russia. Compared to this, what was the mutilated body of a German soldier?

Yet, as *Gospodyni* had said, the Germans were people too: I struggled with conflicting feelings of compassion on one hand and desire for revenge on the other. My feelings became conflicting also with regard to the Russians. They were not so glorious after all. I certainly felt the thrill and joy for their victory, but those whom I had previously thought of as the "sweet luscious liberators" were just the other side of a well worn coin. War was war, soldiers were soldiers; also the Russians sometimes raped, looted, and even murdered with impunity. I was not certain they would treat me any differently than the Germans would have if they found out that I was Jewish. I reached the conclusion that it was not yet safe to disclose my identity.

One night I decided I'd had enough. I was staying with a small contingent of soldiers at a newly-occupied village; in the middle of the night, while the drunken revelry was still going strong, I slipped out of the room where I was staying. The moon was hidden behind clouds, the night was very dark. Mr. Padworski's horse was in a barn with the other horses. The guard at the door was asleep and I led the horse quietly out the back door. All night long I rode, through a countryside that was strange to me, in the general direction of Biesnik until I hit familiar territory.

The Padworskis were glad to see me. The Russians had moved on, taking all their equipment with them, and Mr. Padworski's bed was now back in the house. He was especially pleased I had returned with his horse, for as a result of the war, horses had become extremely rare. A farmer's livelihood depended upon this animal for ploughing and other farm chores. In addition to being useful, horses were symbols of status; and Mr. Padworski now had one of the few left in the village.

One morning in early April I saw someone waving to me from a hill about half a mile behind the barn. From the distance I thought it might be Staszek. As I moved closer I saw that it was, indeed, the son of Balwina. I ran up to him and we greeted each other warmly.

He said, "You know a Jewish man by the name of Peller?"

"Sure. He's my father's friend from Moszczenica. Peller had a wife and two beautiful children."

"When the Germans retreated from here, the Jews that were still alive came out of hiding. This Peller came to see my mother to find out if anyone in the Oliner family was alive and she told him you were alive and that you were to be found here in Biesnik. He's looking for you. That is, he wants to see you and my mother sent me to tell you that."

"I can't believe it. This is wonderful! Sure, uh, come with me. We'll—that is, I'll have to tell Mr. Padworski."

Staszek walked back to the farm with me. Mr. Padworski was recuperating from his illness and doing some light work in the barn. I told him my mother was sick again and needed me. He gave his permission for me to go and Staszek and I left immediately.

As I was walking with Staszek across the Biesnik-Bystra ridges a very peaceful, satisfying, exciting feeling came over me. 'Now there is freedom for me,' I thought to myself. I was extremely happy at the prospect of seeing Peller. We walked very fast and Staszek had trouble keeping up with me.

When Balwina saw me she hugged me and made the sign of the cross and cried and kissed me. "The war is over," she said. "You're safe. You don't have to be afraid anymore. I will send for a man I want you to meet.

In a short while Peller arrived. We embraced and he then told me all about how he had survived the war in a village called Moszczenica in an attic above the stable of a kindly peasant widow. The woman had risked her life in the hope she might convert an infidel to Christianity. Then he told me what was happening in Gorlice. Out of many thousands of Jews only about fifty remained. Peller and several other Jews lived in a large house he had managed to rent from the occupying Russians and the newly established Polish government. He urged me to move in with them saying that now the war was over and it was all right to be a Jew and that in fact the Jews had to band together in order to get what was rightfully theirs: justice, freedom, and a rebuilding of their devastated souls.

I agreed with him. We parted and I made arrangements with Staszek to come back to the Padworski farm and help me pack. Then I returned to the Padworskis and told them my mother's illness was very serious and that she needed me near her, and therefore I could no longer work for them.

Leaving the farm was very painful. I had been as a son to the Padworskis. Mrs. Padworski cried and gave me a gift of grain, which was very valuable at that time. Mr. Paworski gave me some old clothing. He had a very strange look in his eyes when he said the final goodbye. I was wondering again whether they knew my true identity. I couldn't look them in the eyes as I felt a strong sense of shame. If any of the Nazis had found out that I was Jewish, the Padworskis could have been killed. Because of me they had been in grave danger. Although Mr. Padworski had made a number of anti-Semitic remarks during the three years of my service, I sometimes felt that he didn't quite mean what he said. Maybe it was just the tragedy of war that made him say those nasty things. Some truths were better left unacknowledged, given the circumstances of war, I thought to myself. They had treated me like a son and even if they intuitively knew the truth, the fact of my deceit was a painful barrier between us. I had lived a lie and I left the Padworski farm for the last time with tears in my eyes.

Peller was a loving, caring, self-proclaimed leader of the surviving Jews in the city of Gorlice. I lived with him a short while and during this time we spoke only Yiddish because he wanted me to remember my roots. The words rolled off my tongue strangely. Sometimes they dropped heavily to the ground, other times they soared like birds. Gradually, I got the old rhythm back. Jusek Polewski stepped aside and I was Shmulek Oliner once more. Peller became my legal guardian. He went with me to the courthouse in Gorlice and helped me reclaim the land of my grandfather in Mszanka and of my father and stepmother in Bielanka, which I turned over to Balwina and her children. I never returned to Zyndranowa. Rumors circulated that Jews in that part of the country had been put into a ghetto in Dukla. One look at the land of my grandfather in Mszanka and to that of my father in Bielanka convinced me that I didn't want to see my grandfather Isak's farm. I couldn't bear to think of that house—once so full of life—now probably a hollow shell overgown with weeds; a haunted remain of the past, with broken windows, stolen doors, and empty chimneys.

With the help of Peller I went to the Russian military authority in charge of Gorlice and requested to be notified in the event any of my relatives were found alive. In this way I discvovered that a cousin of my father's had indeed survived the war and was presently living in another part of Gorlice. Peller couldn't go with me to look up this relative, so I went alone. The streets were narrow and winding, the houses all jumbled together, and I had some trouble finding where this distant cousin lived. As I entered the hallway of the dwelling which was my cousin's house I heard a woman talking rapidly, loudly, and in a somewhat agitated voice and saw a young Russian soldier inside a room; the door was open and the woman noticed me and looked extremely relieved. She shouted, "Shmulek." She must have heard from Peller about my survival. The Russian soldier saw me and mumbled something under his breath, turned and left, brushing past me. I noticed that the woman was embarrassed thinking about what might have happened had I not appeared on the scene. She immediately composed herself and embraced me saying, "You must be Aron's son, Shmulek." "Yes, I am," I said. Her husband showed up shortly. We embraced and for the first time since Bobowa I had a genuine feeling that I had a remnant of a family again. We started talking about what had happened to our families during the catastrophe. They knew of no other survivors in the Oliner family. This news was very disheartening. Nevertheless, when I left to go home that late afternoon, I felt pretty good. After all, I had found someone who belonged to my family and who cared. I felt useful and important in that I had been able to prevent an unpleasant experience to this woman who was my distant cousin. My stay and frequent visits afterwards were very pleasant.

From May 1945 through December of that same year I stayed with Peller and twenty-five other surviving Jews who lived in the large house he had acquired. During this time Jews throughout Poland were coming out of cellars and stables and various other hiding places and some were trying to reclaim property that was rightfully theirs. During the war many Poles had assumed ownership of these properties and had no desire to give them up.

In the city of Kielce, about one hundred forty-five Jews survived the war. When they started reclaiming their property, the Poles countered by starting a rumor that the Jews were holding Christian children as captives to use in pagan sacrifices. This was all the justification the superstitious Poles needed: riots started and within a week many of the surviving Jews were beaten to death. Some of the Jews who escaped this tragedy went to the Catholic priest who lived there and begged him to go on the radio, denounce the rumor, and intervene on their behalf. Indeed he did go on the air, but what he said was: "I don't sympathize with the rioters. But the practice of blood libel has never been disproved, so I can do nothing."

In Gorlice some Poles resorted to similar excuses in order to defend their usurped properties. Their disappointment that Jews didn't entirely disappear became obvious. Through the heart of the city flowed the river Ropa. The rumor spread that a Christian child had been killed and the body dumped under the bridge. Outside the Peller house a crowd gathered, yelling: "Kill the Jews!" Peller immediately called the police which was under Russian command. Fortunately it just so happened that some of the Russian officers were Jewish. They had the police fire their guns into the air in order to disperse the mob. Peller, not wanting to let a potentially harmful situation simmer, pursued the story of the dead child. He traced it to a Polish prostitute whose child had died. She was paid to leave it under the bridge by the Armia Krajowa (land army). Peller demanded that the culprits be prosecuted and so some of these reactionary anti-Semites had no longer a convenient excuse to kill the Jews.

There was considerable reconstruction going on in Gorlice and to meet my living expenses and get some spending money I did odd jobs. I delivered things here and there, carried messages for the Russian military authority and performed chores on various farms. My travels often took me in the vicinity of the Padworski farm and I may have stopped in to see them, had I not known that Peller had spoken to them about me and told them I was Jewish. Peller said they were not very surprised, but I was too ashamed to face them. Once, I caught sight of Gospodyni and I wanted to run to her. Mr. Padworski, who was with her, didn't look very well and I wanted to do something for him to show my appreciation for the three long years of protection on his farm. Instead, I put my hand over my face so they couldn't see me and turned around, quickly walking in the opposite direction.

My duties as messenger boy for the Russian officers in charge of Gorlice put me in contact with some officers who were Jewish, but denied the fact. Some of them had been among the Russian soldiers who had liberated Auschwitz and they were appalled at the atrocities inflicted upon the Jews during the war. They were particularly horrified at the complicity of some of the Polish informers who used to cripple and maim elderly Jewish women and men and then deliver them to the Gestapo tied together like sheep. Even though these Russians had no particular authority in the matter because there was now a newly constituted Polish government, they decided to pay a visit to a couple of these informers, including the two men called Lega and Krupa.

It was Peller who first told the officers about Lega and Krupa. They had been the ones responsible for the deaths of the Schiff brothers. Also, Krupa had discovered and turned in to the Gestapo the insane man who had escaped from the mass grave at Garbacz—the crazy man Simcha had told me about.

First, Krupa denied he had ever done such things. Then, when he was beaten and almost blinded, he admitted his guilt and begged for mercy, saying he needed the money the Gestapo had given him for his family and that otherwise he wouldn't have acted like this. He protested that the Russian officers had no right to beat him, that they had to go through the Polish courts and that he wanted his gentile, Christian lawyer. They kept repeating they were giving him the same justice he had given old man Menashi and many, many others. They reminded him of the deaths he was directly responsible for, one by one.

Not too far from Krupa's house lived the woman named Polka who had had a Jewish lover. In fact, this lover was one of the Schiff brothers whom Krupa had betrayed. The Nazis had shot the lover right there in the house and made the woman bury him there. Krupa cringed when the Russians went into details. He became white and shaky and crouched low to the floor. Telling the story made the officers madder than they already were and one of the officers crippled the wretched Krupa with a blow on the head with his revolver.

So that was the end of a Polish traitor. His fate didn't bring to life those he had killed, but there seemed some justice in it. One thing the war did was fill me with many conflicting emotions. Sometimes pity and compassion would emerge, sometimes shame and extreme sorrow, other times raw hatred.

In the town of Gorlice I was known as a "tough guy." I went around with a group of older boys who had survived the concentration camps and who had numbers tattooed on their arms. If a peasant was treating a Jew badly we turned the tables. In December I managed to get an apartment of my own. There were a lot of empty houses, but most of them were too run-down to live in. This apartment was given to me by the newly constituted Jewish Committee headed by Peller. It had lice and rats and no running water, but it was habitable and the door even had a lock that worked. I was fifteen years old. Some of the boys I hung around with were in their early twenties and whenever they wanted to make love to some girl they would come to me and get the key to the apartment. "I'll be back in an hour or so," they would say, with a wink, and I felt as a part of their adventures. These friends of mine included friendly Poles as well as Jews, and the girls they managed to pick up were peasants who came to town on market day with their fathers. In all of Gorlice there were only a couple of Jewish girls left alive after the war. One of these girls stayed locked in her room all day long and never saw anyone. She had had a total mental breakdown.

I was proud to be such an important person associating with men and grownup boys. There were times when I looked forward to the future and thought that perhaps the world would open up to me. One day I myself found an attractive peasant girl with very strong features. In order to get her to the apartment I had to bribe her with nylon stockings stolen from the black market. The apartment was broken down and roach infested, without running water or toilet—but then the living conditions of the peasants weren't much better. The girl was interested in the stockings; I gave her the stockings, but since I lacked experience, I didn't get anywhere with her.

Several of my relatives were buried in different parts of the country. Some of the local peasants, who were by and large now willing to prove their friendliness to the Jews, encouraged my distant cousin, Oliner, to exhume the bodies for reburial in a Jewish cemetery. Peller also encouraged us to do this. In fact Peller was able to build in Garbacz a permanent memorial to the massacred people. The monument has the following inscription:

W TYM GROBIE MASOWYM
SPOCZYWAJĄ SZCZĄTKI OKOŁO
1000 ŻYDÓW Z GORLIC I BOBOWEJ
OFIAR RZEZI HITLEROWSKIEJ
ZAMORDOWANYCH BESTIALSKO W
DNIU 14 ŚIERPNIA 1942 ROKU
WYSTAWIENIE TEGO GROBU I
OPIEKA NAD TYM UŚWIĘCONYM
MIEJSCEM MARTYLOGII ŻYDOWSKIEJ
JEST GŁÓWNĄ ZASŁUGĄ
OB. OB. NACHUMA ORMIANERA I
JAKUBA PELLERA PRZEWODNICZĄCEGO
POWIATOWEGO KOMITETU
ŻYDOWSKIGO W GORLICACH

IN THIS MASS GRAVE
REST NEARLY 1000 JEWS
FROM GORLICE AND BOBOWA:
VICTIMS OF HITLERIAN BESTIAL SLAUGHTER
ON AUGUST 14, 1942.
THE ERECTION OF THIS MONUMENT
ON THIS HOLY GROUND
WAS DONE BY NACHUM ORMIANER
AND JAKUB PELLER, THE CHAIRMAN OF THE
COUNTY JEWISH COMMITTEE OF GORLICE.

Lacking sufficient money to acquire caskets, we made burial boxes of wood. A couple of peasants helped us locate bodies and exhume them. The bodies were by this time rotted and the stench was awful. Nevertheless, we took them by horse and cart to the cemetery. One time, I was arrested along the way by the local police for not having permission to transfer human bodies, but I was released soon after. In the end we did succeed in the burial operation.

During this time Peller was also busy. He had traveled, along with others, throughout the countryside gathering money in any conceivable manner. When he had accumulated a sufficient sum, he purchased gravestones and placed them at the other mass graves in memory of the thousands of people buried there. Peller wore a pinstriped suit, riding boots and felt hat and I envied him for his strength and courage and leadership skills. Since the end of the war I had been busy reorganizing the ruin and chaos of my life, all the while trying to avoid confrontation with the village of Garbacz, over which hung the particularly dark cloud of personal disaster. Surviving the war had required a certain spiritual balance which was now, I felt, extremely fragile; I didn't think I could withstand a return to Garbacz. I was afraid—actually terrified—that my cool demeanor would crack under the relentless stare of the spectre of brutal fate.

Sooner or later, of course, I had to visit Garbacz. There was the final resting place of part of my family, at least; and I went there with the naive hope of exhuming the bodies and giving them a decent burial. Imagine the desolate loneliness I experienced while standing in a little wood looking at a small meadow, knowing what lay underneath the grass! I cried out loud, I yelled to heaven. No one heard my yells except the tall trees. I looked up towards the heavens and thought perhaps my family was there. After all, I had been told that there is life after death. There was a breeze that day that blew through my hair. The hopelessness of the task of ever retrieving the bodies overwhelmed me. My family had been taken from me. They were indistinguishable from the mass of a people diabolically slaughtered, and all I could be certain of was that I was a Jew. And yet, I thought, if I was a Jew, why wasn't I buried there with the rest of my people? There was no answer to that question. Life was, in a sense, no more logical than death. There were no ready-made answers; I had to live in order to discover why I had survived. Before I left, I started saying the *Kadish* (the prayer for the dead)…the few words that I remembered. I now felt suddenly good. The dead were at rest and my family forgave me for not dying with them. Peller constructed the beautiful stone: inscribed on it was a statement of the slaughter and the date. I walked back to Gorlice feeling at peace with myself.

Gradually, an unrest grew inside me. I became surly and quarreled with my friends. I got frustrated with my apartment and moved in with the surviving cousins. My cousin and her husband were only too happy to have me. At first I enjoyed their company. It felt good to be in a family situation once again, where a man and a woman live together and make a home. But once again the unrest caught up with me.

I became frustrated with Gorlice, and when I thought of Poland in general a sense of desperation gripped my mind. For me Poland was nothing but a graveyard. Some of my friends seemed to feel the same way and we envisaged the possibility of leaving Poland. "Go west," we counseled each other. "Where there is opportunity, where there is an end to desolation and chaos." Of course, leaving Poland was easier said than done and many of my friends would never make the move.

Perhaps I would not have made the move either, had Peller not been in the habit of visiting the people I lived with. I learned that three of them were planning to leave Poland. They were going to journey west by looping through Germany and, in spite of the fact that I felt sorry for those I was leaving behind, I decided to go with them. In fact, the idea of leaving gave me a great deal of satisfaction: the Germans had marched their armies through the Dukla Gap, and now I, a Jew, was going to walk on German soil.

The German mark was a useless currency in Poland: mere paper and readily available. In Germany, however, General Eisenhower (the Commander-in-Chief in Europe) had reinstated the value of the mark as legal tender. My three friends and I set about collecting marks and stuffing them into the false bottom of a suitcase. When we had gathered a few thousand of these marks we went to the Czechoslovakian border.

As it turned out, Germany was already full of displaced persons and the guard at the Czechoslovakian border turned us back. The money was still safe, hidden in the false bottom of the suitcase, and we escaped by night into Czechoslovakia. Through this country we hitchhiked getting many rides from American GI's and in this way we reached Germany.

My friends left me in a displaced persons' camp in Germany called Fernwald, near Munich. When they were gone, I knew they would not return and my future seemed bleak and hopeless. Forsaken and forlorn, I greeted each day as if it were an unfaithful friend. Only the feeling of unrest which had first come over me in Gorlice spurred me on.

In the displaced persons' camp the supply of food was very limited. As in the ghetto, personal status was based on the amount of luxuries a person had and theft was common. I bummed around a lot and had some dealings in the black market. Many people were lost, wandering from camp to camp. Very often I would take an American Army truck driven by black G.I's to the surrounding camps and search for possible relatives. I never did find any relatives and the return to camp was often depressing.

The displaced persons' camp needed some coal and I was asked to help in getting it. With a couple of men I went to the railroad station and we unloaded coal from a boxcar onto a truck. The truck was easily recognizable as a displaced persons' camp truck, and as we were driving towards Munich to make the delivery, a German boy along the road started yelling, "Hey *Jude, Jude.*" He was about my age and I certainly understood what he meant, Jew, Jew, dirty Jew! My anger was so great I grabbed a piece of coal. I threw it at him and my aim by chance was so good that I hit him in the eye. And I felt good about it. Deep down inside me was a sadistic pleasure that I had managed to hurt a German.

The British government, with the help of the Jewish Refugee Committee of England, decided to accept several hundred refugee orphans from camps throughout Germany. Since I had been unable to locate any surviving relatives, I signed up to go to England. After several weeks of waiting I decided one day to leave the camp and visit a friend of mine who was in another camp called Feldafing, about sixty-four kilometers from Munich. That very day the British Air Force planes arrived to pick up the boys who had signed up for England. Fortunately for me the fog was bad and the planes couldn't take off. Someone telephoned the camp I was visiting and they rushed me to the airport just in time to catch the flight.

In England we were greeted with great warmth and kindness by the British Jews and the government officials. We made the British newsreels. Only in England did life begin for me. In an old mansion, which served as a temporary youth hostel, I was one of hundreds of children given decent food, kindness, and the opportunity to rebuild their spirits. Education was made available to us and at the age of fifteen I took the first small step toward literacy. From about the time I was nine, when the Germans first entered Dukla, until I was fifteen, when they were driven out of Biesnik and defeated, I had lived in a state of darkness, of uncertainty, of primitivity, in a state which was a complete void; I knew only misery, killings, and bad experiences. Reaching England in 1945 was like reaching paradise for me.

EPILOGUE

When I mentioned to colleagues and friends that *Narrow Escapes* was to be published by Paragon House, I asked them what new observations and events would be worthwhile to include in this expanded epilogue. Their advice, my own introspection about the 55 years since the Holocaust, and reflection on what I have accomplished since my arrival in the United States in 1950 led me to focus on two different paths. One path is academic, the other personal. I realize, of course, that it may be very difficult to separate the academic from the personal journey.

For the last 29 years, I have taught courses on the Holocaust, anti-Semitism, race and ethnic relations, genocide, and altruism. I also initiated a general education course at Humboldt State University, "The Sociology of Altruism and Compassion." Students flock to it, not because I am a particularly outstanding teacher, but because there is a great need to hear the "good news" that human beings are capable of kindness, compassion, caring, and social responsibility for diverse others.

In the 1970s, when I first introduced a course on the Holocaust because the Holocaust deniers and detractors were having a field day, it was well received, but it left the students in a state of depression. After all, how do you deal with a course on the Holocaust? You deal with facts, figures, names, concentration camps, gas chambers, and mass execution squads (*Einsatzgruppen*), and you question why it happened, who permitted this sort of bestiality to take place, and where were our Christian neighbors. Eleven million victims were destroyed in concentration camps and extermination camps; a total of 50 million persons, many of them civilians in the former Soviet Union, died as a result of World War II.

A pivotal point in my life that steered me toward studying and speaking about altruism and compassion was a meeting with a young student with a German accent, married to an American, who was a student in my class on the Holocaust. At the beginning of one of those classes, she came to me in tears, saying that she must drop the course, not because I wasn't a good instructor, but rather because she could not stand the guilt about what her people had perpetrated against "my people." I was literally moved to tears by her statement, and I spoke to her, assuring her it was not her fault, there had been a cancer in the midst of the German people called Nazism. (We became friends, and upon graduation she went on to study at the University of Wisconsin's Psychology Department, doing her Ph.D. dissertation on the topic of aggression.) This incident made me think about what happened in World War II besides murder, violence, starvation, gas chambers, and bestiality. It prompted me to undertake a research project on Gentile rescuers of Jews during the war, including my own rescuer, Balwina Piecuch.

Since 1971, when I took the position of Assistant Professor of Sociology at Humboldt State University, I have been known as a "workaholic" by students, faculty, friends, and especially by my wife of 45 years, Pearl. "Workaholic" means that I constantly work at writing or reading in the area of good and evil. In collaboration with Pearl and others, I have written several books on altruism, compassion, and infusing caring into American society. My published articles and books dealing with these topics reflect my life's work, my philosophy, and my abiding belief that the world can be improved.

Gaining complete insight into one's self is, of course, impossible. But, what helps a little are other's observations about one's self. Morton Hunt, the well known social scientist, popular writer, and author of, *The Compassionate Beast: What Science is Discovering about the Humane Side of Humankind* (William Morrow & Company, 1990), spent time with me, interviewed some of my colleagues and reported the following comments:

> "Sam was an incredibly driven person," Paul Crosbie [Professor of Sociology] told me, "And he expected everyone else to be as dedicated and driven as he. That made him tough to work with, but you couldn't get mad at him—his intentions and motives were so obviously good." Jack Shaffer, a professor of psychology and close friend of Oliner's said, "I've often wondered why Sam drove himself the way he did. My guess: many of the Holocaust survivors have a sense of mission because they ask themselves why they're survivors while so many others died. Part of Sam's answer, I think, is to *contribute* something valuable."
>
> Oliner's intimates say that his research healed him. Rabbi Harold Schulweiss of Temple Beth Shalom in Encino, California put it this way: "His work on rescuers was for him the therapy of knowledge. He found the spark of decency in human beings. It was a morally educative experience."
>
> Douglas Huneke, a Presbyterian minister who knows Oliner and has himself interviewed rescuers...says, "Sam had a sense of absolute urgency, of the great importance of the work. It was a compelling passion with him, and a great fulfillment for him."

The well-known psychologist, Gordon W. Allport, in *The Nature of Prejudice* speaks about traits developed due to victimization. He maintains that there are several ways that victims respond including aggression, self-hate, and prejudicc against the out-group. Another response is sympathy. He says, "the mechanism of defense is entirely absent in the case of many victims of prejudice. Just the reverse happens." He quotes a Jewish student, who said, "I sympathize easily with [a Black] who is even more likely to have people against him than the Jew. I know what it is like to be discriminated against. How could I be prejudiced?"

I have been asked many times whether I hate Germans. My answer has consistently been that hate is not part of my being because hate is self-destructive, and it does not help heal the pain. Rather, understanding and compassion do. German colleagues at one conference that I attended in Berlin told me, when they had a glass of wine in them, that they feel very guilty, and that Germany in a thousand years will never erase its guilt. Moved, I told them, "Listen, this is not the way it is going to be. Many people have committed genocide, and healing and forgiveness are possible."

Recently the Australian Parliament apologized to the Aborigines for the abuse, oppression, and murder committed against them.

The German government, headed by various leaders, has also apologized to the Jewish people. Some Christian churches in Alaska have apologized to the native peoples there for the abuses and harm done to them. On September 19, 1999, *The New York Times* published a letter written by Archbishop of New York, John Cardinal O'Connor, to the Jewish community on its High Holy Days. In essence, he has apologized for the Holy Father as well as the Catholic Church and himself. He said, "I pray that as you begin a new decade, and as we begin another millennium in our Jewish/Christian relationship, we will refresh our encounter with a new respect and even love for one another as children of G-d. Working in our own ways, but also working together, let us both remain committed to the fulfillment of G-d's reign. I ask this Yom Kippur that you understand my own abject sorrow for any members of the Catholic church, high or low, including myself, who may have harmed you or your forebears in any way."

In various invited talks around the country in the last 18 to 20 years, I have frequently focused on rescuers and the importance of including them in our history books in addition to Hitler, Himmler, Eichmann and other mass murderers. Invariably, there will be someone in the audience who is a Holocaust survivor, and who confronts me during the discussion period by saying, "Why should you be writing and praising Gentile rescuers who risked their lives for Jews when there were so few, when most people were bystanders or even collaborators?" I admit that, yes, there were bystanders and collaborators, but what of those souls who showed compassion and did not lose their moral direction, who took the compassionate high road, and rescued lives? As I continue in the enterprise of trying to understand not just the nature of evil but the nature of goodness, I find that for me it is self-healing.

The literature indicates that some Holocaust survivors have a tremendously hard time dealing with remorse and survival guilt. Some know that something is not all right for them, and ask the painful question, "Why did I survive and not my loved ones?" There is a gnawing that doesn't seem to leave them, and frequently it seems to inflict their children—not through what the parents say, but through the silence by which they try to "protect" their children from what they went through. On the other hand, studies such as Sarah Moskovitz' book, *Love Despite Hate,* focused on children who survived the Holocaust and did well emotionally and economically. William Helmreich, a well-known sociologist at City University of New York, in his book *Against all Odds* also shows that there are Holocaust survivors who are well adjusted and successful in their trades and professions.

* * * * * *

The first edition of *Restless Memories* ended with my arrival in 1945 in England, where the British Jewish community and the British government greeted us with unusual kindness. They had brought over from the displaced persons camps more than two thousand children who had survived the Holocaust in various ways. Most of them had experienced the extermination camps, and many had seen their parents murdered or sent off to the gas chambers. The emotional state of these orphans varied greatly: some were relatively "normal," while others were neurotic, and some even psychotic. Great credit is due the British Jewish community, especially to those leaders, guides, teachers, and therapists who had the kindness and patience to rehabilitate two thousand "savages" who had survived the Hitler period. Along with several others, I was fortunate to have been sent from one of the youth shelters where we were first housed, to a small, private school called Bunce Court, located in southern England, near Canterbury. This school had been founded by three Jewish sisters who were refugees from Germany. They had escaped Nazi persecution in the late 30's and opened a school both for British-born children and for children from other countries. The principal and founder, Anna Essinger, was a farsighted and truly altruistic human being. She was able to surround herself with staff who understood the traumatized children they were called to educate. Given our condition, it took a great deal of love, perseverance, and determination to help us. They taught us not only reading and writing, but also how to cooperate, how to be kind and concerned for others. I stayed in Bunce Court from 1946 to 1948, and felt very comfortable there. Indeed, these were some of the most memorable and happy years of my entire life.

When I finished the British equivalent of high school at Bunce Court, I moved to London on my own and found a job as a bookkeeper's apprentice. As that did not pan out very well, I found another job as a cabinet-maker's apprentice. I lived in London with Georg and Cidy Hartman who accepted me as a member of their family; they, too, were understanding and willing to put up with my moodiness though I paid them very little money for rent. Those were days of restlessness and loneliness for me. Hoping that I had some family living in the United States, I advertised to see if there were any relatives who would be interested in sponsoring my immigration to America. Saul Oliner, a very distant cousin of my father, responded. This wonderful man sent me a little money and an affidavit of support necessary for obtaining the immigration papers.

On December 14, 1950, I arrived in the United States, having paid my own fare on the *Liberte*—formerly the *Europa*—a famous ship which had once belonged to the Nazis, and was then captured by the French and renamed *Liberte.* My first reaction to the United States was disbelief. It was a place where everyone was in a hurry, where cars went fast and the streets were filled with traffic, noises, and temperamental people. Upon my arrival I was greeted by relatives of Saul Oliner and by my father's cousin Oscar Oliner and his wife Hena, who had both been rescued in Poland by a loving Polish couple. Saul was the largest, perhaps the only, East Coast importer of women's hairnets, and, the day after I arrived, he gave me a job in the business. The nets were hand-made from the hair of Chinese women who sold their hair to a Chinese buyer. My job was to dye and package the hairnets and fill the mail orders that arrived from all over the country. While doing this, I stayed with Oscar in Brooklyn, and I tried to study business and accounting at the City University of New York.

Before my first year in the States was over, I was drafted and sent to Fort Dix, New Jersey. There, after several weeks of basic training, I decided to try to become a translator. I hoped that with my linguistic ability the army would send me to Europe instead of to Korea where a war was being fought. I took some tests and, luckily, passed two (German and Polish) out of three. Several officers assured me that I would undoubtedly be shipped to the European command.

However, as bad luck would have it, I was sent to Korea, where I landed in an infantry unit. We were in the process of being sent to the front lines when a call came from a beleaguered unit of American GI's guarding a large group of captured Communist prisoners on the island of Kojo Do, located off the Korean Coast, near Pusan. We were immediately diverted to that island, where we had to walk perimeter guard and try to contain the rebelling prisoners. Soon after, the U.N. command decided there were too many prisoners on one island, and more prison camps were built on other islands to which I was sent. The first, which had an area of about four square miles, was called Pong Yung Do. At first it was not a very interesting job, but later it became dangerously busy. The prisoners started to break out and even attempted to take over the island, so we had to do intense guarding. One day a horrible massacre of prisoners took place.

Seven or eight months later I asked for a transfer and was sent to the mainland, Pusan, where I again had to guard prisoners. During this time I kept a diary about my war experiences in both Poland and Korea. Those were hopeful days because negotiations were held in Panmunjom where the United Nations and the North Koreans were trying to reach a ceasefire agreement and an armistice. When this was finally achieved months later, it was time for me to return to the United States. I had feelings of great anticipation but also of sadness and uncertainty. While thousands of GI's were joyfully being met by their families when they returned, I arrived and felt lonely again. There was nobody especially happy to see me. I returned to Brooklyn, where I again stayed briefly with my father's cousin, Oscar, and later rented a room at an aged widow's apartment.

It was time for me to try to do something with my life. I decided to make use of the GI Bill and enroll at Brooklyn College. I had no idea what college really meant, and was not prepared for college work; it was a shock. During the first semester, I could not keep up with the work. Also, women were on my mind, and I dated a lot. Finally, Fred Knauer, who had been a GI buddy since the days of basic training, arranged a blind date with a friend of his wife, Judy. That's how I met Pearl, who was finishing her B.A. at Brooklyn College while I was only beginning my college career. Before long, we married and I continued with school while working for Fred Knauer's father-in-law, performing a variety of duties in his small slipcover factory in Manhattan. Working full time and going to school was, of course, not an ideal situation, but with Pearl's patience and help, we survived those tense and difficult years.

I longed to finish my B.A. so that we could move to California. This was a promise I had made to myself while passing through that state on my way to Korea; if I ever returned from the war, that's where I would settle and as soon as I could. There was something about the climate and the general ambiance that drew me to this part of the world.

My dream came true. I did survive Korea unscathed, and I finished my B.A. in 1957. Pearl and I packed our U-Haul truck, hitched it to a small, black 1954 Chevy, and—after a sad and teary goodbye to Pearl's parents, brother and sister-in-law—we drove off to California. Not long after that, I began my graduate career at San Francisco State University where I obtained an M.A. in sociology and my junior college teaching credential. Meanwhile, Pearl taught in a private school in Oakland. Later she obtained her Ph.D in education. Between 1957 and 1971, I took excursions into the business world to supplement our income. First, I co-founded a manufacturing firm called Western Curtains, which I later sold to my partner—my army buddy, Fred Knauer. Then with a dear friend, Tom Simonetti, I purchased Kaufman's Draperies in Berkeley. My intention was to enroll in the doctoral program in sociology at the University of California at Berkeley. This was all somewhat crazy, because it was too much to work for an M.A. and then a Ph.D. and also run a business. Somehow, I always felt that I could handle near-impossible loads. With Tom's patience and Pearl's indulgence, we survived my dissertation while we also expanded Kaufman's Draperies, opening stores in the nearby Bay Area cities of Walnut Creek and Hayward. In 1971, as I was getting close to the completion of my Ph.D. work, I sold my share in Kaufman's Draperies to Tom and his new partners. That same year I obtained a teaching position in the Department of Sociology at Humboldt State University, where I have been ever since. The last twenty-eight years at Humboldt have been very pleasant. My sons—Aron, born in 1961, David, born in 1963, and Ian, born in 1965—have grown into manhood here in Arcata. My experiences with students, colleagues, administrators, and support staff have all been personally extremely rewarding.

In 1976, when I first introduced into the curriculum the course on the Holocaust, I felt it was necessary to explore this enormous tragedy of Western history beyond the scope provided by classroom literature. I had asked myself the question: Was there anything positive or hopeful that happened during World War II? I started thinking back to my own days during the war and how some people were very helpful in my survival. Thanks to Dr. John Slawson of the American Jewish Committee who awarded me grants to begin a study, I became involved in the Altruistic Personality Project. The plan involved interviewing bona fide rescuers to discover their motivation, i.e., why did they risk their lives on behalf of strangers or even "outsiders" during the Nazi occupation? The objective of the study was to interview about 500 rescuers and a comparison group of non-rescuers in order to evaluate possible differences between the two groups.

* * * * * * * * *

I returned to Poland for the first time on March 6, 1982, to establish collaboration on this study with Professor Janusz Reykowski, which involved interviewing rescuers of Jews in Nazi-occupied Europe. I landed at the Warsaw airport and was met by my colleague's daughter, Magda. After a wonderful reception at the Reykowski's apartment, I checked into the hotel Europejski in the center of the city. Subsequently, I found out that this was the hotel to which the Nazis invited Jews from Warsaw to report with their families, suitcases, and money for shipment to foreign countries. These innocent Jews did not know it was a trap, and all of them were shipped to death camps. The Reykowski's did not want me to spend $54 a night for a hotel room, so they suggested I move to a free, small apartment, to which they had access, in the heart of the former Jewish ghetto

There is nothing Jewish left of the ghetto, with three exceptions: the monument to the fighters of the Warsaw Ghetto uprising; a street named after Mordecai Anielewicz, the heroic leader of the Warsaw ghetto uprising of 1943; and—most moving and surprising—the nearby Jewish cemetery. I was amazed to see that it was well kept, and that there was no vandalism on this large, ancient cemetery so close to the heart of Warsaw. I expected that like everywhere else in Nazi-occupied Europe, the Jewish cemeteries would have been desecrated or destroyed and the tombstones used to pave roads and fill potholes on country roads and city streets. I approached a caretaker at the cemetery and asked what the situation was, why things were so clean and well cared for. He told me that a group of American rabbis had recently visited Poland and appealed to the Polish government to care for the cemeteries and other sacred Jewish places, and the Polish government had agreed. I noticed workmen picking up branches and leaves that had fallen on the grass and tombs. What amazed me was to see the beautiful monuments, the tombstones with old inscriptions of very famous names, such as Peretz, a novelist, and the tombs of Ida Kaminska's family, who were Jewish actors. Sometimes during the summer months, the caretaker also told me, young men and women from West Germany come as volunteers to clean the cemeteries. This is their attempt to make up for the devastation that their nation wrought on the Jewish people and the Poles.

Wandering around Warsaw, at the city's center, I came upon the well-kept Nozyik synagogue. Next to it was a Yiddish theatre. On the marquee was the title of a play in Yiddish, *The Rabbi and the Buffoon.* I immediately rushed in and bought a ticket (for 45 cents) for the evening performance. At seven o'clock that evening I returned and was surprised to find, in the lobby, quite a crowd of young and old very well dressed Warsawites. At first, I said to myself, "This play is in Yiddish. How could all these people be Jewish? Have I been misinformed all these years, and are there that many Jews still in Warsaw?" I was too nervous, too excited, to approach anyone and ask. My curiosity was soon satisfied; when the doors to the theatre opened, there stood two women giving out orange earphones to be plugged into the seat arms. Since the play was in Yiddish, there was simultaneous translation into Polish.

I felt somewhat out of place—I was the only person I could see who did not use earphones. It was a spicy play with singing and dancing in Yiddish and some ladies in low-cut costumes. With the exception of one actor, who was also the director and who understood Yiddish, the others were non-Jewish actors whose Yiddish did not sound authentic. The play was about a rabbi who was depressed because of the state of the world, a world filled with war and hatred. To cheer him up, the Hassidim around him dressed up in traditional garb with *paiot* (long sideburns) and *kapotas* (long coats) and tried everything they could think of. They danced and sang some beautiful songs, but to no avail. Finally one of the Hassidim hit upon the idea of taking the rabbi to a circus which had recently arrived in town, and that would surely cheer him up. The rabbi came to the circus and saw the buffoon (clown) who entertained him and made him laugh. Though today's Hassidim would most likely be offended by the scantily clad dancers and singers, I felt that it was a sincere attempt to portray Jewish wisdom and humor.

After my stay in Warsaw I decided to go to my hometown and visit my rescuers, as well as go to other places that I knew so well as a boy. I discovered that Staszek, Balwina's son, had no telephone, so I sent him a cable asking him to call me in Warsaw, which he promptly did. He was very excited and offered to hire a taxi instantly and come for me all the way from his little town in the Carpathian Mountains. I was touched by this very loving but impractical idea, and told him that I would take an express train to

Krakow and a taxi to his home in Gorlice. I got on the express train and found that, contrary to stereotypes and negative images of Poland, the train system was efficient and ran smoothly, maybe better than in the United States.

In anticipation of meeting Staszek and his family, I was rather nervous when I arrived in Krakow. Sad thoughts surfaced because I had not seen him since 1945. In one of his letters Staszek had told me that his mother Balwina had died. The medication I had sent to her several times in the previous months did not save her. The letter went on to say that he had bought a piece of land and built a brick house only a thousand yards away from Garbacz, where a thousand people had been executed, including many members of my family.

I hailed a taxi and found out that the 150-kilometer ride would cost only 5,000 zlotys, about $10. The driver was very talkative, and he soon gathered that I must be a foreigner because of my accented Polish. He asked all kinds of questions about where I was going, why I was going there, how things were in the States, and he talked very freely and critically about the Polish Communist government. The weather was nippy, and though much of the snow had melted, some remained on the roads, especially as we drove into the mountainous Gorlice region. When we arrived in Gorlice, that place I had left 37 years ago, I couldn't recognize it. The town was bigger than when I left. The marketplace (Rynek or town square) had changed; there were new retaining walls and benches and some trees. The town had been more than 50 percent Jewish before the war, but now I could not see a sign of anything Jewish. It had changed so much I could barely direct the taxi driver to the road that led to Garbacz, and Staszek's house. When we finally reached the area, the driver stopped to ask where Staszek Pyrek lived. The woman pointed to a two-story brick house up a small hill, about 900 yards away from Garbacz and about 30 yards off the road.

The snow was melting and the driveway was muddy. Someone at the window noticed me. At the door, a woman greeted me. I tried to wipe my feet, and, as I did, two other women and five children appeared. I didn't recognize any of them. I was extremely excited and asked where Staszek was. They told me that he was still at work, but he would be home within 15 minutes. The women and children stared at me in my Humphrey Bogart coat and my French beret and I could see that they were shocked to see someone wearing a raincoat in the middle of freezing winter. Not knowing what to do with this stranger from America, they took me to the dining room, put my suitcase right down next to the table and, within a minute were offering me hot chicken soup. Of course, they didn't know that the taxi driver and I had stopped in downtown Gorlice for coffee and a sandwich. Though I wasn't hungry, I ate out of fear of offending them. There I sat, having barely taken off my raincoat and cap, eating soup, uneasily anticipating Staszek's arrival.

And then he arrived! As he walked in, I saw how he had changed; he had gone gray and quite bald, but I could recognize his face. We hugged and tears came to my eyes. I was embarrassed to cry in front of three women, and yet I could not help myself. Staszek was also visibly tearful. After he introduced me to his wife, daughter, and daughter-in-law, he immediately suggested that we go upstairs where we would have some privacy and could talk. The house had only three bedrooms and a living room, in which three families lived: Staszek and his wife, his son and his wife, and his daughter and her husband and their small children. The families gave up an upstairs bedroom to me and insisted that I stay with them. I protested that I'd go to a local hotel, but since they were clearly hurt at the mere suggestion, I stayed.

From the second-floor balcony, I could look down the hill into the little Garbacz forest. I spent a few hours contemplating, and sadness came over me from thinking about the mass grave in the peaceful little forest. I was very anxious to go down and visit that grave. Right after dinner and some talk, I decided to go to there. Staszek offered to accompany me. We put our coats on; he had a warm Russian type, while I was still dressed like a Hollywood detective. We walked slowly, in silence. My heart started beating fast and I felt anxious. The thoughts of what had taken place here 40 years ago were almost unbearable for me. I examined the place carefully, retracing the exact steps of the mass murder on August 14, 1942: how they dragged them in from the road only 100 yards away from this forest, how they made them undress...I got teary-eyed again, and Staszek felt sad too. He turned away to let me have some moments to myself.

He waited at the other end of the mass grave, which was approximately 40 by 80 feet. Right after the war Jacob Peller, the leader of the tiny Jewish community in Gorlice that survived the Nazi Holocaust, had raised some money and built a thick concrete wall around the gravesite. There was an iron gate with a Star of David above it and a tombstone (a translation of its inscription appears on page 158). I wanted to take some pictures, but my camera would not work. This was a brand new camera just purchased for me by my son, Aron, before I left for Poland. He had tried to teach me how to use it but something had gone wrong. I was upset because I did want to take some pictures to bring back with me. Staszek had a solution to our problem—just as he did when we were 13-year-old kids. We went into downtown Gorlice and rented a Russian camera from the local photographer; he only wanted a small deposit, and he would not accept any rental payment for it on learning I was Staszek's guest from America. We went back and took photographs. The second day, I returned again, this time to walk around and to think about what had happened there and to pay my respects. The grave itself had somehow sunk; the concrete was cracked and caved-in in several places including the center. As I was standing by the gate, an elderly Polish peasant came towards us, and he and Staszek started talking. He did not know who I was and I wasn't ready to explain it to him. He saw the sadness in my face and started telling me how terrible those days in August 1942 had been. On the day of extermination, he said, the screaming, howling, the attempts to escape were so horrendous that residents of the surrounding farmhouses couldn't stand the terror, the crying, the screaming, and shooting that went on for those long hours. They left their homes and went to a nearby forest. He added that the *Einsatzgruppen* didn't cover up the grave well enough after they were finished, so there was a horrible stench of death emanating from the forest for days afterwards. The peasants themselves volunteered to bring wagonloads of dirt and cover the grave better. Staszek and I walked back to the house in silence. Once inside, he and his wife, Zosia, tried to cheer me up by giving me some whiskey, which did make me feel somewhat better.

On the third day, we decided to drive to the village of Moszczenica to see Staszek's sister, Zosia, who lived on a somewhat decrepit-looking farm. She, her husband, and son greeted me warmly, but unfortunately time was short and we couldn't stay long. I noticed that she and her husband were struggling to eke out a living from the small farm and her two cows. The house was of the pre-WWII style, a kind of log cabin with no indoor plumbing. Unlike her brother, Staszek, she had not been able to improve her life much from the prewar days. We also went to see other places I knew, including my grandfather Herman's farm in Mszanka. The house had been torn down, the land confiscated and turned over to the state, and a new house had been built later by someone who must have somehow obtained the land. I was disappointed, for the past was erased, and the pleasant memories of my joyful moments diminished.

Then Staszek drove me to Bobowa. I wanted to see this place where we were penned in and hungry from June to August of 1942. The town, which was then a ghetto, was still standing but had changed completely. Some of the older shacks had been torn down. There were no synagogues standing. But, I did find the spot where our family had been crammed into a one-room house, even though the building was no longer there. I remembered the little alleys and the hungry people who walked them in the summer of 1942. I asked Staszek to remain behind and let me do the scouting on my own because I did not want him to see my emotions. Walking around, I thought about what had happened. I remembered the crowds, my stepmother's last words to me, the roundup of Jews on that dark Friday morning of August 14. Today a cold wind was blowing and I felt at that moment that I was in a strange, unfriendly world. Then a dog, pleased to see me, walked towards me wagging his tail. I patted his head and left.

I went to the old marketplace. Somehow it seemed much smaller than in August 1942 when the terrified people were being rounded up and hauled away in Nazi army trucks to be taken to Garbacz and massacred. My mood became increasingly bleak. I did not want to stay there any longer. I did not even want to go to the local restaurant for coffee. I asked Staszek to drive me back through Mszanka and to drive through my grandfather Herman's fields where, on my frequent visits, I used to graze his cows. I had an urge to see it once more—it was the place where I had seen my grandfather being beaten and kicked by Nazi agents because he refused to tell them what we had done with the cows they wanted for beef to feed their war machine.

After that we went to Biesnik, where I had lived for three years with the Padworskis at what had formerly been Herman Schiff's farm. The house was gone, and a new brick house built on the same spot. The only thing not changed was the location of the well from which I drew water for three years while serving as a stable boy. There were now also houses on the field where, with Juzek, the knife-stealer, I had spent days grazing the cows. I kept thinking of the Padworskis. Why did I not find the time to see Mrs. Padworski? Her husband had died, and now she lived alone, an old woman. Somehow, my feelings toward them have not yet been sorted out.

When I left Poland in 1945, the rural villages had log cabins, thatched roofs, dirt roads, no telephones, no indoor toilets, and no electricity. Now, 37 years later, I found modern plumbing, rural electrification, hard-surfaced roads, and new houses—most built of bricks and with modern conveniences by the owners. When I had hidden out in Staszek's home in Bystra, it had an outhouse, thatched roof and dirt floors. Now he lived in a two-story brick house with two bathrooms, indoor heating, plumbing, showers, bathtubs and even television. Yes, Poland had changed.

The following day Staszek and I talked and reminisced some more. We walked through the streets of Gorlice and tried to find traces of Jewish existence there. But there were none. What used to be the synagogue was now a factory. A small plaque on it stated, "This building was a Jewish house of prayer." Staszek and Zosia took me to the Gorlice railroad station on a freezing day in March. This parting was tearful.

On the way back to Warsaw, I decided to stop at Katowice, in Silesia, because a friend, Teresa, taught there at the University of Silesia and because it was not very far from Auschwitz. Some years before, Teresa was a visiting scholar at Humboldt State University where I met her. She had invited me not only to visit, but also to give two lectures in her classes. The students were interested, and since these were English classes, I could speak both Polish and English. To test the students' English, I started out with some weak humor in the form of the following joke: "Every man must have a wife because he can't blame everything on the government." I asked them to translate this into Polish immediately as if it were part of a quiz. At first they took it seriously, but then they saw the humor and laughed. Then I tried another one: a comparison between the capitalist and the socialist systems. "In the capitalist system, men are exploited by other men. In the socialist system, it is just the other way around." They did not think this was so funny because they had heard it before. They were very attentive and asked many questions. On the same occasion, I also met the head of the Sociology Department who expressed the hope that I would be willing to teach there for a quarter. I would be provided an apartment and sufficient money for a faculty member in Poland. However, since I was involved in the Altruistic Personality Project, I couldn't accept.

Since Auschwitz and the adjacent Birkenau camp were so close, and because for some years I had been teaching the Holocaust course, I decided to visit it, to see what it looked like firsthand. When I arrived at the famous gates I saw the sign common to every extermination and concentration camp, *Arbeit macht frei,* "Work makes you free." I could not believe the camp was real. It was a huge place; several kilometers long and wide. I counted over 100 barracks. Each would have held over 1,000 people crammed in like fleas in a nest. In some of the barracks, behind glass, there were displays of heaps and heaps of personal items: shaving brushes, clothes brushes, shoes, eyeglasses, Torahs, suitcases with names on them, children's toys, cigarette cases, tin candy boxes with markings in different languages, and artificial limbs. There were mountains of bolts of fabric made from human hair and even Zyklon-B canisters that once were filled with exterminating gas.

Teresa took me to several torture barracks, including the torture chamber and cell where Father Kolbe, along with thousands of other victims, was tortured. There was an approximately 2,000 square yard, brick-walled courtyard adjacent to the torture barracks where approximately 40,000 people were executed over the years after being either tortured or used in experiments. Here I also saw the experimentation barracks where medical experiments were conducted on men, women, and children, and where the notorious Dr. Mengele did his hideous research. I went through the toilet barracks and the various houses of horrors.

To me, all this was holy ground soaked with innocent blood. Finally, I decided to walk into the only intact gas chamber remaining in Auschwitz. Teresa could not go inside. She just waited for me outside. The gas chamber was a room about 30 by 60 feet, built partly underground and not too visible from a distance except for the tall chimney. As I walked in, a feeling of despair overwhelmed me because I could hear in my mind the voices of people screaming and choking to death. No words, no picture, no movie, no documentary can convey the feeling of it, the scratches on the walls, the phony shower heads, the holes in the ceilings which were the "showers" through which Zyklon-B was poured. Next to the gas chamber was the crematorium. Every half hour, bodies were dragged from the chambers, emptied of hair and gold teeth, then tossed into the crematorium. Nearby was the gallows where Commandant Hess of Auschwitz was hung after the war. There was a huge, vivid photograph of him in a glass case.

Before we left Auschwitz, I saw some people taking flowers to the execution wall beside the torture room and experimentation barracks. I was told that the Pope visits that wall when he comes to Poland. Before leaving Auschwitz I wanted to see, for the last time, that execution wall. Standing there, in that courtyard before the wall, I had a very eerie feeling, and I found myself turning toward the sky and asking the old/new question: where was God? Then I noticed the tall birch trees surrounding the huge and solid, two-story brick barracks. I thought of the horrors these trees had witnessed. I have read and heard that the birds never flew or nested in those trees during the days of horror. Strangely enough, even now—40 years later—I couldn't see any birds in those trees. As we walked out of Auschwitz on our way to the adjacent camp of Birkenau, I noticed once again the signs on the fence that said *Achtung!*—the German word of warning that the wires were electrified.

As bad as Auschwitz was, Birkenau was even more depressing. There we saw approximately 300 wooden barracks. People had been crammed into them like sardines, and I could not imagine how anyone could survive in the wooden bunks infested with typhoid bacilli and lice and without adequate food or clothing. The only source of heat was a brick oven, with a chimney through the roof, at the center of a barrack. It was almost never used, however, because there was seldom any wood. Can anyone imagine what it was like, the cold winds blowing in from the vast plains, the freezing winters with snow and ice, and these scantily dressed people trying to feed the oven so they could live another day, another hour? As I walked along these miles of barracks, the wind was blowing hard. I was wearing sweaters, a raincoat with a lining, and a beret, shoes, and warm socks. How did those people survive without decent nourishment or proper clothing, doing hard labor and always faced with the fear of dying that same evening or the next morning? How did they cope? In one building I saw a display of thousands of photographs of deformed people on whom the Nazis had experimented. I gazed at the forlorn, frightened looks on their emaciated faces—looks expressing the deepest trauma and disbelief. How was this possible? Now, 40 years later, the documentation was such that we understand only too well how this could happen; the world just stood by. The Allies knew about the extermination of Jews and others, much of the European world knew, many Germans knew, the American Jews knew, Pope Pius XII knew—but very few people cared enough or, more importantly, *did* enough to stop the mass murder. Thank God for a few thousand Gentile rescuers, because otherwise I don't see how we could ever put aside this distorted image of humanity. I am now convinced that those who contemplate war, the generals, the dictators, the warmongers, all should be brought to Auschwitz and Birkenau and forced to walk around and look at these pictures and the displays of objects taken from the four million victims. I would like that those people who deny the existence of the Holocaust visit these places and walk around and maybe even stay a day or two so that they might absorb the horror evident even now. I know that this is wishful thinking.

After walking through Auschwitz and Birkenau, I went to the museum at the entrance of Auschwitz and bought books and photographs related to those places. My purpose was to show them to my students, not to make them feel bad or guilty, but because I wanted them to know that Auschwitz is a special reminder of unspeakable horror for the Jewish people, not simply a place where four million people died, most of them Jews. I wanted them to understand that Auschwitz is a symbol of man's inhumanity to man, and that we should remember it, not only to honor the eleven million dead, but so that such a tragedy not be repeated, not ever.

Teresa and I returned to Katowice. The next day I returned to Warsaw to do some more work on the Altruistic Personality project with Janusz Reykowski. Once more, I walked the streets of Warsaw to gain a better impression of life there. There were lines to buy meat, wine, clothing, candy, and cosmetics. Poland did not have many consumer goods. In restaurants, waiters and waitresses were in no rush to wait on you, and by American standards things were inefficient and slow. For example, I went to buy a map in one of the many bookstores where Marxist literature was on sale. It took me a long time. First, I had to look for the map and tell a clerk I needed a map. Then, I paid the cashier who gave me a receipt, and, finally, I went back to the clerk who went back to the storeroom and got me the map! I suppose a system like this at least provides, in accord with socialist standards, enough jobs.

I finished my business with Janusz, including arrangements for the final translation of the Polish research questionnaire that we used to interview rescuers for the Altruistic Personality Study. One of the last things I did before my departure from Warsaw was to visit the Jewish Historical Institute. What I walked into was a neglected building, in need of repair and new paint, but some remodeling was going on inside for setting up additional displays. The Institute was right next to an orange skyscraper that stood on the ground where one of the oldest Warsaw synagogues used to be. The Jewish Historical Institute's function is to preserve records of Jewish civilization and culture in Poland. It is part of the Polish Academy of Science and, therefore, is a state institution. The staff was very helpful and very warm, particularly one secretary who had survived the war in Russia. She treated me with great kindness, offering me coffee in her modest little office while I waited to meet with the Director of Archives. She told me about her children who are married to gentiles. Her son, an engineer, earns about 14,000 zlotys a month, totally inadequate to feed a family of four. She told me that the museum serves several functions. It is in charge of some valuable archives, including the original Ringelblum papers. These were written by a famous historian, Emanuel Ringelblum, during the tragedy of the Warsaw Ghetto and were buried in two milk cans and an iron box. After the razing of the ghetto, and during subsequent rebuilding of that section of Warsaw after the war, workmen found these buried treasures. From them the world learned what had really happened during the uprising.

Other purposes of the institute are to help students and scholars with their research, and to serve as an arm of Yad Vashem, an organization that, among other things, documents the activities of rescuers and awards medals to those who deserve them. At the Institute, too, I had the pleasure of meeting Ringelblum's brother-in-law, now Professor Emeritus of History, who provided me with more information about the ghetto uprising and his famous brother-in-law.

One of the most fascinating stories was one the secretary told me in response to my questions about what kind of Jews live in Poland now. The impression I got from her, and from sources outside the Institute, was that there were three types of Jews still in Poland. One group was the aged, who received modest government pensions; such people had nowhere to go and were waiting to die in their ancient homeland. The second category included those who deny their Jewish origins and are intermarried; their children did not know anything about Judaism, because it was much more comfortable to blend into the contemporary Polish scene. Finally, there was one last category of Jews, if indeed they could be called "Jews." In the final tragic moments, as they were being taken to Treblinka and other German extermination places, Jewish mothers pleaded with Polish women to rescue their infant children. According to estimates, between 10,000 and 20,000 Jewish babies were rescued in this manner by kind and humanitarian Polish women. These children grew up as Catholics. They did not know who they were, and the new parents who loved and cared for them did not want them to know. Still, sometimes neighbors or others told these rescued children that, in fact, they were not the biological offspring of those parents but, rather, Jewish children who were given to Polish people to save their lives. Occasionally, on their deathbeds, parents confessed to children that they were Jewish by birth. These individuals, who were now in their 40s, were beginning to inquire about their roots. It should be noted that, under the Communist regime in Poland, there wasn't much literature about the Holocaust. Consequently, these persons could learn very little about their roots; but now they would come to the Institute from time to time to learn more of the Holocaust and try to trace their origins. According to some estimates, in 1982 the Jewish population in Poland was approximately 20,000 to 30,000, including those identified as Jewish as well as those who might be called crypto-Jews.

My impressions of this first visit to Poland since the war were bittersweet—painful memories and joyful moments. I do not yet fully understand the link between my present life and that other world I once knew. I remember Balwina burning the egg, her eyes red and swollen after I appeared on her doorstep. Her words move through me. "Only by living will you honor your family…." Then, later, through a sputter of tears, "I will miss you. Be careful. If you ever…if it's safe—but only if it's safe—try to come back some night and visit and tell me where you are…."

I want to go to her door in Bystra and say, "Balwina. Here I am. It's Shmulek."

My life now is safe in America. I am grateful for my life with Pearl, my three sons, my friends, and my work. Sometimes, the faces come back. I hear my stepmother's last words as she was taken away on the military truck. Even the ordinary scenes seem extraordinary: Mr. and Mrs. Padworski reading the newspaper. I still have a mixture of feelings towards them and the Polish peasant boy, Jusek. Was it really me?

When I left Poland, I promised to bring Staszek and Zosia to my home in California for a visit.

******

In 1984, after several months of trying to get visas and send them tickets, Staszek and Zosia arrived at the San Francisco airport. Neither spoke a word of English and they had to make numerous plane changes on the way. They appeared utterly wiped out, and what was in store for them was a six-hour auto trip to Arcata, which is near Eureka on northern California's Pacific coast.

Soon they rested up and adjusted to my home. Pearl does not speak a word of Polish, but for the eight weeks they were with us, everybody communicated beautifully, especially with regard to preparation of meals. In the kitchen each knew what the other was intending. Through loving gestures each understood what was going on. I, myself, had fun because it gave me "extra power" to be the official translator at mealtimes, during visits to see friends, and at St. Bernard's Catholic Church. Staszek and Zosia were observing Catholics so every Sunday I drove them to this nearby Eureka church, and I attended with them. Quickly, they made good friends with some of our friends and were invited to their homes for parties. Again, I played the major role as translator. Even jokes were exchanged in such manner that as I translated them, people actually could laugh. Staszek was full of jokes, some of them a bit irreverent to Polish priesthood.

We visited many places including the beautiful redwood forests here in northern California and took trips to San Francisco. They became friends with our three sons. Staszek, being a restless human being, was looking for something to do, so he built a tool shed for us from old lumber. It still stands to this day. We invited a number of Polish speaking students from Humboldt State University to our home so that Staszek and Zosia would have some company. In Poland at that time, clothing was not readily available and was poorly made, so we shopped for clothes for them to take back home. We packed several suitcases with clothing and other items including presents for the children. We provided Staszek with funds to purchase a cheap, second-hand vehicle when he returned to Poland, so when I saw him again on another trip there, he drove me around in his little Fiat.

I felt very good about their visit. Both Pearl and I thought they were wonderful guests, and I felt in some minor way I was able to repay Staszek for the risks he and his family had taken for me during those Nazi years. In our discussions, he was able to remind me of events that I had either forgotten or suppressed. I felt close to Staszek and was sorry when they had to go back to take care of their family and return to their respective jobs.

* * * * * * * * *

In 1989, as a result of the sponsorship of a conference by the Polish Academy of Science under the leadership of Janusz Reykowski, the Noetic Science Institute of Sausalito, and the Altruistic Personality and Prosocial Behavior Institute, Pearl and I had an opportunity to go to Poland once again. The conference had some publicity, and I was interviewed by a major Polish newspaper, *Polytika*. A certain Mr. Teodor Gocz in Zyndranowa, a village two miles from the Slovak border in the Carpathian region of Poland, read this interview and subsequently got in touch with me. He informed me that he knew me as a little boy and that we played together at my grandfather Isak's house in Zyndranowa. Additionally, he informed me that, of the four houses that before the war had belonged to members of my family, only one remained standing, although it was in terrible disrepair. This house had belonged to Zalman Polster, grandfather Isak's brother. These were my relatives who had been murdered in a mass grave near Barwinek, in a little forest very close to the Slovak border along with 700 other Jewish souls.

Mr. Gocz invited me to come to Zyndranowa to see the Zalman house. Then he surprised me by telling me that he would like to see this little wooden house made into a regional Jewish museum. I was very happy about the possibility of the museum because it would serve as a memorial to my murdered relatives. Another reason to put an effort into this museum was that I felt that the Jews, who had lived in Poland for a thousand years, had been physically virtually wiped out and completely deleted from Polish culture. Poles needed to learn of Jewish contributions to Polish literature, art, and science. Hence, the museum should not only be a place of commemoration of past events, of Jewish artifacts and photographs, but also a history of the Jewish past in Poland as an integral part of that society. Gocz sent me photos of the Zalman house and I recognized it. Soon I began to send funds, and the remodeling and repair began.

In 1992, Pearl and I, on our way to Moscow, went to see Mr. Gocz and the Zalman house. I remembered what it looked like before the war. It was there that I had been lovingly served cookies and milk by my relatives. It had been in total disrepair as Mr. Gocz had said. In fact, the building was falling to pieces (see photo front cover). Mr. Gocz, a kind soul and a member of a minority group in Poland known as the Ruthenians or Lemkos, said he wanted to make this into a Jewish museum because he believed that minority people of this region, the Jews and his own, must be commemorated and remembered. I determined, then and there, that more funds would be raised in order to rebuild this hut and make it into a museum. Including a new roof, windows, and foundation, in all it took several years to rebuild and was dedicated in 1994.

While Pearl and I were in Zyndranowa, Mrs. Gocz took us to the nearby forest where my grandfather Isak, his family, and my siblings Moishe and Feigele were murdered on August 13, 1942—one day earlier than the mass murder in Garbacz. When I saw the monument, something came over me. I knew I would have an emotional crisis. I asked Pearl and Mrs. Gocz to leave, to move away a few hundred yards. I walked over to the stone and read the inscriptions. Suddenly, I broke out into loud screaming, and tears flowed from my eyes.

After a while, Pearl and Mrs. Gocz returned, also teary eyed. They had heard my lament.

* * * * * * *

In 1994, I was again invited to Zyndranowa by Mr. Gocz, this time for the grand opening of the Jewish museum. I went alone because Pearl couldn't go. I left Arcata on June 8 and arrived June 9 in Amsterdam. My thoughts wandered. I asked myself, why am I going to Amsterdam since my destination is Poland for the grand opening of my family museum? Perhaps it was because I wanted to relive my pleasant experience of 1975 when I was in Amsterdam and Copenhagen. Amsterdam is beautiful, and I would call it a people's city. There are more bicycles than cars. Pedestrians and streetlights lend a feeling of safety, even late at night. This is what I remembered of my last visit to Amsterdam, and I thought that I would experience the same thing. I felt I needed some pleasant, light interlude before I again went to Poland to relive painful memories. For me, beautiful, green Poland holds memories of mass executions, and most of the country is dotted with hundreds of mass-execution graves and major extermination camps built by the Nazis.

On the way to Amsterdam, I struck up a conversation with a Mr. Koopel, a Dutch engineer. We talked about the current political and economic situation in the European Community, nationalism, and how he felt about the united Europe. While he thought that a united Europe is inevitable, he also was lamenting the possibility of losing individual cultures to a mass kind of polyglot culture. Upon arrival at the Amsterdam airport, I asked him what would be the best way for me to get to my hotel, which was an inexpensive hotel in the Center City. He offered me a ride, an extremely pleasant surprise. He had flown to England for the day to do business, and he had his car parked at the Amsterdam airport. Interestingly enough, his home was only three blocks away from my hotel.

Exhausted as I was upon checking into the Acca Hotel, I decided to take a walk, and indeed, the excitement was still there as I sat down at a sidewalk cafe and ordered beer and pizza. Certainly, not the best diet in the world for someone who has relatively high cholesterol. I decided to get "cultured." I saw three museums in the next three days. The Rijksmuseum, the Museum of Modern Art which is called Stedelijk, and Vincent van Gogh's Museum.

I wanted to experience the Anne Frank museum, so I walked 17 blocks alongside the canals to the Anne Frank House. Though it's been greatly enlarged since I saw it in 1975, there was not enough space for the crowds of visitors to stop long enough to scan the dozens and dozens of books written about her or the many translations of her diary. I could hear the voices of young and adult tourists speaking in English, German, Italian, French, and even Polish. On display, alongside the translations of her diary, were several books and articles that deny the existence of the Holocaust and call her diaries fakes. These are hate publications that come from various hate/racist groups not only in Europe but the United States and Canada as well. As I was walking around, I noticed the famous bookcase that had acted as a false door to Anne Frank's hiding place. I thought about the Dutch betrayer, who received the equivalent of $1.80 for each person he betrayed, and I imagined the Gestapo knocking on the door, and the screaming, and the arrest of the innocent that ensued.

The next day I wanted to go to the Jewish Historical Museum where quite a bit of Chagall art is exhibited. There are also religious articles and displays telling the sad story of the Dutch Jews being shipped out to their death. Unlike the Anne Frank House, this museum was not very well attended.

Everyone in Amsterdam spoke English; not only tourists but also the hotelkeepers, restaurant owners, waitresses, taxi drivers and bus drivers. It seemed to me that Holland was already part of the English-speaking "globalized" world. Amsterdam, as I experienced it in '75 and on this trip, was very crowded with tourists. The canal rides were still as exotic as ever. I heard that there are over 2,500 houseboats on the canals in which people live. I learned a bit of the history of Amsterdam—it is named after the river Amstel. The city was once a marsh and small lakes, and during the 15th, 16th and 17th centuries the canals were built. Along the canals one can discern social class and rich neighborhoods. Houses along some canals, built 200 or 300 years ago, are very elegant, while in other parts of the city, houses are decrepit, and because they are built on pilings, a lot of them are leaning and collapsing and are propped up by logs. Some of them have been boarded up and condemned. At night, by the canals in some sections of the city, one can also see rats strolling along the waterfront and frequently not hurrying too fast to get away from pedestrians.

Occasionally, one sees sad scenes among the young—tourists who are on drugs. There were some people totally sprawled out on the sidewalk, deaf to the world. I guess from drugs or alcohol. One particular young man had written on his forehead, "I'm a loser"; he was barely walking. I looked at this young man and wondered if his mother knew what he looked like. Would she be glad to see him? And what went wrong that he became so self-destructive?

I also went to a very beautiful museum located outside of Arnheim in a wooded area. It was the Kroller Mueller Museum, and had paintings and sculptures not only inside the museum itself but also outside in the beautiful gardens and lawns. There, a disappointing incident occurred. It was a Sunday and I had taken a bus from the Arnheim railroad station to get to the museum, a distance of approximately 24 kilometers. I forgot to ask when the last bus would return to the railroad at Arnheim. It left without me, and I was stuck in the wooded park outside the museum. Fortunately, a bus filled with young French tourists took pity on me and gave me a lift to the railroad station so I could get back to Amsterdam.

It was time to leave for Denmark. In Copenhagen, the weather was dull, rainy and miserable. I decided not to spend a lot of money on a taxi to get to the Ascot Hotel, which is in the heart of Copenhagen. At the airport I consulted with somebody who told me to take a certain bus which took me directly into the heart of Copenhagen within a block of the hotel. The city was beautiful. I remembered it very pleasantly from back in 1975 and I wanted to see whether any of these feelings would be rekindled. There are miles of walking streets, lots of pedestrians and hundreds of shops and restaurants that are open all night. People walk around in peace without having to breathe exhaust fumes.

During my walk, I saw all kinds of performances on the street. A group of Peruvian Indians playing their beautiful native instruments had CD's for sale, and people were buying them. Another performance I found most unusual: a group of little children, dancing and singing, who turned out to be evangelical proselytizers. Not only did tourists and onlookers give them money, but the children gave the onlookers a little booklet of the gospels. I thought it an interesting way to try to convert people to Christianity.

I saw many museums in Copenhagen, including the famous Thorwaldsen Museum of Sculpture. I may have seen 1,000 paintings on this trip, paintings by Paul Gaugin, Monet, Van Gogh, Matisse, Picasso, and others. I really wanted to familiarize myself with these great painters. I tried to imagine how these artists must have felt as they recaptured the various themes and images in their heads. I went to the States Museum, which is one of the largest museums that I've ever seen. It consists of sculpture and a combination of modern and classical painting by the great masters. I also saw the Museum of Resistance. Denmark has a heroic history of resistance against the Nazi occupation. I had planned to take a traditional tourist bus to key points in Copenhagen. Unfortunately, it was all sold out. I asked the bus driver, "Who is your competition?" She said, "Our competition is also sold out," and she added, "They're also part of our own company." They did manage, however, to apologize profusely in their charming Danish way

I went to the Jewish section, saw the synagogue and talked to people about the community. During World War II, the Danish saved most of their Jewish citizens from the Nazis. A secretary at the synagogue assured me that there is no anti-Semitism in Denmark. In her opinion, the Danish do not distinguish between Jewish citizens and Christian citizens in their country. But, in reality anti-Semitism is beginning to show its ugly head, largely brought in from outside by hate groups, skinheads, and other European Neo-Nazi groups.

When it was time to leave for Poland I hailed a taxi; the driver turned out to be a Polish Jew. We spoke Polish to each other for the forty-five minutes it took to get to the airport. We talked about the situation of minorities and ethnic groups. I was curious to find out how he got to Denmark from Poland. He said that in the late 1960's the communist leader, Wladyslaw Gomulka, used anti-Semitism as a tactic to further entrench himself into power. The economic plight of Poland was blamed on the Jews. There is a small Jewish community in Denmark, he explained, and its size has increased since 1968 as a result of the political anti-Semitism in Poland, which resulted in thousands of Jewish survivors leaving. Some of them ended up in Denmark, some in Sweden, and others migrated to other parts of the world.

Arriving at the Warsaw airport I discovered it had been totally rebuilt since my last visit in 1992. It's much more efficient, much less bureaucratic, with shorter lines, and passport control was very efficient and quick. When they see an American passport, they don't even bother asking any questions. As in 1982, Zula and Janusz Reykowski were waiting for me. They received me very warmly and cordially, and immediately took me to Zula's mother's apartment—a tiny little place where Pearl and I had stayed before. Zula's mother had been conveniently shipped off to visit relatives in Lodz. When I pressed them why I had to stay in an apartment rather than in a small, inexpensive hotel, they said that Zula's mother had planned to go to Lodz in any case. I wondered about that. I came to the conclusion that their kindness and caring were showing. As often as they could, the Reykowski's tried to feed me, care for me, make sure I wasn't wanting for anything. They are very kind, compassionate, and true friends.

I saw that Poland had become a different land. It seems that everyone is a merchant. Anyone can buy anything and everything in Warsaw. Not only are there department stores and grocery stores, there are also thousands of small vendors who have little kiosks and benches. Sometimes they're just standing in tunnels, tram stations, and underpasses selling anything from ties to handbags. Much of the goods is foreign made. That in itself is part of the problem, the Poles import everything rather than manufacturing much. One Pole told me that he's a little afraid for the future of Poland because, "during World War II, the Western powers sold us to Stalin. Now with the fall of the Soviet Union, the West has bought us." His implication was that every "giant and middle-sized corporation" is trying to do business in Poland because they see an opportunity to exploit consumerism. Many Western companies have opened up branches in Poland: Coca Cola, McDonalds, Burger King, Pizza Hut, Taco Bell, and hundreds of others.

I walked around Warsaw a lot. I went to the Polish National Museum and the Polish Military Museum, which displays episodes of Polish military heroism and an assortment of weapons. I went to see the Nozyik synagogue again. It was the only synagogue in Warsaw at the time. It was very cautiously guarded. A little old lady peeked out through a small window by the entrance and said, "The synagogue is not open until eight o'clock." I wasn't able to go at eight that night when it was open. On the main gate of the synagogue, I noticed in big letters written the word, "MAFIA." I had also noticed other anti-Semitic graffiti on several residential buildings in Warsaw. Near the synagogue there is the state-sponsored Yiddish theatre where I saw the *Rabbi and the Buffoon* in 1982. I didn't have enough time to go to see the current play, which was a comedy by Sholen Asch. I also noticed a Jewish kosher restaurant in the vicinity. Life was just buzzing.

Crime too had become extensive in Warsaw. Six or seven years before when I was in Poland, it was very, very safe. Now car theft, vandalism and drugs are major social problems. "This is progress in the name of capitalism," said one passenger to another on a Warsaw tramcar.

I went once again to the Jewish Historical Institute and Museum where I asked permission to videotape some of the Holocaust displays. They promptly allowed me to do so but suggested that I make a small donation of money to the museum, which I agreed to. The displays were much the same as I've seen in previous years, but now I had a chance to tape more details of the horrors and humiliation which the Nazis had photographed during those dark years.

The train ride from Warsaw to Zyndranowa and Gorlice was comfortable; the Polish countryside is mostly flat, green and beautiful, filled with small farms and grazing cattle. The only other passenger in the first class compartment was a young woman in her early thirties. We spent almost three hours talking until we arrived in Krakow. Her name was Zosia Garfunkle. I asked, "Isn't that a highly unusual name, Garfunkle?" And she said, "yes, it's of Jewish origin." But she hastily added that she was Catholic. She proceeded to tell me that her father, as a six-year-old boy, had been hidden during the Nazi occupation and then converted to Catholicism. Her grandfather was taken to Auschwitz and never returned. I asked her how she felt living in Poland and what she was studying. She said she was studying Hungarian, which is a relatively unknown language internationally, especially as to its origin. The reason she was studying it was that there was demand for translators and secretaries due to commerce and trade with Hungary. She was studying in Warsaw, but resided in Krakow. I questioned her about minorities and ethnic groups, and she said that there was indeed racism and anti-Semitism in Poland. Even though most people think of her as a Catholic, she said, occasionally they make anti-Jewish jokes in front of her in order to upset her. They may actually suspect, she said, that her origin is Jewish even though she's a practicing Catholic. Zosia was troubled by such remarks and jokes. I kept thinking how sad that there may be many hundreds of people like Zosia's father who, as children, were converted so they could survive. (In 1982 the secretary at the Jewish Historical Institute had informed me that there were many such former Jews as Ms. Garfunkel.)

An article appeared recently in the *New York Times* (Roger Cohen, "For a Priest and for Poland a Tangled Identity," October 10, 1999) that provides a dramatic example of such a child who did not know that he had Jewish roots. A Polish priest named Romuald-Jakub Weksler-Waszkinel recently discovered that his biological parents were Jewish, and that a Polish Catholic couple saved him from certain death in Majdanek. From 1943, his Catholic parents, Piotr and Emilia Waszkinel, brought him up, doted on him, and were very proud of him. Once somebody had yelled at him "Jewish orphan"; upset, he had gone to talk to his mother about it and asked her what is a Jew? She said, "Good and wise people will not call you that, there is no need for you to listen to bad people."

When he was 17, he decided to become a priest. His father begged him to change his mind, but he persisted. Shortly after, Piotr died from a heart attack. In his guilt and grief, this future priest's faith wavered, but he managed to renew his conviction. He was ordained a priest in 1966, and he is now a teacher at Lublin's Catholic University. As the years went by, he came to suspect the truth that he was Jewish. In 1978, when his mother was seriously ill, he confronted her, asking who he really was. She told him the story—how his Jewish mother, trapped in a ghetto, had contacted her and begged her to take her infant son and save him. Emilia could not remember the names of his family members but knew his father had been a tailor in the nearby town of Stare Swieciany. Although he told nobody, he did write to the Pope, who responded in a very loving, kind way. He also never considered abandoning the priesthood. Many years later, he discovered that his biological father's name was Jakub Weksler. In his house he has photographs of both sets of parents, and he wears a Star of David with a cross inserted. He says, "That is my life as I see it. The cross is love. Without love, it is the Roman gallows. Jesus is not responsible for the wrongs perpetrated in his name, and I would like to resemble him, if only a little."

Father Weksler-Waszkinel, the article notes, is extremely upset about Polish anti-Semitism and the old canards still in existence. He says, "'Too many people still believe a reference to a Jewish stereotype as enemy of Poland pays politically. Too few find any place for Polish war guilt." He notes, "It is good to see all the Israeli students at Majdanek. But I wish they went around in the company of Polish kids. In Israel, wrong things are said about Poland. And here, the stupidities about Jews persist. I am in the middle and I know that what is needed is contact, understanding and love.'"

Most Jews, after learning about their roots, stay in the life they're accustomed to, where they are loved by their adopted parents and where they feel safe. Some Jews convert back to Judaism and form Jewish survivors' clubs. Since the fall of communism in 1989, the situation has changed for the better for Polish Jews. There are newer, more optimistic estimates about the Jewish population in Poland—between 30,000-80,000. There appears to be an interest in things Jewish. Jewish foundations, including the New York based Ronald S. Lauder Foundation, spend money in Poland to encourage Jewish education. So does the Joint Distribution Committee, which helps young Jewish people to find their Jewish roots and their Jewish identity. Several Jewish organizations and clubs have thus come into being during the last few years. In Warsaw the Raoul Wallenberg School for Jewish children and the Maccabi Fencing Club were established. There is also a research center for Jewish history and culture at Jagiellonian University in Krakow. Jewish foods, such as matzos and kosher vodka, Jewish cultural festivals in Krakow, bookstores, and restaurants—in which young Catholic Poles too are interested—are cropping up. Jewish tourists from Israel, Western Europe, and America are on the increase. There's an American-trained rabbi who is the head of the Lauder Foundation and is responsible for its activities. Jews in Poland, who used to hide their identity, such as Kostek Gerbert, an important journalist with Gazeta Wyborcza, a leading newspaper in Warsaw, now openly speak about their Jewishness. Now under a democratic Polish government, there is possibility for Jewish survival in Poland.

The members of the Jewish community obviously do not belong to a single ideological mooring. Some are orthodox, others are agnostic, and yet others know nothing about Judaism. There is hope that Judaism might reestablish some minimal number of Jewish institutions fostering Jewish cultural life in Poland. There is a museum being built near the monument of the heroes of the Warsaw Ghetto uprising of 1943. It is called the Museum of the History of the Polish Jews. Adam Michnik, who is Jewish and a former member of Solidarity, is currently the editor-in-chief of the most famous newspaper, *Gazeta Wyborcza.* In his paper, he takes on racists and anti-Semites in Poland.

In Krakow, that June of 1994, as the train pulled into the station, Staszek and his son-in-law, Wiesiek, were waiting for me. The weather was hot, humid and polluted as we embraced and then drove off in Wiesiek's car, a Polonez (Polish made). The Poles had not enforced any anti-pollution laws in the 1980s. The traffic was atrocious. I was glad to get out of Krakow. As we were driving along country roads to Gorlice, we talked about Staszek and Zosia's visit to our home a few years before and about whether the shed he built still stood firm.

We got hungry and stopped to get pizza, which is something new in Poland. As we continued on, we discussed economic conditions in Poland and about how prices were rising constantly. The Polonez had over 200,000 miles on it, and though they didn't tell me, I could see that they were worried it might "conk out" at any time. As we neared Staszek's home in Gorlice, he asked me if I wished to stop in the village of Mszanka where my Grandfather Herman had lived. Even though I knew nobody was alive and the house no longer stood, I wanted to see the place of my youth again. My thoughts raced back to June 1942 when the Nazis ordered my Grandfather Herman, his wife, and me to leave Mszanka and report to the Bobowa ghetto. I remembered how I felt when a neighbor, using his horse and wagon, took us to the ghetto. I hadn't seen that village for years, even though I had been to Poland a few times.

As we were turning off to Mszanka, the engine stalled. We couldn't go any further. Staszek and Wiesiek were embarrassed. We were at least half a mile from the nearest farmhouse. Fortunately, the peasant/farmer was in the nearby fields, and Wiesiek walked over to him and asked if he had a telephone. He did, so Wiesiek walked another quarter to half a mile to the man's home and made a phone call to his friend, who arrived in another 25 minutes with an old, beat-up car. I thought, "How can an old, beat-up car pull another old, beat-up car?" As they started hooking up the Polonez to his friend's car, I noticed they had a rope. I said, "Oh my God, this is going to tear. There's no way they can make it." I was proven wrong. It was a very strong rope. We drove about eight kilometers that way. So, rather than continuing to Mszanka, we turned around and went straight to Staszek's home.

When we finally arrived, all the family was waiting for us. We kissed and hugged, and I was introduced to the five grandchildren. Even though we had eaten pizza two hours earlier, before I could catch my breath, I had to sit down and eat very rich and fattening chicken soup. Staszek and Wiesiek also sat down; the women served us while they ate in the kitchen. In Staszek and Zosia's house live two other families: his son, Olek, with his wife and children; and his daughter, her husband (Wiesiek) and their three children—a total of eleven people living in one small, two-story house. But, there were now plans for their son Olek, his wife and two children to move out very soon to a newly built home. During my visit, I had many discussions with these young grandchildren, all of them beautiful and clever, who asked me questions about America and expressed a desire to visit the States. I said that some day it might be possible.

Every time I come here, I stay in the same room, with the window overlooking the mass grave. Somehow it's reassuring that the little forest has not moved or been cut down. I walked over there, took some photographs, and said the Kaddish over the dead to make myself feel good. I stayed with Staszek's family for two nights, in their crowded home where the atmosphere was so warm and pleasant. I was constantly on display, and I couldn't rest because I had so much on my mind—namely the main reason for my trip to Poland, the dedication of the regional Jewish museum in Zyndranowa.

Fortunately for me, the Reykowskis decided to come to be with me during the dedication, and also to take a few days of vacation in the nearby village of Szymbark not far from Staszek's home. There, the Polish Academy of Science has a government-owned substation, now a research station for meteorology, climate, and water supply. They rent out some rooms to vacationers, and the Reykowskis rented three for three days.

On June 24, Staszek took me to Zyndranowa, where I met with Gocz (see photo page 144). We embraced and exchanged news and pleasantries. I reaffirmed my impression of Teodor as a warm, caring, authentic person. We went over to the hut; indeed, it had been improved greatly since Pearl and I saw it in 1992. One room that had been a stable for cattle during the winter was totally converted into museum. There I saw displays of photographs and Jewish items and objects, but they were still working very hard trying to clean-up, fix things, and hang yet more objects—mostly blown-up photographs of Jewish people. I had brought with me a suitcase full of artifacts from the United States such as prayer shawls, candelabra, and other items which Gocz and his assistants promptly put on display for the next day's grand opening. The dedication was supposed to be at 2:30. I thought to myself that I might have to say something in Polish. That possibility made me rather nervous.

When I arrived for the grand opening on Saturday, June 25, 1994, I discovered that I didn't have a tie on. Fortunately, I found one in my pocket. A moment later, I was rushed to meet the Minister of Culture, who had come from Warsaw especially for this grand opening. I met the county supervisor, the city mayor, the village elders, priests, honored guests, poets, and a Jewish musical group that would later play some very sentimental and sad Jewish music. Suddenly, all this hit me. I wasn't prepared for this kind of ceremony, for so many people. After numerous greetings, welcomes, and sentimental, warm, and endearing expressions by Mr. Gocz and the Minister of Culture, the door to the museum—formally named the Zalman Jewish Museum—opened. I was given flowers. Then I was given bread and salt—which is a symbolic greeting to someone who comes back home.

Inside the museum, everything was clean, the pictures hanging, the small room crowded with people, among them the Minister of Culture, the village elders, the supervisor, the mayor, myself, Zula and Janusz Reykowski, and Staszek, Zosia, and some of their children. Janusz was standing by me—my "security blanket"—for I feared that I might slip and not remember some Polish word during the speech that I would have to give.

My tension was immense. I thought about what I would say. My hand was shaking as I held a couple pieces of paper on which I had previously prepared some notes in case I was asked to speak.

I was asked. I began in Polish:

I am honored by your presence. I want to thank you for coming from near and far away to be here today for this special occasion. Mr. Minister of Art and Culture, Mr. County Supervisor, Mr. Mayor, Mr. Elder of the Village of Zyndranowa, honored guests, and members of the parish, I am grateful that you are here. I want to express my deep appreciation that you're all here to witness this special historical event, the opening of this regional Jewish museum.

This museum does not only honor my family, people of the Jewish faith, but also other people who were murdered in this region by the Hitlerian murderers. I have a strong hope and feeling that this museum will be a memorial, not only to the citizens who lived here but also to Poles in general, to remind them how sad recent Polish history was. It must be remembered that Jews who lived here for over 800 years made a major contribution to Polish civilization and culture. I hope that the young generations will come here and learn about the recent past. As an American philosopher by the name of Santayana said, "Those who do not remember the past are doomed to repeat it in the future." I believe that, as time goes by, you wonderful citizens of Zyndranowa will be visited by a number of people, including tourists, who will learn much from you and the museum about the people who lived in these territories before the war. This museum, for me, symbolizes rescue of memory. Because without memory, there's a danger of not knowing what preceded us. I shall never forget my martyred family. And this museum will help to preserve their memory, not only their memory, but that of other Jews who have paid the price for the "crime" of being born Jews. For that reason, I wish to repeat my heartfelt thanks, not only to Mr. Gocz and his family, but to the entire remodeling committee and the parish members.

And now I have been asked to say something about my own survival during the war. As you gentlemen and ladies know, part of my family lived here, but the other part of my family lived near Gorlice. Because my father remarried after my mother died here in Zyndranowa and was buried in Dukla, I went with my father and stepmother to live in a village called Bielanka. In June 1942, we were ordered, as were other Jews, to leave our homes and everything else and report to the ghetto, Bobowa. Dozens of villages in that manner were cleaned out and sent to the ghetto. There we lived in a state of misery and hunger and fear and deprivation. Occasionally, I would sneak out from Bobowa Ghetto to buy some food for the family. In August of 1942, only two months after we arrived there, the liquidation of the Bobowa Ghetto took place. Giant Nazi army trucks arrived at the Bobowa town square. Nazi guards, some spoke Ukrainian, chased us all out from our homes, houses, and apartments to the Rynek. There, they loaded us onto trucks, and took us to a pre-dug, mass grave in a suburb of Gorlice called Strozowska, which contained a small, little forest called Garbacz. There, people were undressed and forcibly thrown and murdered into their grave. A thousand people were murdered in this one mass grave in a period of one day.

I, fortunately, did not get there, because my stepmother's last words before leaving to go to those trucks was for me to run and hide and save myself in order to tell the future generations what had happened. I did that in a state of fright, fear, and stupor. I wandered around the countryside for two or three days. Then, I thought of a friend called Balwina Piecuch in the village of Bystra, which was very close to where my grandfather lived in the village of Mszanka. I came to her. She already knew what happened. She took me in. She comforted me. She gave me hope. She changed my name and taught me the Catechism and told me that I must survive in order to tell about this. I pretended to be a Catholic boy, and found work as a cowboy/stable boy in a village called Biesnik. Balwina couldn't keep me hidden because of certain Polish traitors, known as Szmalcowniki, who made their living betraying Poles who hid Jews.

My good friend, Staszek, who is standing here by me, Bawina's son, frequently acted as my brother and tried to authenticate my story with my new employer. I worked for a couple in Biesnik, who happened to have rented a Jewish farm. The Jews were exterminated. They rented the farm from the German authorities. It was due to Balwina Piecuch, a compassionate Polish woman, and her children that I am here today. I am alive because of Staszek Pyrek, who acted in the role of my brother, who helped me convince my employer in Biesnik that I, indeed, was a Pole and a Catholic.

I want to conclude these remarks here today on this very special occasion by saying that it is somehow fitting that someone in Poland saved my life and now a wonderful, caring group of people had such a wonderful vision to save the memory and culture of the people of the Hitlerian mass murder. The museum is just the beginning. These rooms will be filled soon with important Jewish cultural objects from this region.

I once again thank you from my heart, Mr. Gocz, as I thank the members of the parish. You wonderful people have suffered much. You who are the ethnic group known as Lemko in Zyndranowa. I thank you once again for making this museum a reality. I thank you very much for caring. For me, this historical moment bodes well for this museum and the future. For those others who are present from near and far away, you honor me by being here today. And I thank you, also, from the heart.

During the talk, I had tears in my eyes and choked up. As I glanced at the audience, I saw their tears well up, too. That had a circular effect. I had to pause for a brief moment because of all the cameras and the heat and all the memories that came back to me. This was the place where I used to come as a little young boy for cookies and cake.

As soon as I finished my speech, dried my tears, and relaxed somewhat, Mr. Gocz arranged for a Jewish poet and musician to take part in the ceremony. The musician played a beautiful violin repertoire of sad Jewish songs, and the poet, a blind woman, began to recite the poem in a very sad and emotional way, as only Russians can. The beat and style resembled that of the Russian poet laureate Yevtushenko. The content dealt with the questions of "Where was God? Where were the people when the tragedy was occurring, as the world stood by, and innocent people perished?"

The musician accompanied her, and when she finished her poem, he continued to play. Next there was an Israeli Jewish poet who spoke perfect Polish. The essence of her beautifully presented poem was that Poland was once truly a home for Jews; she enumerated the names of famous Polish Jewish artists and writers who made great contributions to Polish art, culture, music, science, and philosophy.

Following that presentation, we left the very packed, hot room. I had promised the journalists present that I would see them after the ceremony—in fact, I gave them numbers, telling each in what sequence they could talk to me for a few minutes! Mr. Gocz and his assistants, meanwhile, had arranged a beautiful table covered with white tablecloths in an empty room of the Zalman House. On the table were wine and vodka, cheeses and fish, and bread. The room was small. Mr Gocz couldn't invite the entire crowd that now was standing outside the small museum, so he invited the "important guests"—the Minister of Culture, the poets and musicians, the county supervisor, the village elders and local town mayors, the priests and ministers, Janusz and Zula, and rescuer Staszek and Zosia. I sat at the head of the table and discovered I was expected to perform some sort of Jewish ceremony. It occurred to me that in a traditional Jewish home one says a prayer over bread and wine, and then one says another prayer thanking God that he made this occasion possible for all of us to meet again. I said the prayer, which I knew in Hebrew, over the bread. We lifted our glasses, toasted each other and broke bread. Much discussion followed, mainly dominated by the Minister of Culture, Jan Jagiello, who said that he had not quite known how rich and beautiful the Lemko culture is, and pointing out that Poland has many ethnic groups, including Russians, Lithuanians, Latvians, Germans, Gypsies, and even the handful of Jews who still remain. He promised that he would try to preserve ethnic diversity in Poland.

This was a festive meal, but I was too nervous to eat, and I was feeling guilty that so many people were outside in the heat with no access to food anywhere in the immediate vicinity of the museum. I later discovered, however, that many of them went to the nearby public school building where festivities to celebrate the Lemko spring festival, *Od Rusal do Jana*, were being held the same day. There at the school were concessions with all kinds of Polish kielbasa and drink, including Coke. When I too arrived at the festival, I was labeled one of the "important" people who had to go on the stage and be presented with an award from the village of Zyndranowa. I tried to say a few words in the Lemko language, a dialect of Ukranian, which the people appreciated and applauded. I sat down on a bench next to Janusz and Zula to observe the performances—singing, dancing, and local instruments, and a beautiful Gypsy troupe that danced and played violin.

The Lemko are ethnic Ukrainians who felt oppressed by Poles when the Poles thought they had nationalistic ambitions for independence after World War II. The Poles frequently had problems and violent confrontations with minorities, both before the War and right after. The real history of the conflict between the Poles and Lemkos, I have yet to learn. Nevertheless, they were driven out from their villages in 1947 and 1948 by the Polish government, and during the last 25 years have returned from the Eastern Territories to which they were expelled. Stalin gave these former Eastern German territories to Poland after World War II, and the Poles expelled the East Germans there to West Germany. Stalin also lopped off a large piece of Eastern Poland and gave it to his Soviet Union.

I gave several interviews with television networks and newspaper reporters, most of them Polish. Fortunately, Janusz was standing by, so when I was short of a word, I just could look at him and he would whisper it to me. The interviewers asked about how I survived, how this village had changed, what I remember about the past, etc. I wondered why there was so much interest in such a small museum. Why did the media converge on this small village? One conclusion I reached was that there were genuinely altruistic reasons as well as the possibility of a human-interest story. In addition, there is the newfound interest in Jews and Jewish culture by the younger Polish generation.

German television interviewed me at great length, in English. Their topics were similar to those of others—my feelings, my impressions, and the purpose of the museum. Why should there be a tiny little museum in an isolated, out-of-the-way village near the Slovak border? My answers were about the same—namely, that there was a Jewish presence and culture in this area, that future generations should be educated about their history, and that, because of the location, there might be frequent tourist visits. They, too, will benefit from education about the past and the Jewish presence in Poland.

At another moment during the Lemko festival, a woman came over and gave me a hug. She said she remembered my family, and she had found a picture of my grandfather, Isak Polster, and one of his house. She asked me to come with her and meet the person who had the picture. This came as a total shock to me because I had been looking for photographs of my family members for years without success.

I wanted these pictures very badly, so I climbed up a little hill among the crowd to find the woman who had these photographs. Immediately, I realized that in order for me to get the photographs, the holders would need some reward, a little bit of money; this was not an act of pure altruism. In a semi-embarrassed way, I pulled out some money from the inner pocket inside my pants, (where I kept it for safekeeping from potential pickpockets). I had to find the appropriate bills; I pulled out two fifty-dollar bills and gave one to each to get those photos. Looking at the pictures brought tears to my eyes. I recognized my tall grandfather, Isak, and the chestnut colored horse with a white spot on his head that he was holding onto. As a child of seven and eight, I used to ride that horse.

All day I had appointment after appointment. I gave yet another speech at the festival. Because it was easier for me to speak Polish than Ukrainian, I said a few words of appreciation in Polish. I also had a meeting with the committee for reconstruction of the museum, at which the Reykowskis were present. I gave Mr. Gocz and the Committee some suggestions about what I thought still needed to be done in the museum. They most graciously agreed. Much, of course, will depend upon my ability to raise more funds to send them. It was my belief that another $8,000 to $10,000 would get the museum fully operational with proper display cases and a supply of cultural articles such as candelabras, prayer shawls and other items, and more enlarged photographs of people who had lived in the region. Enlargements of the two photos that I received from the woman in Zyndranowa would become part of the display.

I left Zyndranowa feeling happy that, with Mr. Gocz' help, I had been able to establish this little regional museum. I felt that Great-uncle Zalman would approve. Before leaving I again promised that I would help out to make the museum more viable. Once again, there were hugs and goodbyes. I had put my eyeglasses down somewhere and couldn't find them. As we left in the Reykowskis' car, I was thinking it was lucky I had another pair in Warsaw. Suddenly, we heard a loud car horn and saw a car chasing after us. It was Mr. Gocz. He had found my glasses. I felt very satisfied that so much had been accomplished. I had even found out that my grandfather's Lemko name was Itsko, not Isak, and that's what the villagers had called him. I knew him as Isak Polster, which is what the Poles would have called him. My father, instead of being called Aaron, was affectionately called Urko by the villagers in Zyndranowa.

I now had to return to Warsaw, but first needed to go back to Staszek's home to say goodbye. Once again, I was treated with special tenderness. Several members of the family had attended the museum ceremony, and I think they felt sorry for me because they witnessed me having such a difficult time. As I was talking to the family, my thoughts wandered again to the Garbacz cemetery, the mass grave. Once more I picked up the mini-cam, and as I walked through the little forest, I turned it on and filmed the walls of this mass grave wherein lie 1,000 murdered people, many of them members of my family. The day was beautiful. Birds were singing and the sky was clear. Instead of taking part in the joy of the moment, I said Kaddish, the prayer commemorating the dead. Then I went back to Staszek's house.

I returned to Warsaw with my friends, Janusz and Zula Reykowski, their daughter, Dorota, and her friend, Olah, who had also been present at the grand opening. Zula had been the major photographer during the grand-opening ceremony, taking still photographs and recording some of the various proceedings with the mini-cam. Again, we drove past the Garbacz Cemetery. In Kelce, a major city where the Reykowski's had relatives, and where a pogrom took place after the war in which 56 innocent Jewish victims were killed by rightist Poles, we stopped for lunch. The Reykowski's relatives treated us to a royal feast in their little garden cottage not too far from their main apartment. One of them, Janusz's cousin, gave us an interesting lecture about the life, habits and culture of honeybees. From there we headed straight to Warsaw, back to my little apartment—Zula's mother's apartment.

Zyndranowa was still on my mind. I realized there was still much to do to make this museum a reality. Many things were still needed. I began thinking about how I might help Mr. Gocz obtain them, so before I left Poland, I sought out the counsel of Jan Jagelski, who is in charge of Jewish cultural monuments in Poland, and who is an important member of the Jewish Historical Institute in Warsaw. When I telephoned him, he informed me that he would be glad to see me in a few hours because, at the moment, he had to take a group of Polish teachers to the Jewish cemetery. The purpose was to educate these teachers about Jewish culture and the recent Jewish past. I decided to avail myself of an opportunity to go there again with someone so knowledgeable and asked him if it would be okay to come along and simply listen to what he had to say. He agreed, and indeed I learned much from him. For instance, the cemetery was established in 1806 and is one of Europe's largest. It contains 100,000 tombstones, which have been preserved. Ironically, during World War II there weren't any bushes or trees left standing on this sacred ground because people cut them down for fuel. Now, fifty years later, trees have sprung up between caskets, tombstones, and mass graves. The only "true forest" in all of central Warsaw can be seen in the Jewish cemetery. It's a beautiful and tragic place. I learned that the great sages (Hassidim) had special tombs, and they were buried without their wives; their wives had to be buried in a separate place while their sons lay next to the fathers. Mr. Jagelski took us to a mass grave in the middle of the cemetery where the Nazis executed hundreds of people from the Warsaw Ghetto. In the distance, we could see a group of kids from the United States lighting candles on various monuments. It reminded Mr. Jagelski of the interesting, sad story of Janusz Korczak, the renowned children's doctor, who had written numerous books. He was in charge of a Jewish orphanage in the Warsaw Ghetto. When the liquidation of the orphanage took place, Dr. Korczak walked into the Treblinka gas chambers with the children in order to comfort them during the last minutes of their lives. He preferred to die with them rather than save himself.

To me, this is the essence of Jewish heroism. It seems to me that it is easy to run and save one's self; real heroes stay with those who cannot save themselves and comfort them to their last breath.

The monument to Korczak recently began to melt down. It seems that the statue was built of plastic. Aware of the legend about the doctor, visiting youth from the West would come to see the famous hero's monument and, innocently, would light candles. One day when they left, the candles started melting the monument. Mr. Jagelski stated he would have the Koczak monument moved to a more prominent place and rebuilt from more proper material.

After the tour through the cemetery, the Polish teachers left. I went to see Mr. Jagelski in his office at the Jewish Historical Institute, where I explained my two major concerns about the museum in Zyndranowa. He informed me that he had heard about Zyndranowa and knew Mr. Gocz to be a very fine and honorable person.

I asked him, would there be any possibility for the Zyndranowa museum to become affiliated with the Jewish Historical Institute in Warsaw, which also has a museum. I felt that such an affiliation would more likely insure its future. I realize that Mr. Gocz, his immediate family, and certain members of the parish have good hearts and want to see the little museum flourish. But once they pass on, what's to stop other members of the Zyndranowa parish from thinking it over and perhaps deciding that a Jewish museum is inappropriate in their village? Perhaps this little house, which now the parish claims as theirs, could better serve as a "bed and breakfast" or for some other purpose. I have fears that someone in the future might pack the cultural objects and these photographs of Jewish life in that region into boxes and throw them into an attic. I felt that an affiliation could assure its continued existence. Mr. Jagelski informed me this could be done only if the parish agrees to be affiliated with the Jewish Historical Institute. He gave me encouragement. He suggested that we should draw up some kind of memorandum of understanding with Mr. Gocz and the parish. I agreed to do so and to have a Polish lawyer look it over. I hoped that Mr. Gocz and the parish members would see this as a very fair and equitable understanding to be reached between us all. Mr. Jagelski also made it clear that the Jewish Historical Institute had no funds, and if any funds were needed to maintain the museum, they must come from elsewhere. I assured him that I would try my best to provide funds to keep the museum operational.

My second concern was where to obtain more Jewish artifacts, since we didn't yet have enough to fill the three rooms, plus small storage room and hallway. He told me that there were many Jewish objects sitting in Polish homes, in attics and cellars, which Polish people had obtained at the time of the liquidation of the Jews. It would require that someone systematically look through the towns and villages in the Carpathian Region. That, too, was possible, but it would take time to accomplish. I thanked him for his kindness, and we promised to keep in touch.

That evening, as on my previous visits to Warsaw, Zula and Janusz gave a party for me before my departure. Early the next morning, Zula took me to the airport. Leaving Poland is always sad for me because there are so many memories—both the pleasant memories of staying with the Reykowskis, of seeing Staszek and his family, and of Mr. Gocz, and the warm people of Zyndranowa, and the sad memories and experiences that, occasionally, still haunt me. As I boarded the plane, I left the past and these feelings behind me, and I began to think of returning to my family. My first stop in the United States would be in Montclair, New Jersey, where my son David, his wife Liz, and our 10-month-old beautiful grandson, William Jonathan, live. It has been a joy to see that Liz and David are such very caring parents.

* * * * * * *

In early 1998, I was especially looking forward to another trip to Montclair because not only had David and Liz given us a second grandson, Harrison, but I had recently discovered I have a second cousin in Lakewood, New Jersey.

On March 31, I met Joseph and Jean Gerhard at a very joyful and loving first visit to their home. I had not known of Joe Gerhard's existence, nor he of mine. Through a happy circumstance his son, Dr. Harvey Gerhard, traced me, and we established contact.

Joe was born in September 1914 and grew up in Jaslisk, near Dukla. He knew my family substantially better than I did since he is 17 years older. He remembered me as a young child. He attended school in a country that was mostly Catholic, and where religious indoctrination and prayer were part of the curriculum. When it came time for the students to pray to Jesus Christ, the two or three Jewish kids in the classroom would say "praise the Lord" instead of saying "Christ." This was their way of avoiding antagonism from the Polish students and teachers.

When he was 17, Joe went to work in the lumber mills. His father was a builder of homes, specifically of homes for Polish immigrants who came back to Poland from the United States after World War I. In 1939, when World War II broke out, Joe was in Jaslisk, and the Germans immediately took him and other skilled Jews to work in the woods for the war effort. In June of 1942, the Nazis expelled all the Jews from nearby villages, including Zyndranowa, and sent them to Dukla where they lived in crammed quarters with Dukla's Jewish families. One day in August of 1942, a young boy came running into the woods telling all the Jewish men to return immediately to Dukla. They took hundreds of Jews and assembled them there on a nobleman's estate, which was surrounded by a big fence—a fence that was still standing in 1998. They separated out the young people who worked at the quarries or in the woods from the older men, women, and children who were put in another group guarded by Germans and Ukrainians.

They all had to face the wall, and if anyone turned around they were shot. Joe Gerhard was in one line with his younger brother, and his sisters were together with their mother. His older sister had an eight-month-old baby with her. One of the Germans walked over to his younger sister, and because she looked healthy and attractive, he told her she should remain because she would work well in the kitchen. But she didn't want to. She said that she wanted to go with her mother. His father, who had recently had stomach surgery, was still very ill and was standing in pain in the rain. One woman had an umbrella. She opened it up to protect herself from the rain. A Nazi came over and said, "You will not be needing this. You will be flying to heaven," and he shot her on the spot. Joe told me the older people, including my grandfather Isak, his wife, Raisel, and Uncle Zalman, were loaded on trucks and taken to a nearby mass grave where they were executed. However, my uncles Mordecai and Mendel were part of the work crew.

There were two quarry companies in Dukla: Ludwick and Walde. The managements were German. Young men were forced to go to the quarries and smash rocks to be used to fix roads. During that time they stayed at night in four large, vacated Jewish homes in Dukla. Because Zalman's son, Mordecai, refused to work hard, he was shot before the eyes of the workers. So were two other young men who refused to work hard. In 1943, the prisoners from the Walde Company were taken from the quarries and moved to a camp not far from Plaszow, where the famous camp of Oskar Schindler was, and where they worked in a factory building car engines, which were being converted from gasoline to wood. There was an oven-like stove in the back of the car that could boil water that produced heat and steam, which enabled the car to move. This conversion, Gerhard believed, was not yet successful, but was at an advanced experimental stage.

Why I was so thrilled to meet Joe Gerhard was this—he was able to tell me more about my family and about life at Zyndranowa. Joe assessed my father as a happy-go-lucky man with striking looks and a small black goatee beard. My mother, Shaindel (Jaffa), was beautiful and very gentle. She offered Joe candy from her little country store every time he showed up in Zyndranowa. He described the other families that lived there, including some I did not even know about. Besides my grandfather, Herman, who lived in Mszanka, there were his brothers, Zalman and Isak, and their sister, Fremed, who all lived in Zyndranowa. I found out that Joe's mother, Rosa, and my mother, Shaindel were first cousins. Thus, he and I are second cousins.

He described exactly what my Uncle Mendel looked like. Mendel had a gentle, kind personality, some pox marks on his face, and was blind in his left eye. He had no idea what had happened to Uncle Mordecai, but Mendel, who was sent from the Ludwick Company to Rzeszow, survived. He moved to Hungary after the war, something I had not known. From Hungary he moved to Israel where he died in 1968 in Tel Aviv. I much regret that I only found out about this lately, because if I had known, I would have searched for him while he was still alive.

Joe and his two brothers managed to survive the war. He met his wife, Jean, in Stuttgaard, Germany. Jean had also had horrible experiences including living in the large Lodz ghetto and later being sent to Auschwitz, where she worked as a seamstress for the Nazis.

Joe related an incident that happened to him during the Nazi occupation. The Zyndranowa border police used German shepherd dogs to help them guard the Slovak border. These dogs were killers. Joe and a group of other Jews at one point were being used as the victims to train the dogs to attack and kill people on command. He describes the kindness of one policeman who told them, "This dog will kill you if I let him go. But I won't let him go, so just run and drop down on the ground and pretend to be dead. I will come with the dog and make sure he doesn't bite you." In the midst of this unspeakable cruelty, this was an act of compassion by only one man. Before hearing this story, I thought I had heard of every form of human degradation and bestiality, but it appears to me that not until the last Holocaust survivor passes away will these stories cease to be told.

Joe Gerhard described the gentleness of my tall grandfather,

Isak, and told of the horse that Isak rode. (They appear in a photograph in this book.) He knew Zalman very well, and was pleased to hear that the little museum was being established in Zalman's house. He expressed the wish the if he cannot make it back to Zyndranowa to see it, maybe some of his children may.

I have been in contact with Mr. Gocz since the dedication of the museum, and he tells me there have been busloads of tourists, and he has had prominent signs erected to point visitors from the main road to the museum.

* * * * * * * *

As I stated earlier, it is not easy to separate the academic from the personal. On a personal level, I am a busy grandfather to four grandsons. William and Harrison live with their parents in Montclair. Evan and Daniel and their loving parents, Aron and Kristen, live in Walnut Creek, California. Pearl and I often visit with our youngest son and his wonderful fiancée, Valerie, who live in Chicago and who are about to get married.

In academics, my primary focus continues to be on the nature of good and evil, and as an educator I have, for a number of years, been researching and studying in these areas. I have taught, authored and co-edited articles on the nature of the evils of genocide, racism, and anti-Semitism. Under my supervision, some graduate students have written their theses on these general topics. On the nature of goodness, Pearl and I co-authored and edited several books including *The Altruistic Personality: Rescuers of Jews in Nazi Occupied Europe; Embracing the Other; Toward a Caring Society;* and *Who Shall Live: The Wilhelm Bachner Story,* which I co-authored with Kathleen Lee. I have also contributed chapters on altruism and prosocial behavior to several edited books and have published articles on these topics in journals. More recently I have undertaken studies on Carnegie Heroes, that is, U.S. and Canadian people who risk their lives on behalf of strangers; military heroes; Jewish rescue and resistance groups; moral exemplars and Hospice volunteers.

These studies help me better understand the nature of good

and evil. The British Broadcasting Corporation recently produced two documentaries based on our research on altruism, one titled "To Give or Not to Give" and the other "Rescuers Speaking." These documentaries help to disseminate the need for caring and compassion in pedagogically appropriate ways, and they show us that there *are* ordinary people who are heroes, there *are* caring people, and that alienation, neglect, and indifference need to be thwarted. It is my belief that we must sensitize people to the terrible consequences of being a bystander. Elie Wiesel, who won the Nobel Peace Prize, teaches us that the real enemy of humankind is not war or racism or prejudice, cynicism, and neglect, but is *indifference* to war, prejudice, racism, cynicism, and neglect. This, too, I profoundly believe.

What lessons have I learned from the Holocaust? What kind of useful knowledge have I gained? I cannot say the lessons are all positive. As I look around the world since the Holocaust, I see the substantial number of genocides that have been committed—Biafra, Campuchea, Rwanda and Burundi, Bosnia, Kosovo, and East Timor. But I also see that our "globalized" world has recently become more sensitized to the wholesale destruction of minority groups in sovereign states. The United Nations decided to intervene in Kosovo as well as East Timor to stop those massacres, which is a good sign. My hope is that this is the beginning of a conscientious and caring world community that will no longer permit unfettered mass destruction by dictatorial leaders. We must be on the lookout for malicious dictators who would massacre their own people within their borders.

The Holocaust has taught me—and, I hope, my students—what the consequences are when people fail to regard other ethnic and racial groups as members of the human family, and when they do not treat them as brothers and sisters. We must reverse the ancient propensity for believing that we need not concern ourselves with people who are different, "not like us." We need to be on guard against "troubled" spots around the world, where economic and political conditions have deteriorated to such a point that states are ripe for a demagogic leader to turn up and "save" the people by selling them a destructive, nationalistic, and racist ideology. People may follow such a leader when there is desolation and chaos in their country. Our vigilance should be strengthened, and economic, social, and moral support should be rendered to such groups of people. If necessary, limited military intervention should be undertaken in order to save innocent lives from certain mass slaughter. It is important to strengthen the United Nations so that it can foster the notion that we *are* one global people, that we need to help each other, and that aggression and war are not an option.

We have in the United States, between our colleges, secondary, and elementary schools, eighty-five to ninety-five million students, "a captive audience." Here is an opportunity for serious and concerned educators to promote change by including in the curriculum the ethic of caring and social responsibility. This should not be at the expense of science, reading, writing, and arithmetic but in addition to it, using appropriate pedagogical approaches to educate about the consequences of prejudice, neglect, ignorance, stereotyping, and discrimination. Teaching prosocial behavior is not an impossible undertaking; it just takes vision and an effort to change institutions to become, themselves, more concerned with the issues. Institutions, including the workplace, educational institutions, and religious institutions, should recognize the urgency for this and put additional effort into it. It is clear to me that just as bigotry, prejudice, discrimination, sexism, racism, and anti-Semitism have been taught by institutions, individuals, and hate groups, so it is possible to teach about altruism, caring, and social responsibility for diverse others.

There is a great need to establish a sense of global community. The social sciences must take the lead, recommending appropriate ways for institutions not only to remedy injustices and prejudices but to take a positive approach to building a truly diverse and multicultural community. It is time we de-emphasize material acquisition and seriously look for a new moral vision. It is time to do more to diminish cynicism, separation, and alienation that polarize us. This can happen, but only if social problems are attacked at many different levels simultaneously, including the political, economic, and spiritual levels. We must learn that we cannot be bystanders in the face of evil because when we are, it means that we give permission to the physical and emotional destruction of some people.

There is a Hebrew saying, *Tikkun Haolam*, which means, "mend the world." I believe that solutions to our problems are possible because there is no alternative, and I will continue to believe and teach that they are.

Bibliography

Allport, Gordon. 1981. *The Nature of Prejudice.* Reading, MA: Addison-Wesley Publishing Company.

Cohen, Roger. 1999. "For a Priest and for Poland a Tangled Identity." *The New York Times,* October 10.

Helmreich, William. *Against all Odds: Holocaust Survivors & the Successful Lives they Made in America.* New Brunswick, NJ: Transaction Publishers.

Hunt, Morton. 1990. *The Compassionate Beast: What Science is Discovering About the Humane Side of Mankind.* New York: William Morrow and Company, Inc.

Moskovitz, Sarah. 1983. *Love Despite Hate.* New York: Schocken Books

O'Connor, John Cardinal. 1999. "Letter to the Jewish Community." *New York Times,* September 19.

Oliner, Samuel P. and Kathleen Lee. 1996. *Who Shall Live: The Wilhelm Bachner Story.* Chicago, IL: Academy Chicago Publishers.

Oliner, Samuel P. and Pearl M. Oliner. 1988. *The Altruistic Personality: Rescuers of Jews in Nazi Europe*. New York: The Free Press.

Oliner, Samuel P. and Pearl M. Oliner. 1995. *Toward a Caring Society: Ideas into Action.* Westport, CT: Praeger.

Oliner, Pearl M., Samuel P. Oliner, Lawrence Baron, Lawrence A. Blum, Dennis L. Krebs and M. Zuzanna Smolenska, eds. 1992. *Embracing the Other: Philosophical, Psychological, and Historical Perspectives on Altruism.* New York: New York University Press.

Photo 1994
Gate to Garbacz mass grave.

Photo 1992
Garbacz mass grave and monument (see inscription page 158).

Photo 1992
Zalman's house before remodelling.

Photo 1994
Zalman's house after being rebuilt. Now a regional Jewish museum.

Dr. SAMUEL P. OLINER (Ph.D., University of California at Berkeley) is Professor of Sociology at Humboldt State University and Founder and Director of the Altruistic Personality and Prosocial Behavior Institute. He is the author of several dozen publications on the Holocaust, altruism, prosocial behavior, and national and international race relations. He has appeared on numerous national television shows and has lectured widely in the U.S. and several other countries on the topic of rescuers of Jews in Nazi-occupied Europe.

His books include *Race, Ethnicity and Gender: A Global Perspective* (Kendall/Hunt Publishing, 1997, co-editor, Phillip T. Gay), *Who Shall Live: The Wilhelm Bachner Story* (Academy Chicago Publishers, 1996, co-authored with Kathleen Lee), *Restless Memories* (Judah L. Magnes Museum, 1986), *Toward a Caring Society: Ideas into Action* (Praeger, 1995, co-author, Pearl M. Oliner), *Embracing the Other: Philosophical, Psychological, and Historical Perspectives on Altruism* (New York University Press, 1992, co-editors, Pearl M. Oliner, Lawrence Baron, Lawrence A. Blum, Dennis L. Krebs, and M. Zuzanna Smolenska) and *The Altruistic Personality: Rescuers of Jews in Nazi Europe* (Free Press, 1988/1992, co-author, Pearl M. Oliner). In 1998 he completed a research project on the topic of rural race and ethnic relations titled *Tolerance and Intolerance in Rural America* which was funded by the Anti-Defamation League of B'nai B'rith. Recently, he completed a research project interviewing Carnegie Heroes in order to examine their motivations for risking their lives on behalf of others. The results of this study will be reported in a forthcoming book, *Extraordinary Act of Ordinary People: Faces of Heroism and Altruism,* which deals with heroism and altruism in a variety of settings.